Excavations at Glasgow Cathedral 1988–1997

Stephen T Driscoll

with contributions by
Susan Bain

and

Donal Bateson, Kevin Brady, Paul Buckland, Adrian Cox, Irene Cullen, Gertie Ericsson,
Richard Fawcett, Jane Fletcher, Katherine Forsyth, Dennis Gallagher, Helen Howard, Lorna
Johnstone, Sarah King, Helen Loney, J Hugh McBrien, Jennifer Miller, David Park, Susan
Ramsay, Melanie J Richmond, Julie Roberts, Robert S Will, Eila Williamson

Illustrations by
Marion O'Neill and Keith Speller

THE SOCIETY FOR MEDIEVAL ARCHAEOLOGY
MONOGRAPH 18

ISBN 1 902653 66 1

Edited by Christopher Gerrard
Published by The Society for Medieval Archaeology
Printed in England by Maney Publishing

This publication has been made possible by a grant from Historic Scotland
in collaboration with The Society for Medieval Archaeology

The Society for Medieval Archaeology Monographs are available from
Maney Publishing
Hudson Road
Leeds LS9 7DL
UK

Cover: *Glasgow Cathedral at Sunset*, by C R Mackintosh (1890).
Courtesy of the Hunterian Art Gallery, University of Glasgow

MANEY
publishing

SOCIETY FOR MEDIEVAL ARCHAEOLOGY MONOGRAPH NO. 18

EXCAVATIONS AT GLASGOW CATHEDRAL 1988–1997

By Stephen T Driscoll

We are delighted to enclose, on behalf of the Society for Medieval Archaeology, the latest publication in their Monographs series, along with a leaflet giving further details including price and how to order this publication.

We would be pleased if you were able to review this in your journal and ask that offprints/copies of the review are forwarded to the series editor (to whom queries should also be addressed):

Dr Christopher Gerrard
Monographs Editor
Society for Medieval Archaeology
Department of Archaeology
University of Durham
South Road
Durham
DH1 3LE

Many thanks
Liz Rosindale, Editorial Manager, Maney Publishing

8 October 2002

Please reply to:

☐ **Hudson Road, Leeds LS9 7DL, United Kingdom** *(registered office)*
  Telephone +44 (0)113 249 7481 · *Facsimile* +44 (0)113 248 6983 · *Email* maney@maney.co.uk

☐ 1 Carlton House Terrace, London SW1Y 5DB, United Kingdom
  Telephone +44 (0)20 7451 7300 · *Direct* 73___ · *Facsimile* +44 (0)20 7839 2289

☐ Maney Publishing North America, 44 Brattle Street, 4th Floor, Cambridge, MA 02138, USA
  Telephone (toll free) +866 297 5154 · *Facsimile* +617 354 6875 · *Email* maney@maneyusa.com

Maney Publishing is the trading name of W.S. Maney & Son Ltd *Web Site* www.maney.co.uk

Registration Number: 1922017 England *VAT Number:* 640 6260 62

**To my parents
who took me to
church regularly**

EDITOR'S NOTE

Since 1966 the Society for Medieval Archaeology has published 17 monographs. These have appeared on a regular basis every two or three years, with a slight hiatus in the mid-1990s. Whatever the choice of theme, the series has always retained its size which was designed originally to mimick the format of the journal, though there have been flirtations with hardback, colour, double-column text and styles of citation. To some extent these variations reflected differences in the product and its market, as well as swings in printing costs and publishing fashion.

In 2000 the Society reviewed the purpose and presentation of its monographs and took soundings from its committees and the wider profession. It became obvious that the old format did not meet all needs with equal success, in particular those of modern excavation reports. The new monograph style presented here for the first time is intended to remedy those shortcomings.

The Society is always willing to consider proposals for new monographs, especially where these extend the range of scholarship covered so far in the series (eg in areas such as Anglo-Saxon settlement, artefact studies, environmental studies, field survey, fortifications, historiography, landscape, monasteries and theory). Authors and editors should contact:

Christopher Gerrard

Monographs Editor
Society for Medieval Archaeology
Department of Archaeology
University of Durham
South Road
Durham DH1 3LE

CONTENTS

LIST OF FIGURES

Appendix

SYNOPSIS

An extensive programme to renew the heating and electrical systems of the cathedral provided the opportunity for a substantial investigation of the interior during 1992–94. These excavations were conducted by Glasgow University Archaeological Research Division (GUARD) and revealed valuable evidence for three of the earlier phases of cathedral building, beginning in the early 12th century. Outside, the cathedral environmental improvements associated with the landscaping of Cathedral Square in 1989, allowed the Scottish Urban Archaeological Trust to investigate the sites of the western towers. A series of minor watching briefs was also occasioned by the renewal of services during this period, and contributed a modest amount of new information. Taken together the excavations have revealed new information about the history and development of the cathedral, which can be summarised under four broad headings:

1. Pre-12th-century activity. Few areas produced deposits which pre-dated the sequence of cathedrals, but amongst those early features were burials, the earliest of which can be dated to the 7th–9th centuries.

2. Sequence of cathedral building. The excavations revealed significant details about the position and scale of the two earliest phases of cathedral building and information about the construction of the building in its final state including the demolished west towers. Among the most dramatic discoveries were fragments of wall paintings and architectural masonry from the late 12th-century cathedral. This greatly enhances our understanding of the decorative programme of the second phase of cathedral building and our appreciation of its architectural significance.

3. Medieval use and burial practice. The most conspicuous features below the floor of the church were burials which date from the early Middle Ages to the late 19th century. They probably constitute the longest excavated sequence of burial at any Scottish church and reveal significant changes in burial rites and preferred location of burial over time. These burials also provide important information about aspects of the changing use of the church. Particularly noteworthy is the association of particular burial places with nave altars, where prayers could be offered on behalf of those buried. Two unique bronze mortars, presumably ecclesiastical objects, were found buried in the lower church.

4. Post-medieval building and burials. Following the Reformation the interior of the cathedral was progressively reconfigured to accommodate three congregations. Evidence of the arrangements in the nave survived well enough to allow its layout to be reconstructed. As burial within churches came to be forbidden the areas where burial was permitted became increasingly restricted to those parts not used for worship: the central crossing area and east bays of the nave, the treasury, the towers, and later the crypt. At the same time the treatment of the body became more complex and the coffins more elaborate.

SUMMARY

This monograph describes the most extensive modern excavations undertaken at any Scottish cathedral. The investigations at Glasgow Cathedral between 1988 and 1997 located the first cathedral, dedicated in 1136, and provided new information about the form and interior decoration of the second cathedral, which was begun in the late 12th century but never completed and was intended to house the translated remains of St Kentigern (Mungo). Excavated burials, of 7th–8th century date onwards, confirm the presence of an earlier cemetery while the numerous burials excavated in the nave provide unique insights into the populations and burial practices of medieval and post-medieval Glasgow.

RESUMEN

El presente volumen describe una de las excavaciones modernas más extensas de cuantas se han realizado en una catedral escocesa. La investigación arqueológica de la catedral de Glasgow tuvo lugar entre 1988 y 1997 y permitió localizar el primer templo edificado, dedicado en 1136, junto con nueva información sobre la forma y decoración interior de la segunda catedral, comenzada a finales del siglo XII e inacabada, diseñada para albergar el cuerpo de San Kentigern (Mungo). Los enterramientos excavados, de los siglos VII-VIII y posteriores, confirman la existencia de un cementerio previo, a la vez que las numerosas tumbas excavadas en la nave nos informan sobre las prácticas funerarias y aspectos antropológicos, patológicos y forma de vida de los habitantes del Glasgow medieval y post-medieval.

RESUME

Denne monografi beskriver de mest omfattende, nyere udgravninger foretaget af nogen skotsk katedral. Undersøgelserne af Glasgow katedral mellem 1988 og 1997 stedfæstede den første katedral, indviet 1136, og gav nye oplysninger om udformningen og den indvendige udsmykning af den anden katedral, der blev påbegyndt i det sene 12. århundrede skønt aldrig fuldendt, og som det var hensigten skulle huse de overflyttede rester af St. Kentigern (Mungo). Undersøgte begravelser, dateret til 7.–8. århundrede og frem, bekræfter tilstedeværelsen af en tidligere begravelsesplads, mens talrige begravelser undersøgte i skibet giver enestående indsigt i befolkning og begravelsesskik i Glasgow i middelalderen og den efterfølgende tid.

ACKNOWLEDGEMENTS

Fieldwork: a great many friends and colleagues participated in the excavations, but Bob Will (supervision), Keith Speller (drawings and photographs), Mel Richmond (finds manager) and Sarah King (on-site skeletal analysis) deserve special mention for providing fieldwork continuity. Similarly, many contributed to the post-excavation analysis, but special thanks are extended to Irene Cullen, Susan Bain and Kevin Brady for their contributions to the report preparation, editing and archiving. Illustration of the excavations was by Keith Speller, illustration of the finds is largely the work of Marion O'Neil with help from Jill Sievewright and Caitlin Evans. Dr Eila Williamson helped to research the historical background. Jane Fletcher, Adrian Cox (SUAT), Morag Cross and Dr Colleen Batey (Glasgow Museums) also made significant contributions. Joehari Lee contributed a personal set of excavation photographs.

The Revd William J Morris, Peter Rintoul and Friends of Glasgow Cathedral, and the wider community of Glasgow Cathedral made us welcome during our fieldwork and provided a comfortable working environment. The Historic Scotland custodians and Direct Labour team made a huge contribution through the provision of access to the building and for their support handling the spoil. The cathedral architect, Bob Hyslop, proved a helpful manager of the building works. The conservation work on the stones was undertaken by Nic Boyes, and photographed by Chris Hutchins. The bronze mortars were photographed by David Henrie. The project has benefited at every step of the way from Dr Richard Fawcett's enthusiasm, supervision and scholarship.

During the preparation of the finds studies I consulted with a number of individuals who generously supplied me with information and opinions. On the bronze mortars Dr David Caldwell (National Museums of Scotland) and Michael Finlay; on the sculptured stone Ian Fisher and Neil Cameron (Royal Commission on the Ancient and Historical Monuments of Scotland); on the personal seal Alastair Campbell of Airds, Abbot Mark Dilworth OSB, Dr T A Heslop (University of East Anglia), and Gilbert Márkus OP; on the false teeth Dr Henry Noble, on the musket balls Dr Stephen Wood (Scottish United Services Museum). I especially appreciated the interest of my most dedicated visitors, John Durkan, Archie Duncan and Hugh McBrien, who all contributed valuable advice during the course of the excavation and over the ten years it has taken to bring this to print.

David Park and Helen Howard, who analysed the painted stone, would like to thank Nic Boyes and Dr Richard Fawcett of Historic Scotland for their assistance, and Sharon Cather for her help with all aspects of the study of the fragments.

Historic Scotland provided the financial support for the archaeological work conducted within the cathedral as part of their programme of improvements to the heating and electrical services. The Historic Scotland Conservation Centre undertook the conservation of the architectural masonry, including the painted fragments. The post-excavation analysis and the preparation of this report was made possible by substantial grants from Historic Scotland. Throughout the process of preparing this monograph the Inspectorate of Ancient Monuments has provided valuable advice and encouragement.

Finally, I must thank Katherine Forsyth for the expert finishing touch she applied to the final version. Her contribution is evident in some of the finds discussions, but is found throughout the report. Without her help this report would have taken much longer to appear and would not have been as coherent.

Stephen T Driscoll
Glasgow University
29 September 2000

1

INTRODUCTION

S T Driscoll

1.1 HISTORICAL BACKGROUND

The historical traditions enshrined in the earliest *vitae* of St Kentigern maintain that Glasgow's ecclesiastical origins are to be found in a small cemetery on the bank of the Molendinar Burn. This cemetery was supposedly consecrated by St Ninian and subsequently adopted by Kentigern as the centre of a see established in the kingdom of Strathclyde in the 6th century. The 12th-century *vita* of Kentigern succinctly asserts the antiquity of the see of Glasgow and its connections with the earliest evangelists of northern Britain. Although the *vitae* probably embody some authentic material, the 12th-century reworking of the tradition material is so substantial that all details relating to Glasgow's history prior to the foundation of the see by Earl David (between 1114 and 1118) must be treated with extreme caution. From the 12th century, the historical records become increasingly abundant and allow the rapid development of the see to be charted in some detail. In this Introduction the most important of the documentary sources are briefly reviewed and the major features of the cathedral chapter described. Historical issues relevant to a full understanding of the archaeological evidence include: the status of the bishop and the organisational structure of the chapter, the burgh and its changing relationship to the cathedral, the post-Reformation alterations and modified usage of the cathedral, and the consequences of the restoration work which began in the 19th century. Most readers will probably also find it helpful to have a summary of the architectural development of the extant cathedral, given that all the archaeological work has been framed by the building's present condition.

Apart from Kentigern himself, there is no record of the bishops of Glasgow prior to the 11th century. About 1109 Thomas, Archbishop of York, ordained Michael as bishop of Glasgow. This ordination appears as one in a long sequence of efforts by the bishops of York to assert their authority over the church in Scotland (Durkan 1999). Serious doubt exists as to whether this Michael or his York-ordained predecessors had a significant presence in Glasgow. Apart from the accounts generated in York, nothing is known of these bishops. Nor is there any material evidence from this period at Glasgow; an archaeological blank which is most telling given the great quantities of sculpture known from Govan at this time (Driscoll 1998). According to the contemporary Scottish documentation, the first bishop, John Ascelin, was established in Glasgow between 1114 and 1118 by David I, who at the time was ruler of Cumbria (Barrow 1996, 6; Watt 1991, 54–55). The exact moment of David's endowment is not clear (Shead 1969; Driscoll 1998, no 2), but as early as *c*1114 David began to provide monies towards the construction of the cathedral (Barrow 1996, 8; 1999, 53–54). Further details of the endowment of the cathedral do not come until 1136, when on the occasion of the dedication of the first cathedral, the results of an inquest instigated by David were recorded. Barrow (1999, 60) believes that the inquest was probably held by David between 1120–21 or 1123–24, but Shead (1969, 223) suggests that the actual enquiry could have taken place somewhat earlier, between 1109–14. The inquest enumerated the extensive holdings of the church of Kentigern, which included lands in the later Barony of Glasgow, the Upper Ward of Clydesdale, Tweedale, Teviotdale, Annandale and probably in Nithsdale. This rich endowment was supplemented by the grant of Govan

FIGURE 1.1

Prospect of Glasgow Cathedral from the north-east from John Slezer's Theatrum Scotiae *(1693). The earliest detailed image of the cathedral and precinct. The cathedral shows signs of post-Reformation neglect, but all the main elements of the cathedral (towers, bishop's castle and the manses) still survive. Reproduced by kind permission of Glasgow University Library*

to the cathedral in 1128–36, again probably on the occasion of the consecration of the new cathedral (Barrow 1999, 72). Also to mark the consecration, the cathedral was granted the royal estate of Partick and various other sources of revenue (Barrow 1999, 80–82). From 1136 onwards the cathedral's history is relatively well known owing to the survival of extensive archives which have been available to scholars since the late 19th century (Figure 1.1).

The earliest building was an ambitious Romanesque church, which when completed was probably the most substantial masonry building in western Scotland. On the limited evidence produced by the excavations, the scale of building is hard to substantiate. Rainer Mentel (1988), on the basis of similarities in plan (1998), has argued, however, that the 'giant order' in the Jedburgh Abbey choir (Thurlby 1995) was modelled on the early 12th-century cathedral at Glasgow. If this is true then Glasgow 'marks the starting point of the development of Romanesque architecture in Scotland' (Mentel 1998, 48). Glasgow's first cathedral may have fallen some way short of its immediate Romanesque rivals, the great eastern monasteries of Kelso, Holyrood, Dunfermline and St Andrews, which in 1136 were

either still under construction or recently completed (Fawcett 1994b, 26–41; Cruden 1986, 26–54, 102). The construction of a major church was entirely appropriate for a diocese fashioned from a former kingdom. As far as can be seen Glasgow's diocese corresponded with the former kingdom of Cumbria. It extended south-east to Tweeddale and Teviotdale, south to Annandale and Carrick (skirting the diocese of Galloway) and north to Renfrew and the Lennox (Figure 1.2). The bishop of Glasgow was the principal ecclesiastical authority over all of the western territory then under the dominion of the king of Scots.

While this study is not intended as a history of Glasgow Cathedral, a number of topics relating to the cathedral's development will be outlined here. This historical overview has been grouped under five headings, which will provide a context for the archaeological discussions to follow. The first topic concerns the authenticity of the traditions surrounding the origins of Glasgow and the activities of Kentigern. The second topic considers the position of the bishop and the organisational structure of the chapter. The third topic is the burgh of Glasgow and its changing relationship to the cathedral. Fourth, the post-Reformation

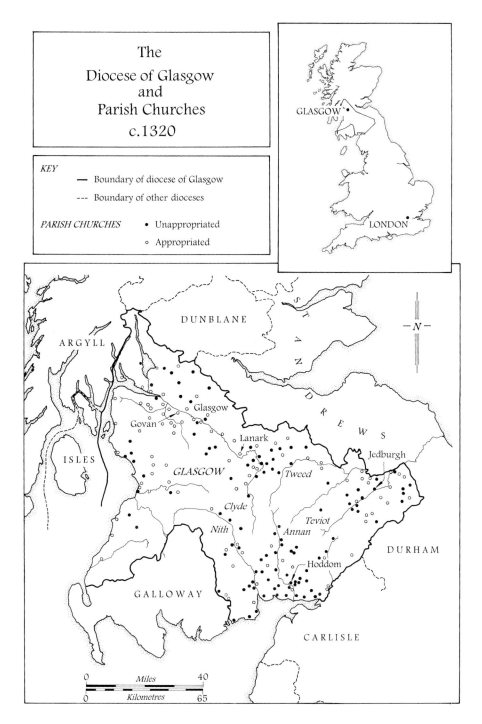

The
Diocese of Glasgow
and
Parish Churches
c.1320

KEY
— Boundary of diocese of Glasgow
--- Boundary of other dioceses

PARISH CHURCHES   • Unappropriated
                   ◦ Appropriated

FIGURE 1.2

The diocese of Glasgow. Dots indicate parishes held before c1320. See map compiled by
Norman Shead for the Scottish Historical Atlas *(1975, 155) for details of parishes*

alterations and modified usage of the building are outlined. Finally, the key consequences of the restoration work, which began in the 19th century, are noted.

The Kentigern tradition

Using pre 12th-century church dedications as an indicator, it is clear that veneration for Kentigern was strong in Cumbria (Redford 1988, 220–221).

Kentigern, also known affectionately as Mungo, has been described as the most important of all the northern saints of Britain (Figure 1.3) (Bowen 1969, 83–84), as evidenced by the eight dedications in English Cumbria (Barrow 1996, 6, no 25). Amongst these Kentigern dedications is the early medieval foundation in Annadale at Hoddom, which was a centre of some importance in the 12th century (Scott 1991). Whatever the importance of these sites for the cult of Kentigern, during the 12th century Glasgow

3

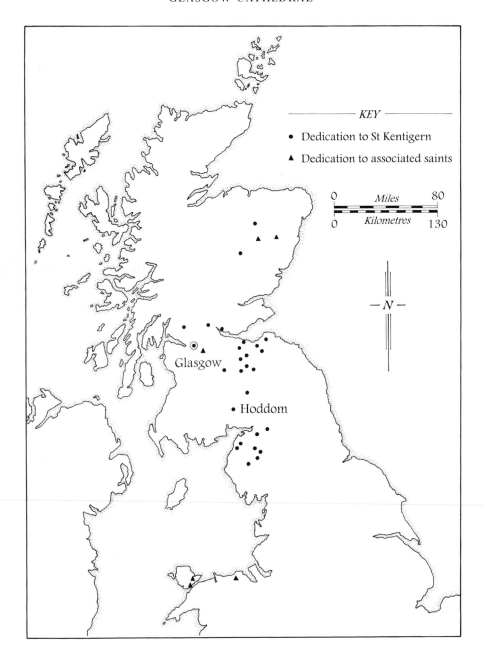

FIGURE 1.3

The extent of the cult of St Kentigern as indicated by dedications to the saint (circles) or associated saints (triangles). After Bowen (1969, 84) with additions

established itself as the most significant centre for this vigorous cult. The clearest indication of this vigour is found in the two 12th-century lives of Kentigern which were commissioned by successive bishops of Glasgow (Forbes 1874).

These lives draw upon early medieval material, the historical value of which is difficult to assess and opinions differ widely even as to the date of the earlier strata embedded in the 12th-century versions (Mac-Quarrie 1997; Jackson 1958). The consensus is that aspects of an authentic 7th-century Kentigern tradition survive within the existing *vitae*, but the degree to which they have been doctored does not inspire confidence in the uncorroborated detail. For instance,

a comparison of the earlier fragmentary *vita*, compiled during the episcopacy of Bishop Herbert (1147–64), with the version by Jocelin of Furness, completed during the episcopacy of Bishop Jocelin (1175–99), shows a strong hand at work updating and sanitising the *vita* for a late 12th-century audience (Gardner 1998). Because of the uncertainties surrounding the *vitae*, only the barest details concerning Kentigern can be accepted as historically correct. Reduced to its essence the tradition maintains that Kentigern was the grandson of the British king of the Lothians, that he was educated by St Serf at Culross and that he became a monk. He travelled to Glasgow to bury a holy man named Fergus at the site of an existing cemetery. As a consequence of political disruptions he travelled widely through Cumbria and lived at Hoddom as well as Glasgow. At the time of this death, around 614 (MacQuarrie 1997, 118), his biographers present him as founder of Glasgow Cathedral, presumably bishop of the northern British. Kentigern was buried at Glasgow and his tomb became a focus of devotion.

The degree to which the tradition has been re-worded by Jocelin of Furness and his predecessor means that details relating to this late 6th- to 7th-century church at Glasgow, even simple comments such as the presence of an old cross (Forbes 1874, 110), must be regarded with extreme caution. Probably all that can be accepted without too much doubt is that the cathedral lies near to the site of the early medieval church. This church, almost certainly of timber, was the focus of a cemetery and was served by a Christian community. The landscape setting of the cathedral, its streamside position, its sacred grove (Durkan 1998, 137) and its holy well (built into the existing building), certainly conform to our expectations for a 'Celtic' monastery, but tell us little about the status of this site. The massive size of the parish suggests, however, that Glasgow served as a mother church for the middle stretch of the Clyde and would have served as a suitable seat for a bishop (Durkan 1986a; 1986b; 1998; MacQuarrie 1992).

Whatever the truth about the original status of Glasgow and the subsequent period when Govan seems to have been the principal religious centre on the Clyde (Driscoll 1998), the 12th century saw a burgeoning interest in the cult of Kentigern, no doubt heavily encouraged by the newly written *vitae*. Enthusiasm for the cult is clearly apparent in the flurry of building work, which saw a succession of three major campaigns of enlargement within the space of a century and culminated in the completion of the existing cathedral. Less than 50 years passed from the dedication of John's cathedral to the beginning of major enlargements in 1181 during the episcopacy of Jocelin (1174–99). This work was delayed by fire but had progressed enough for a part to be dedicated in 1197, however it was never completed and was replaced by an even larger building which was begun around 1200. As the excavations showed these success-ive phases of building and enlargement were all within a relatively limited area, and the fixed point through-out was probably the presumed site of Kentigern's burial. This rapid expansion in the late 12th century is one of the remarkable aspects of the cathedral's history, which coincides with the growth in importance of the burgh itself under the lordship of the bishop.

Bishop and chapter

For most of its history Glasgow was the second most important see in Scotland, after St Andrews, but at times the bishops of Glasgow were the leading ecclesi-astics in the kingdom. This importance is reflected in the frequency with which the bishop served as a royal official. There was a natural political dimension to the construction and leadership of a see which by c1320 included 206 parishes (Shead 1975; 1988). With the establishment of the cathedral, the bishop became the most powerful lord in Cumbria, and his influence extended far beyond Clydesdale to include the Lennox and the Borders. The bishops were fundamental to the government of the west, but they followed more wide-ranging briefs. The first bishop, John (1114–18 to 1147), served as a papal envoy whose main goal was to secure recognition that the Scottish church was independent and outwith the authority of the archbish-opric of York. The bishops of Glasgow also acted as brokers in awkward internal affairs such as the revival of the see of Dunblane. Perhaps the most regular, consistent contribution to governing Scotland made by the bishops was as chancellor: no fewer than eleven held this office (Dowden 1912).

The importance of the see is also reflected in the size and nature of the chapter, which from an early date adopted the practices of Salisbury. The needs of the chapter, particularly with respect to the liturgical rites, had a strong influence on the design of the cathedral church itself. It seems fairly clear that Glasgow Cathedral and its chapter were modelled upon the secular cathedrals developed in northern France, which were a prominent feature of the Norman world (for example, Bayeux, York, Lincoln and Salisbury) (Barrow 1996, 8–9). The cathedral chapter bore little resemblance to 'Celtic' or, indeed, to Benedictine monasteries, although the canons did fulfil similar liturgical roles. The college of canons maintained a rich programme of worship and catered for the pastoral needs of pilgrims, but they also had parochial responsibilities. Members of the chapter held prebends (incomes) from the parish in exchange for seeing to the pastoral needs of the parishioners. From a royal perspective one of the main advantages of this sort of organisation was that it was free of interference from a religious order. It was not however free from outside influences or organised for the convenience of the bishop or the king.

The chapter was initially composed of at least six canons governed by 'old and reasonable customs', but by the time of Bishop Herbert (1147–64) the number of canons had grown to 25 and been formally consti-tuted (Barrow 1996, 10–11). In 1259 Glasgow Cathe-dral obtained from the dean and chapter of Salisbury an account of constitution and customs, but adopted only those regarded as useful (Dowden 1912, 66; Glasgow *Registrum* i, doc 205–211, 164–171). This constitution had only recently been codified at Salis-bury Cathedral, so its adoption indicates a close relationship between the two cathedrals. It also reflects a determination to construct a well-organised adminis-tration for the diocese, an aim effectively accomplished by the end of the 13th century (Shead 1976; 1988; Ash 1990).

The influence of Salisbury extended beyond administration matters to the essence of the cathedral's purpose. From 1259 the organisation of worship in the cathedral followed the Sarum Rite. This had significant architectural implications. Fawcett (1990a, 109) has suggested that the liturgical requirements for an architecturally distinct choir were behind the decision to construct the great 13th-century eastern limb with its multiple altars. This is because at the heart of the Rite is a calendar of saints to be celebrated on a given day and detailed patterns and protocols for movements in and around the church to the altars dedicated to particular saints (Bailey 1971, 17–18). In this respect Glasgow was not unusual, because the Sarum Rite was extremely popular at the great churches throughout Britain and on the Continent. Certainly part of the motivation behind the building works of the late 12th and early 13th century was to create a cathedral where elaborate and formal worship could be focused around the tomb of St Kentigern.

Architectural history

Over the years there have been various guides to the cathedral of varying quality (for example, Davidson 1938; Radford 1970; Fawcett 1985a) as well as general appreciations of the building. There have been numerous architectural studies starting in the 19th century (MacGibbon and Ross 1896; Eyre-Todd 1898) and numerous notes and articles on the history of the building, which frequently drew upon the excellent surviving documentation (for example, Stones 1969; 1970; Durkan 1970; 1986b). This brief account of the architectural development of Glasgow Cathedral will follow Richard Fawcett's authoritative accounts, which represent significant advances on earlier studies of the fabric (1990a; 1996; 1997). The archaeological excavations provided considerably more detailed information about the extent and progress of the various building campaigns, but have confirmed the three main phases discussed by Fawcett (Figure 1.4). It is conventional to describe the phases by the name of the bishop during whose rule the work was done. This convention has been followed here, not least because there is virtually no knowledge of the identity of the medieval architects.

The first cathedral was dedicated in 1136 by Bishop John (Figure 1.4a). No remains of it exist *in situ* above ground, nor were any architectural fragments known prior to the excavation. It had always been assumed that it lay under the existing building and this proved to be the case. The west front of John's church lay at the third pier of the existing nave and its east end probably included the area of St Kentigern's tomb. If so it would have been *c*40 metres long (see Section 3.2).

This first cathedral began to be enlarged around its eastern end during the reign of one of Glasgow's most significant bishops, Jocelin (1175–99). During the last quarter of the 12th century Jocelin managed to persuade the pope to grant Glasgow special status as a 'daughter' of Rome (1175), and was rewarded by the king with a grant of control over the burgh (1175–78). Jocelin commissioned a new *vita* of Kentigern, and by 1181 was 'gloriously enlarging' the cathedral itself (Fawcett 1990a, 108). By 1197 enough of this enlarged church had been completed to allow it to be consecrated (Duncan 1998). One fragment, consisting of a length of wall with an engaged shaft, survives in the SW corner of the crypt (Figure 1.4b). It is enough to suggest a cruciform east end built on two levels, presumably to create a platform for the high altar above a crypt which encompassed the saint's tomb (Fawcett 1997, 2–3, 10). Comparison with the later work suggested that the second cathedral too was never finished and this was confirmed during the excavations. From comparable structures, it may have been intended to be 45–50 metres long.

Judging from the architectural details, work on the third major phase of building was begun shortly after the consecration of Jocelin's cathedral in 1197. Fawcett argues that the transepts of Jocelin's church were truncated, new non-projecting transepts were set out to the west and the nave was greatly expanded (Figure 1.4c). On stylistic grounds, this new layout of an aisled nave and non-projecting transepts can probably be attributed to Bishop Walter (1207–32) (Fawcett 1990b, 150; 1997, 22). Work on this design began and the walls of the nave were completed to at least the height of the window sills, before there was yet another change in plan. This new change saw the eastern limb greatly expanded, but the layout of the nave, including the rhythm of the bays, remained unaltered (Figure 1.4d).

The enlargement of the eastern limb is attributed to bishop William de Bondington (1233–58) (Fawcett 1990b, 150; 1997, 25). It accommodated a more spacious choir, more altars and, above all, a more magnificent setting for the tomb of the saint who founded the see of Glasgow (Wilson 1998). The chosen plan, with an ambulatory and space for four altars at the east end, seems to have been inspired by a type favoured at a number of Cistercian abbeys and also employed at Lichfield Cathedral. It is hard to know how quickly the building progressed, but the gift of wood by Maurice of Luss for building the bell tower and treasury in 1277, suggests that work on the transepts was nearing completion by this date (Glasgow *Registrum* i, doc 229, 191–192). The nave was probably nearing completion around the end of the 13th century although the Wars of Independence may have caused some interruptions, not the least because bishop Robert Wishart (1271–1316) was alleged to have diverted building materials to construct siege engines (Fawcett 1990a, 109).

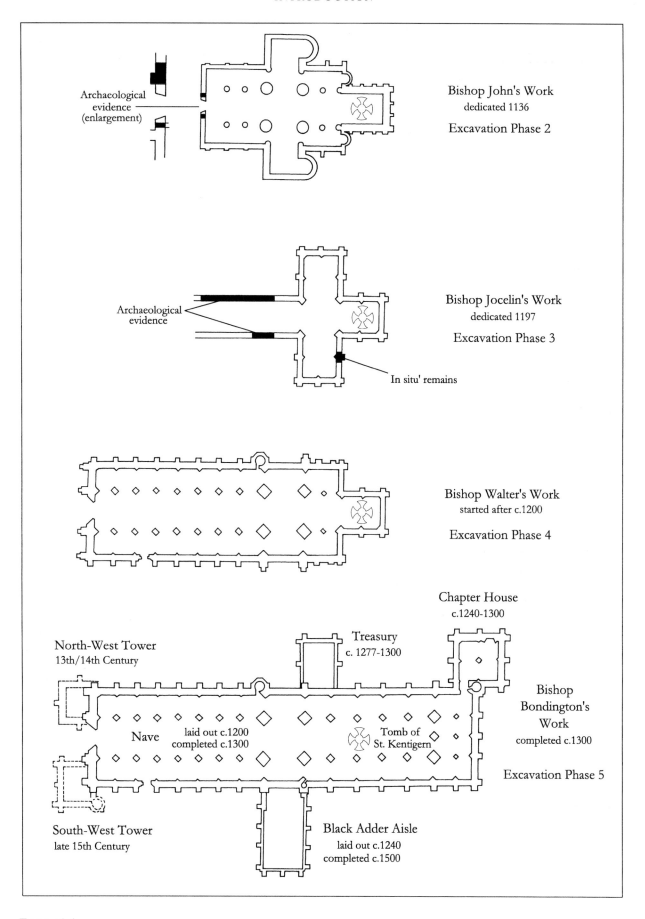

Archaeological
evidence
(enlargement)

Bishop John's Work
dedicated 1136

Excavation Phase 2

Archaeological
evidence

Bishop Jocelin's Work
dedicated 1197

Excavation Phase 3

In situ' remains

Bishop Walter's Work
started after c.1200

Excavation Phase 4

Chapter House
c.1240-1300

North-West Tower
13th/14th Century

Treasury
c. 1277-1300

Bishop
Bondington's
Work
completed c.1300

Nave   laid out c.1200
completed c.1300

Tomb of
St. Kentigern

Excavation Phase 5

South-West Tower
late 15th Century

Black Adder Aisle
laid out c.1240
completed c.1500

FIGURE 1.4

Conjectural plans of the four successive building programmes from the 12th to the 14th century

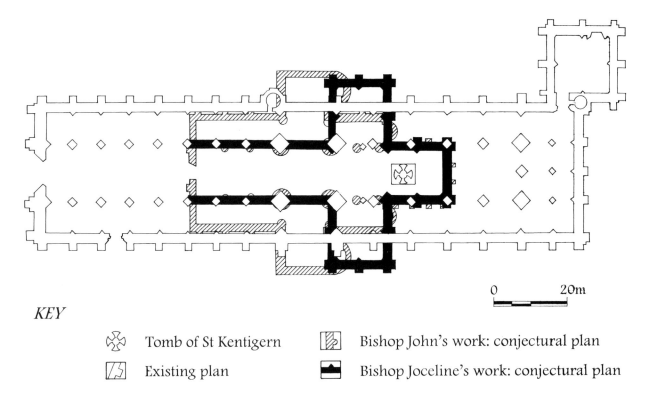

KEY

⚜ Tomb of St Kentigern   ▨ Bishop John's work: conjectural plan

▨ Existing plan   ▬ Bishop Joceline's work: conjectural plan

FIGURE 1.5

Diagram showing the relationship between the conjectural plans of the early cathedrals and the final plan

A number of structures were designed to project from the main body of the church as part of the 13th-century work. A two-storied chapter house was placed against the NE corner of the choir while at the SE of the choir a two-storied sacristy/treasury was built. The enigmatic structure known as Blackadder's Aisle was not so quickly completed. This projection of the south transept was apparently dedicated to the holy man Fergus who features in the *Life of Kentigern*, but although laid out in the 13th century it was not completed until the 15th century by archbishop Robert Blackadder (1483–1508) (Fawcett 1985c). The towers have a similarly chequered history. As far as can be said on the basis of 19th-century drawings and surviving architectural fragments, the NW tower was begun in the 13th or early 14th century, but the SW was apparently not added until the 15th century (Fawcett 1990a, 109; Macaulay 1997). The 15th century saw a considerable amount of repairs and embellishments, most notably to the chapter house and central tower, but apart from those to the two western towers none of them have archaeological implications (Figure 1.5).

The burgh and the cathedral

Texts relating to the later Middle Ages are relatively plentiful, making it possible to reconstruct a nearly comprehensive picture of Glasgow from its surrounding ecclesiastical landscape (Figure 1.6) down to the location of forgotten altars in the nave (Durkan 1970; 1986a; 1986b; 1998). The altars attracted secular endowments, especially during the 15th century, which established a link between powerful families and specific parts of the church and may have included burial privileges. Over time the endowment of the cathedral chapter grew as new parishes were granted to the church by prominent landowners, many of whom retained an interest in the appointment of canons.

One of the greatest gifts presented to the bishops of Glasgow was dominion over the burgh and rights to the revenues, fines and tolls which in most other burghs belonged to the king or to secular lords. These rights were granted to Bishop Jocelin (1175–99) by William I the Lion in 1175–78 (the earliest known charter creating a burgh in Scotland) and proved a great incentive to successive bishops in promoting the development of a strong market and fair. This gave the bishops a deep interest in the prosperity of the burgh, which was manifest in numerous ways, from defending Glasgow's trading rights against challenges from Rutherglen, Renfrew and Dumbarton, to furnishing bridges to promote trade: a timber one by 1285 and a stone one by 1410 (Pryde 1958). The establishment of the university in 1451 represents a further stage of urban development (Mackie 1954), which contributed towards the metropolitan status, finally confirmed on Glasgow when it was elevated to archiepiscopal status in 1492 (Pryde 1958, 138–139).

As the burgh grew, the activities of its citizens became visible within the cathedral, in particular

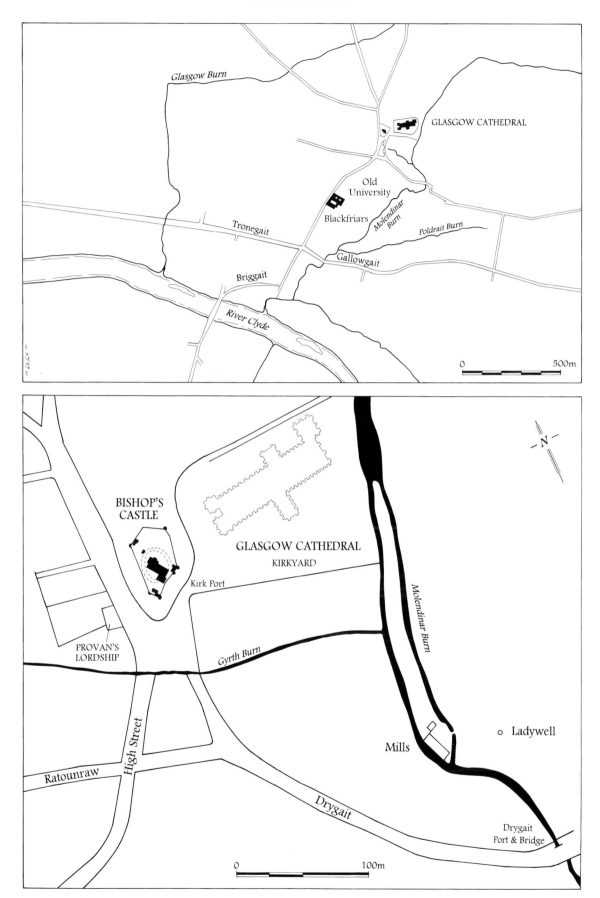

FIGURE 1.6

Location map of the medieval city of Glasgow and the cathedral precinct

through the endowment of altars. The parish had an altar, probably to St Kentigern, in the nave. The altars were used as meeting places by the trade corporations and for consistory court hearings (Durkan 1970). The notices of grants provide the most direct indication of devotional activity by those outside the chapter. The earliest references relate to the 13th-century cathedral, which may reflect the growth of a secular urban population. The earliest mention of such a gift occurred in 1290 when it is noted that Robert, a bygone citizen of Glasgow, and his wife Christina had given property '*in augmentum luminaris Beate Marie Virginis in le crudis majoris ecclesie Glasguensis*' (McRoberts 1966, 46; Glasgow *Registrum* i, doc 237, 198). By this time Glasgow was also attracting a significant number of pilgrims, the most famous of which was King Edward I of England, who on 28 August 1301 offered oblation at the shrine of St Mungo and the tomb, implying that they were located on separate levels (Fawcett 1990a, 113). Duncan (1998) has presented a detailed argument that Kentigern was never translated. Bishop Jocelin was refused permission to translate the saint in 1197 at the time of the consecration of the new cathedral and the establishment of the Glasgow Fair. This indicates that the tomb believed, already in 1136, to contain the mortal remains of Kentigern was still undisturbed in 1197 (and remains so to the present day). Although there is no pre 12th-century evidence it is quite possible that this tomb is indeed, as Jocelin and his predecessors believed, the burial place of the historical Kentigern. Following Duncan's argument there could never have been a feretory to contain the saint's corporeal relics, although, of course, there were non-corporeal relics of Kentigern.

Post-Reformation changes

Uniquely of the mainland Scottish cathedrals, Glasgow survived the Reformation substantially intact to become an important and increasingly intensively used place of worship during the 17th and 18th centuries. The cathedral, however, did not come through the political unrest of 1559–62 unscathed. In 1560 the precious treasures and archives of the Cathedral were removed to Paris for safekeeping (McRoberts 1959, no 97). It is presumably at this time that the cathedral was 'cleansed' of furnishings such as altars and sculpture and any remaining valuables may have been hidden away. The fabric of the cathedral suffered from vandalism and petty plunder at this time. By 1574 it was in sufficiently bad condition to attract the attention of the Glasgow town council:

> the greit dekaye and ruyne that the hie kirk of Glasgow is cum to, throuch taking awaye of the leid, sclait and wther grayth thairof, in this trublus tyme bygane sua that sick ane greit monument will alluterlie fall doun and dekey without it be remidit

(Burgh Records i, 20, quoted in McRoberts 1959, 147).

The condition was serious enough to encourage the town council to raise a tax of £200 for repairs to the cathedral in that same year (Renwick 1908, 305), but the process of repairing the cathedral and modifying it for Presbyterian worship dragged on for years. In 1578 the lead of the cathedral roof was repaired (Chalmers 1914, 88). In 1583 the Kirk Session gave instructions 'to big the auld consistorie windowes with stanes' (Renwick 1908, 310), in 1584 instructions were given to remove the 'auld stanes quhair the pulpet stud afore' (Renwick 1908, 311) and in 1588 it also ordered some ash trees in the High Kirk yard to be cut down to make forms for folk to sit on in church (NSA, 111). Once the fabric had been secured and the old liturgical apparatus had been removed, attention turned towards seating and the insertion of lofts in the aisles. In 1591 the Deacons of the Crafts 'appeared, and declared none of them were willing to big Lafts in the Quire of the Kirk, and thereupon the Session protested they were at liberty to grant liberty to any who should sue for liberty to big Lafts there' (Gordon 1866, 129). In 1608 the Magistrates decided 'on building a Seat for the College, at the expense of the College: also, to change the King's Seat, and the Pulpit, from the places they have been so long in' and the Session nominated 'My Lord Bishop, Provost, Bailies, &c., to see the whole Seats in the Hie Kirk reformed' (Gordon 1866, 133). As the population grew, the demand for seating increased so that in 1656 the Session requested the Magistrates 'to make more room in the Hie and Laigh Kirk, in regard they do not contain them that come to hear, Sabbath and Week Days' and reported 'that the Magistrates and Council has made an Act that the Kirks should be enlarged by Lofting and otherwise, as shall be convenient' (Gordon 1866, 173; Chalmers 1914, 22). From an early date interest in the fabric extended beyond the main body of the church. The repairs of 1588–89 to the NW tower (Renwick 1908, 306) imply that it was still in use at this date.

Initially attention was focused on the choir which in 1635 was transformed through the erection of a partition on the *pulpitum* into the High Church or, as it came to be called, the 'Inner Church'. As the population increased over the 16th and 17th centuries additional space for worship was required. The cathedral eventually came to house three congregations: in addition to the Inner Church, the Outer High Kirk was made by partitioning the west end of the nave, and the new Barony of Glasgow parish used the crypt (Fawcett 1990a, 110). Throughout this period the cathedral remained the most important public meeting place in Glasgow and even hosted the nationally important General Assembly of 1638, which effectively challenged the authority of Charles II (Mason 1988).

The Outer Kirk congregation, which had been worshipping in the nave since 1587, eventually secured a distinct architectural space in 1647 when a stone wall was erected at the east end of the nave (Durkan 1970, 49, pl 3; Fawcett 1990a, 110). Work on the interior was to follow. In 1648 it was recorded that 'the Session earnestly desire the magistrates may cause repair the Outer Hie Kirk, and put up a pulpit in it' (Gordon 1866, 169–70). The partition was a massive wall, but originally it did not extend to the roof so, in 1659 the magistrates were 'spoken to for making a partition wall in the Outer Kirk, or lofting it above, in respect of the great prejudice comes to the minister and hearers by cold' (Gordon 1866, 174). Unfortunately for the parishioners it appears as though these improvements were not made until 1713, when the wall was raised and new doorways introduced (Burgh Records v, 506). Modifications continued to be made into the 19th century, by which time the Corporation was responsible for the upkeep of the churches. In 1812 the west window was re-opened and new seats installed (Fawcett 1997, 35). The congregation of Outer High Church continued to use the nave until 1835.

Records have survived of a number of modifications to the crypt which have archaeological implications. Prior to the establishment of the Barony congregation in the crypt (the 'lower' or 'Laigh Kirk') in 1595 (Chalmers 1914, 21), one of the magistrates, the second minister and others were instructed to inspect accounts of *penitentis* money and to arrange for removal of pavement from the crypt to the College Kirk in 1588 (Renwick 1908, 317; Gordon 1866, 323). Presumably the stones contained inscriptions associated with or of interest to the College. This was only the first of several changes to the floor level of the crypt, which are associated with its use for burials. In 1753 William Crawfurd of Possil erected a railing to his burial place in the 'south east corner of the Barony Church Isle in the arch where the well is. . .' (SRO, CR4/144, folio 26). But shortly after this, in 1798, the Barony congregation ceased to use the lower church (Chalmers 1914, 21) and the whole crypt was transformed into a burial place. This involved introducing about one metre of earth over the floor and the erection of railings to mark out the lairs (Old Scots for a 'burial plot', often intended for a family) (Figure 2.53). In 1843 the accumulated earth was removed from the lower church and, as part of the restorations to the crypt and the chapter house, the original levels of the floors were restored and the windows were opened up (SRO, MW.1.188, Part III, Letter from Campbell to Lords Commissioners of HM Woods and Forests, undated). Significantly from an archaeological perspective, this included the repaving of the crypt (SRO, CR4/144, 7 April 1843).

Modern restoration

In the 1830s there was a growing appreciation of the architectural significance of the building which led to the execution of detailed architectural drawings and the publication of proposals for restoration work

(Honeyman 1898). Alongside this interest in the fabric a notion was advanced that the building was Crown property and this was accepted in 1835, by which time there was only a single congregation using the choir (Fawcett 1990a, 111). Major programmes of demolition and reconstruction were undertaken in the 1840s and 1850s, which included the removal of the western towers in 1846 and 1848 (Macaulay 1997), all traces of the Outer Kirk including the partition, and the lofts from the choir (1852) (Fawcett 1990a, 111). This latter action was not well received by the more conservative churchmen.

During the 20th century there was an active building programme which attempted to combine conservative restoration work with operations which allowed the cathedral to remain in active use. From an archaeological perspective the most unfortunate phase of this work was the installation of a central heating system via a system of subfloor ducts in 1914–16. These brick-built ducts were approximately 1m deep x 0.8m wide and ran along the aisles on the nave, choir and crypt. No archaeological observations were made during the extensive disturbances caused by the construction of the ducts, but when they were rebuilt in 1994 a record was made of the exposed sections. The one positive result of this work was that it brought to light the first archaeological evidence for the 12th-century cathedrals in the form of the well-know painted voussoir (Radford and Stones 1964), which is discussed below (see Sections 3.2 and 3.3).

1.2 ACCOUNT OF THE EXCAVATIONS

Previous archaeological investigations

There have been a number of excavations in the cathedral, all but one of which have been associated with construction work or burial. The one purely research-driven excavation was undertaken by Peter MacGregor Chalmers in 1898 (Chalmers 1905). His research objective was to discover the apse of an early church which enclosed the site of St Kentigern's tomb as preserved in the configuration of the crypt. MacGregor Chalmers opened up trenches just to the north and south of the tomb. He reported the presence of an apse, which confirmed his expectations. Unfortunately the re-excavation of his trenches revealed no trace of earlier building works of any shape.

A small-scale excavation was undertaken by the late Alastair Gordon on the occasion of the installation of electrical ducts in the west end of the crypt in 1978. Although working in tightly confined trenches, he identified a drain, presumed to be associated with the altar at the tomb of St Kentigern (Gordon 1980).

Recent work

The exterior trenches

The excavations reported upon here are the consequence of two distinct programmes of works at the cathedral. In 1988 excavations were carried out by the Scottish Urban Archaeological Trust (SUAT) as part of a scheme to landscape the cathedral precinct in anticipation of Glasgow's year as 'European City of Culture' in 1990. Excavations were confined to two areas on either side of the main west door. These excavations were sponsored by Strathclyde Regional Council and took place over eleven weeks during the summer. A separate programme of excavations, undertaken by SUAT in 1987, allowed substantial portions of the original bishop's palace to be excavated. This showed that until the 14th century the bishop's palace stood hard by the existing west door of the cathedral (McBrien 1988). Although each of these excavations was undertaken under different circumstances they were all limited to investigations only in those areas which were to be effected by improvement works.

The interior trenches

During the winter of 1992–93, the Glasgow University Archaeological Research Division (Driscoll 1993) was commissioned to excavate a series of trenches around the interior in advance of the installation of new heating and electrical systems (Figure 1.7). Trenches were located where new ducts were to be installed below the floor in the nave, choir, crypt and session room (or treasury). These works were sponsored by Historic Scotland and benefited from the support of the Historic Scotland works squad.

The first area to be excavated in 1992 was a trench in the choir running N–S behind the present communion table and immediately west of the easternmost columns. Little was expected here, because the trench lay over the vaulting of the crypt, and, apart from architectural fragments, no significant discoveries were made.

Two trenches were dug in the crypt, both running N–S (Figure 1.7). The E trench was located just to the west of the Lady Chapel and the W trench was located immediately to the west of the tomb of St Kentigern, with the exact locations being determined by the configuration of the piers. The nominal dimensions of the trenches (1.2m wide x 1.0m deep) were designed to satisfy the requirements of the heating system ducts, though the precise trench shape was determined by the staggered run of the floor slabs, some of which were undermined by graves and had to be removed for safety reasons (Figure 1.8).

Initially work in these trenches focused on the modern burials and the back-filled trenches dug by Peter MacGregor Chalmers in 1898. These modern features had removed earlier archaeological deposits, but a few features did survive. These trenches were excavated completely to the natural subsoils, which left the foundations of the existing building standing proud. The foundations were constructed of reused masonry, so when trenches were cut through the foundations for the heating ducts, they were cut by hand. The work was undertaken carefully over a period of many weeks by members of the Historic Scotland works squad. All of the removed stones were examined for carved features or painted surfaces.

The excavations in the nave began with a trench running along the south side of the north arcade (Figures 1.9–1.11). The trench could not be completed before Christmas, so it was temporarily covered over for the holiday season. In January a second trench was opened along the north side of the south arcade. Because of the earlier start, the excavations in the northern trench were more exhaustive. The old ground surface was found to follow the natural slope of the site, so the archaeological levels containing the earliest deposits were relatively close to the floor level in the west end but became increasingly deeply buried under graves and made-up ground towards the crossing. An attempt was made to completely excavate these trenches, but the depth of archaeology was too great. In the event, efforts concentrated on the northern trench and the locations of critical features were targeted. At two places in the N trench, the excavations were taken to depths of over two metres. These were to examine the conjunction of walls near the third column and the old ground surface at the extreme east end of the trench. Elsewhere, the excavations were not much deeper than one metre, thus most of these trenches were not completely excavated. Special attention was taken to avoid leaving incompletely excavated burials and no burials were left partially dug unless they lay well beyond the trench edge.

A small trench was excavated from the session room across the lower flight and the half-landing of the north crypt stair. Initially this was intended to be a small trench to take electrical cables only and thus was much smaller than the others (0.3m wide). Very little was recovered from this trench. The installation of the electrical panel in the session room required a further excavation, which did reveal several burials.

Overall the excavations lasted for 10 weeks and involved on average seven archaeologists. All of the excavations were done by hand, using trowels for the most part. Attention was focused on recording architectural elements and burials. All features were extensively recorded using photographs and measured drawings. There was no systematic programme of environmental sampling, but samples were taken from all suitable contexts such as hearths and waterlogged ditches. For experimental purposes samples of soil were taken from the abdomens of a small number of burials to look for gut remains. The team's bone

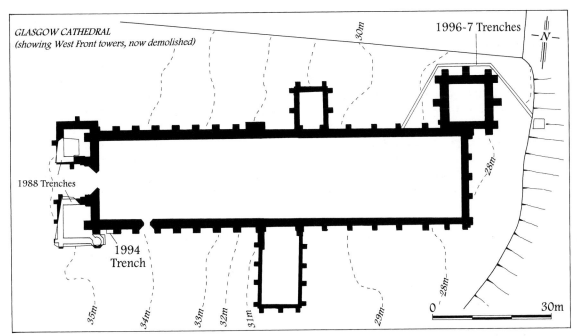

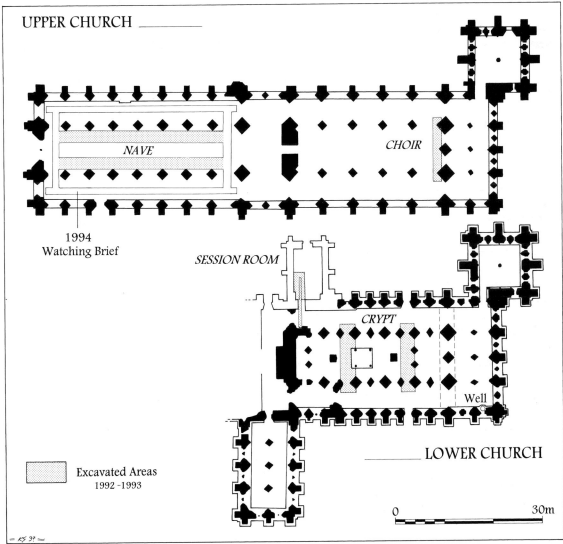

FIGURE 1.7

Plan showing the locations of all excavation trenches

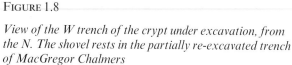

FIGURE 1.9

The N nave trench under excavation, from the W

FIGURE 1.8

View of the W trench of the crypt under excavation, from the N. The shovel rests in the partially re-excavated trench of MacGregor Chalmers

specialist was on site for the entire excavation, which allowed damaged or fragmentary remains to be recorded *in situ*. Certainly this enhanced the quality of the burial records.

From a purely scholarly perspective there were two factors which limited the value of the excavations. Firstly, to allow the cathedral to continue to function, the trenches could not be greatly extended beyond what was required for the works programme. Where opportunities were created by the fortuitous run of the floor slabs the trenches were extended latterly. This was particularly valuable in the crypt where extensions revealed the bronze hoard and allowed the late 19th-century excavations to be fully understood. The second limitation was that not all of the trenches could be bottomed. In part this was due to lack of resources, but more significantly many of the deposits in the nave were too deep to be excavated without shoring the trenches. For most of the length of the nave the excavations were taken below the level of the works programme, but it was possible to examine the deposits completely in only a few locations. Clearly it would have been desirable to fully excavate the nave trenches,

but it is doubtful whether the deeper deposits could have been interpreted in such narrow trenches.

Following the main excavations, the old ductwork from the early 20th-century heating system was demolished. This provided an opportunity to glimpse the deposits in areas outwith the formal excavations. By cleaning the exposed sections a number of useful observations were made.

During the excavation the cathedral remained open to the public. Although no special arrangements were made for visitors, it proved possible to keep interested members of the public informed about the progress of the excavations. In addition to casual visitors, a number of distinguished scholars and churchmen visited the excavation. In this respect the 1992–93 excavations were similar to the MacGregor Chalmers excavations of 1898, which attracted the interest of an impressive set of visitors, among them Archbishop Eyre, the Minister Rev Muir, the Principal of the University, the Professor of Ecclesiastical History and distinguished Scottish antiquaries (Stones 1970, 147). Almost a century later it was gratifying that so many contemporary scholars took the trouble to view the excavations and offer gentle advice. These included the Minister and a cardinal (then archbishop), four professors and many others.

FIGURE 1.10

The full extent of the nave excavations, from the W. Copyright J Lee

1.3 THE RECORDING SYSTEM

A continuous number system was used for the recording of the stratigraphy. The context numbers were assigned in blocks to specific areas (001–005 in the choir, trench code CH; 101–150 in the crypt East, trench code CE; 201–252 in the crypt West, trench code CW; 301–458 in the nave North, trench code NN; 501–603 in the nave South, trench code NS; 651–72 in the Session House, trench code SH; trench code WT 1000–1160 have been used for the tower trenches. Minor excavations and watching briefs outside the cathedral are designated ED for E of SE door and ND for N of the NW tower.) In the field, burials were given individual numbers for the skeleton, coffin, grave fill and grave cut if they were present, however, for the sake of simplicity in the text only the skeleton number is used to describe a burial, unless attention is being drawn to a specific feature. Finds were allocated a separate number system (sf 1–1000).

Multi-context plans, of which there were 26, were drawn at a scale of 1:20. Sections and elevations, of which there were 25, were drawn at a scale of 1:10. Figure 1.11 provides a key to the location of the nave sections. The photographic record comprises a comprehensive set of 35mm black-and-white prints and colour slides, recorded on *pro forma* sheets. A small number of additional shots were commissioned in a medium format from Joehari Lee.

The archive

The archive comprises the original documentation noted above and material generated during the post-excavation process. The latter comprises context listings, in both context and phase order, small find record sheets, an interim report and the various specialist research reports. The archive is deposited at the National Monuments Record of Scotland, Edinburgh, where full texts of all specialist reports are available.

1.4 POST-EXCAVATION RESEARCH PROGRAMME

Although it was widely expected that the excavations would discover a large number of burials, the complexity and quality of the evidence greatly exceeded expectations. As a consequence the post-excavation programme was longer and more extensive than originally anticipated. The post-excavation research design established research priorities which focused on the medieval evidence, especially the structural remains. A second priority was to analyse the burials in detail, because it was such a good assemblage and to allow the bones to be reburied in due course. Effort was thus directed towards the evidence relating to the least well-documented aspects of the cathedral: its architectural origins and the medieval lay population.

The material dating to the post-medieval period was the least well-served by these research priorities. Most of the small finds are post-medieval in date and the vast majority of these are bits of coffin furniture or related to burial. Although the quantity of these fittings is large, they were scarcely ever found *in situ* and often were in poor condition. Although the best of coffin evidence was examined, there is room for more work here because so little has been done in Scotland to date. For instance, we could have undertaken a more detailed topological study of the coffin grips, but decided not to because the chronological control was poor.

A second area where further research would probably produce interesting results concerns the identities of the burials. In the nave it may be possible to identify families by their relationship to the altars of particular saints or by reference to the memorials fixed to the walls and roofs of the aisles. There is more abundant evidence about who was buried in the crypt. There is probably sufficient information in the crypt inscriptions, burial registers, lair plans and other documentation to allow the social context of these 19th-century burials to be recovered in some detail.

1.5 PHASING

A scheme of phasing has been imposed upon the archaeological data to make it more manageable and

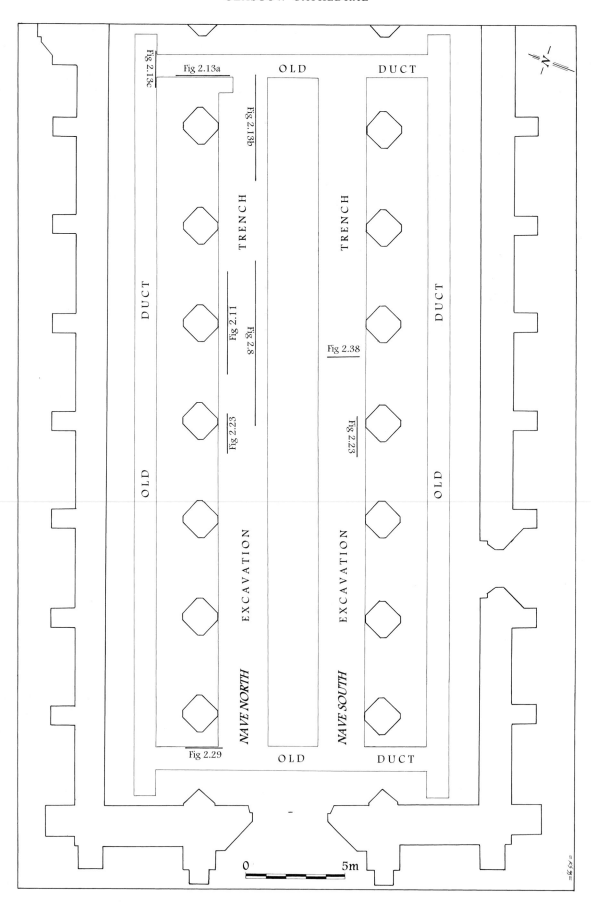

FIGURE 1.11

Location of the trenches excavated in the nave and their sections

to allow comparisons to be made between areas (Figure 1.4). The phasing is closely tied into the architectural activity, so the phases are not of equal duration nor are their boundaries defined with equal precision. Also it will be recognised that phases 5 and 6 pertain only to the nave.

Because the phasing derives from the building programmes, it has some inherent limitations. The principal constraint is that although the recorded consecrations give a specific date at which part of the building could be brought into use for worship, that date cannot be applied to the completion of the building as a whole. Perhaps more frustrating is that few detailed records of the progress of the construction of the final cathedral exist (phases 4 and 5), so the construction chronology is heavily dependant upon art historical assessment. It is acknowledged that the phasing presumes that the major structural remains have been correctly identified with the appropriate, documented building programme. This is not a straightforward problem and is addressed as the specific archaeological material is presented.

Phase 1: pre 12th-century activity

An area of old ground surface towards the west end of nave which was not too heavily used for graves was cut by two shallow (?drainage) ditches and a substantial hearth, dated by radiocarbon to AD 670–1020. A portion of an oriented burial seen below the earliest cathedral was radiocarbon dated to AD 660–890.

Phase 2: cathedral of Bishop John (early 12th century)

The footing courses of what appears to have been the western wall of a masonry building of the same orientation as the existing building is identified as the cathedral of John, the first bishop, dedicated in AD 1136. A burial disturbed by the construction of the second cathedral produced a radiocarbon date of AD 1047–1280 and was presumably interred in the nave of the first cathedral.

Phase 3: cathedral of Bishop Jocelin (late 12th century)

Portions of the north and south walls of a second phase of building operations underpin the columns of the present nave. These walls include architectural fragments from the earlier cathedral. This nave is assumed to have belonged to the building consecrated by Bishop Jocelin in 1197, but was never completed. Sculpted architectural masonry and fragments of wall painting found elsewhere in the excavations greatly extend our knowledge of the decorative programme of this phase of cathedral building.

Phase 4: early 13th-century cathedral

The aisle foundations of the nave begun around 1200 utilised the walls of the previous incomplete nave as the foundations for the arcade and were extended half the length of the nave. The foundations for a temporary timber-framed west front probably mark the end of the first building campaign in the nave. The extended eastern arm of the cathedral including the crypt was probably started around the 1240s and completed by the 1260s. The rubble foundations of the existing crypt incorporate the demolished fragments of Jocelin's cathedral. There is scant evidence for medieval burial in the central area of the crypt.

Phase 5: completion of the laying out of the nave (mid 13th century)

The architectural evidence strongly suggests that work on the nave was suspended around 1240 while work progressed on Bondington's extended eastern limb. About 1280 work on the nave resumed. The timber partition was removed and the pier foundations were extended westward. Deep deposits of white sand, the spoil of stone working, and spreads of mortar were used to raise the floor in the east half of the nave. The construction of the NW tower began shortly after the completion of the nave, in the early 14th century.

Phase 6: burial activity in the nave (13th–17th centuries)

Once complete, the nave became a focus for popular lay devotions, most conspicuously represented by burials. Burial was extremely dense in the middle bays of the nave, but it was possible to identify a few designated burial places, family or fraternal burial lairs. A personal seal, dating from around 1300, was recovered from one of these lairs. Evidence of coffin furniture indicates that burial continued in the nave. This late burial was largely confined to the east bays of the nave, outwith the areas actually used for worship.

Phase 7: post-Reformation structures and burials (17th–19th centuries)

Foundations of the structures provided for reformed worship in the western portion of the nave were the most conspicuous evidence of the changes made to the building following the Reformation. These changes led to the restriction of burial to the area of the crossing. Reformation unrest probably accounts for the burial of two massive 13th–14th century bronze mortars in the crypt. In the early 19th century the lower church was used for burial.

Phase 8: modern refurbishment (1835–present)

Evidence for the 'restoration', begun after 1835, includes the demolished foundations of the towers and of the internal partitions in the nave, paving in the crypt and fragments of plaster used to repair the damage to the capitals in the choir.

1.6 THE RADIOCARBON DATES

Three radiocarbon samples were selected to provide some absolute dating support for the stratigraphic sequence. In particular it was hoped that the dates could give an indication of the age of the earliest activity on the site, which pre-dated the building works. Secondly, the samples were selected in order to assess the age of the earliest phases of building work, believed on historical grounds to date from the 12th century. The early masonry exposed during the excavations did not contain any definitive diagnostic features, so the chronological interpretation of the masonry was largely dependant on brief historical notices. The samples were analysed at the Glasgow University Radiocarbon Dating facility at the Scottish Universities Research and Reactor Centre, East Kilbride (see Appendix).

ARCHAEOLOGICAL STRUCTURES

2.1 THE NAVE
by S T Driscoll

Two trenches were excavated in the central part of the nave in 1992–93. Both ran the length of the nave on the side of the main arcade towards the central space. The nominal trench dimensions specified for the heating ducts were 1.2m wide by 1.1m deep, but opportunities were taken to excavate deeper to investigate particular features. The N trench was the first excavated and it was dug more intensively than the S because questions relating to many of the common features were resolved in the N trench. In addition to the main N and S trenches, detailed observations were made as the old ducts in the aisles and at the E and W ends of the nave were removed in 1994. The full extent of the excavated trenches and the old duct trenches is shown above (Figure 1.11). Midway along the nave the natural slope of the cathedral site falls away sharply to the E, towards the Molendinar Burn. The lie of the land has implications for the survival of early features. At the W end the old ground surface, containing features pre-dating the nave, was located immediately below the bedding for the paved floor, while to the E the build up of deposits above the original ground surface was 2.5m deep.

Phase 1: pre 12th-century activity

A number of features was recorded which pre-date the construction of the first cathedral. These include burials, two ditches, a hearth and a single posthole. The ditches and hearth had been disturbed by later burials but survived well enough to make it clear that they represent activity prior to late 13th-century building works. This is supported by radiocarbon evidence.

At the W end of the trench were two ditches which ran roughly parallel and crossed the trench at a slight SW/NE angle (Figures 2.1 and 2.2). Both ditches (362 and 402) cut the natural clay (329) and were positioned about 3.5m apart. They both widened slightly to the north as they crossed the trench. The westernmost of the two (362) had been partially cut away by a grave (330) but its width could be seen to vary from 0.92m where cut by the grave, to 1.1m at the north baulk. The ditch had steeply sloping sides with a rounded base and a depth of 0.4m. The grey brown silty clay fill (363) contained flecks of charcoal, some burnt bone and a small proportion of little angular stones. The second of the two ditches (402) had a similar width, varying between 0.86m at the south baulk to 1.2m at the north baulk. Although the upper part of the ditch had been cut away by grave 399, the ditch survived to a depth of 0.15m and was filled with bands of silty and sandy clay (403) (Figure 2.3). The uppermost fill was of redeposited natural clay. Fill 403 contained an iron coffin fitting (sf 533) and three iron nails (sf 532), both of which must derive from the grave. The ditches seemed designed to carry water away from the crown of the precinct to the NW. Their alignment corresponds to the drains seen under the towers (see Section 2.5). Water in this part of the site remains a problem; on wet days water seeped into the old ducts in the NW corner of the nave. In addition to serving as drains the double ditches may represent a boundary for the early medieval churchyard.

Immediately to the E of ditch 362 was a spread of burnt soil and charcoal (359) (Figure 2.4). This hearth consisted of a concentrated spread of charcoal (0.15m deep) which was overlain by a thin spread of relatively

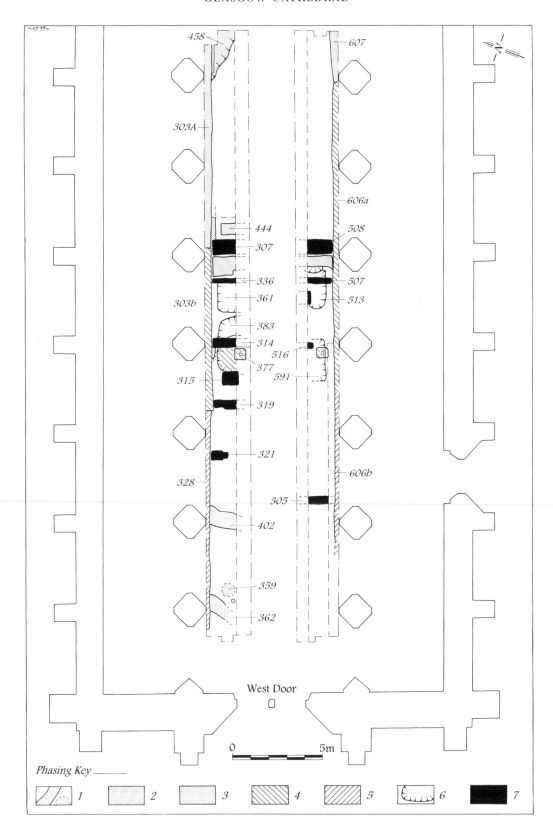

FIGURE 2.1

Phased plan of major features in the nave. 1: pre 12th century, 2: early 12th century, 3: late 12th century, 4: early 13th century, 5: mid 13th century, 6: 13th–17th centuries, 7: 17th–19th centuries

clean orange clay and surrounded by a halo of orange/grey clay and ash with frequent charcoal inclusions. The charcoal concentration was exposed through the clay at the centre of the feature. The hearth had been disturbed to the NE by a grave cut (337). A sample of the charcoal composed of barley and oats, and wood

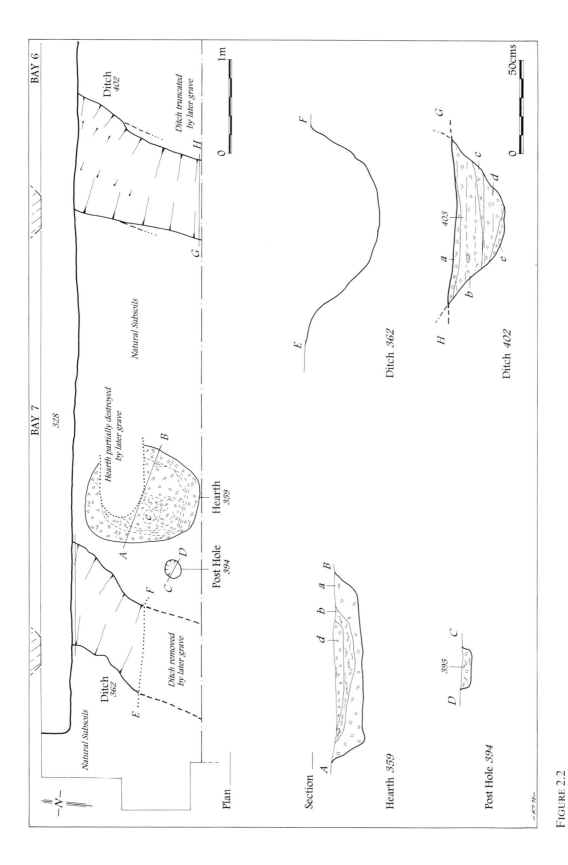

FIGURE 2.2

Detailed plan of phase 1 features in the nave (N trench; for location of sections see Figure 1.11)

21

FIGURE 2.3

View of ditch 402 from the S. The small scale stands on the base of the ditch

FIGURE 2.4

View of hearth 359, cut by a later burial, with ditch 362 to the right of the north arrow

from hazelnut, oak, alder, hazel, cherry and yew trees was dated using conventional radiocarbon techniques. It has produced a calibrated age range of AD 772–980 (GU 7301). Possibly associated with these features was a small single posthole (394) located between ditch 362 and the hearth. It had a diameter of 0.2m and a depth of 0.06m. The posthole fill (395) was grey black soil with some lumps of clay and contained large charcoal flecks.

Burials

The earliest feature on the site was a grave (456) which pre-dates the cathedral by some four or five centuries (Figure 2.5). It was discovered by the third bay where it had been cut by the earliest wall (368) on the site, believed to be part of the early 12th-century cathedral (see phase 2 below). The skeleton (sk) 455 had been further disturbed by the 13th-century foundations but survived further disturbance because it lay some 1.5m below the present floor level. Although only the left arm could be excavated, the presence of the pelvis and spine make certain that this was a grave and not stray bones. The skeleton was orientated E–W, but no sign of a coffin was noted. The grave cut penetrated only a short way into the natural and appears to have been quite close to ground level at the time of the construction of the 12th-century wall 368. The condition of the bone was notably poorer than the 13th-century and

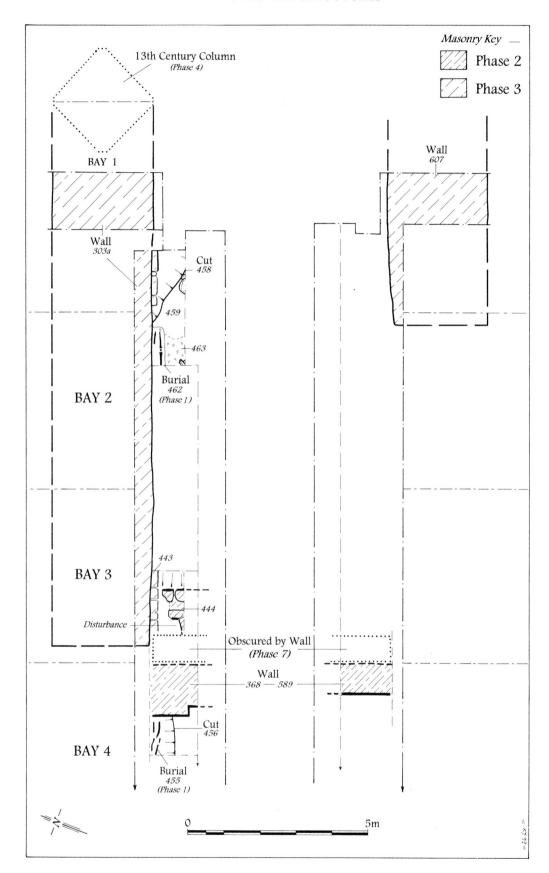

FIGURE 2.5

Plan of radiocarbon-dated burials and phase 2 and 3 structures in the nave

FIGURE 2.6

View down the deepest part of the excavation in the nave, near the crossing. The legs of burial 462 are visible in the bottom right corner. Just to the left of the feet the oblique shadow is cut 458

later burials which is consistent with the calibrated radiocarbon date of AD 677–860 (GU 4746).

There are at least two other early graves in this trench. Sk 462 was seen in the first bay at a depth of 1.3m (Figure 2.6) and had been cut by the works of the second cathedral. The calibrated radiocarbon age for this burial is AD 1169–1263, so it could date to either phase 1 or 2. Two further burials (367 and 370) were disturbed by the construction of the nave foundations and partially embedded in the mortar of the wall 328. They are certainly pre-13th century but they were not radiocarbon dated.

Finds and dating evidence

Few artefacts were recovered from these features and none could be used to date the foundation. The nails from the upper fill of ditch 402 seem to derive from later coffins. The general layer of grey silt or loamy clay (556) contained a single iron nail, a piece of iron slag and two sherds of Scottish East Coast White Gritty Ware (hereafter SECWGW). This fabric is dated to between the 12th and 15th centuries and must represent material trampled into this context as activity increased in the early 12th century. The dating therefore relies largely on stratigraphic relationships and the radiocarbon evidence.

Interpretation

Grave 455 provides the earliest evidence for activity at the cathedral site. This badly-preserved, E–W orientated grave is presumably part of a cemetery associated with an early medieval church. The two ditches in the

N trench were probably intended as drainage ditches, although the fills were not particularly stony (such as to promote drainage) so they may also have served as boundary ditches. Neither ditch was observed in the S trench, so it is impossible to comment on their wider significance.

Phase 2: cathedral of Bishop John (early 12th century)

The earliest masonry building fragments consist of a wall (368/589) running N–S between the third and fourth bays of the nave (Figure 2.5). These features had been substantially demolished, but one or two courses of wall above the foundations survived. Unfortunately this wall had been disturbed by later construction in medieval (wall 303) and post-medieval times (wall 307). The post-medieval wall 307, which served as the E wall of the Outer High Kirk, obscured the east face of wall 368. Resources allowed this early structure (368) to be investigated in detail only in the N trench, but substantially the same wall 589 was observed in the S trench. Apart from features associated with the wall few other deposits could be assigned to this phase as generally the excavations were halted before reaching the required depth.

The clearest view of the early wall was seen on the W side where later graves (especially 361) had exposed the wall face and removed some of the wall core. The wall was built of dull red sandstone ashlar, which had been finely dressed and was tightly jointed (Figure 2.7). The base course was marked out by a simple chamfer (0.09m deep). The only structural feature was a simple buttress-like projection (0.9m wide x 0.25m deep). The core of the wall consisted of dark grey sandstone rubble bonded in a pale brown lime mortar.

FIGURE 2.7

*The junction of three walls in the nave. The chamfered
plinth of the earliest wall 368 under the metre scale is
thought to be the W wall of the cathedral consecrated in
1136. To the left is wall 303b, which is abutted by post-
medieval wall 307*

A wall (589) which apparently corresponds to wall
368 was noted in the south trench (Figure 2.5). It had
a chamfered plinth set on an alignment corresponding
to that of wall 368. The two walls occupied parallel
alignments and were constructed of similar material,
although they do not line up. This suggests that the
stretch of walling in the N trench comes from near the
corner of a doorway where a greater thickness might
be expected. The E face and full width of wall (589)
was also obscured in the S trench by the construction
of wall 508 which corresponds to wall 307 in the N
trench. A mortar spread (603) immediately west of
wall 589 may represent the fill of the construction
trench for the wall. Disturbed, disarticulated bones
were contained within the mortar and the construction
of the wall must have disturbed an earlier grave. The
mortar spread overlay a layer of brown silty clay
containing charcoal and sand (602) and a burial (600)
partially exposed by a later grave (513).

The full width of the wall 368 could not be determined with confidence because of the position of a
later wall (307). This post-medieval wall was set into

the core of the early wall and it was not clear how
much of the core had been removed (Figure 2.8).
Minimally we should assume a width of between
1.5–2.0m. A spread of moderately compacted mixed
brown mortar with small rounded fragments of white
sandstone and clay was traced by excavating E under
wall 307. This spread ran into another less substantial
N–S running masonry structure (444). Only the
foundations survive but they are clearly rougher in
build than was seen in the chamfered stretch of wall
and, although the facing stones were of similar pale
red sandstone to wall 368, here the core was of crushed
white sandstone (Figure 2.9). On the E face of 444 a
short stretch of a chamfered edge survived. Despite
the difference in core material and the apparently
coarser finish of wall 444, it is possible that 368 and
444 are both elements of the same structure, ie the W
wall of a building with the same orientation as the
existing cathedral. If so this would make the wall 3m
thick.

A spread of mixed, pale brown mortar (446)
extended E from wall 444 and may well represent
spillage during the construction process. Above this
was a sequence of fine-textured light grey sand and
charcoal-rich lenses (445). This accumulation may
indicate that the wall stood in the open for some time,
although whether during construction or after demolition could not be determined. The earliest deposit of
post-demolition rubble here was a compact layer of
yellow-brown mortar containing fragments of stone
rubble (442) which appears to derive from 444.

To the W of wall 368 a layer of compact mixed
brown-grey silt (437) accumulated against the wall
face (Figure 2.10). The surface of this layer exhibited
evidence of burning in several places which suggest
that this represented the contemporary ground surface
following the completion of the structure. This putative ground surface sealed the grave (456) containing
burial 455 which provided the early medieval radiocarbon date discussed above.

The other features associated with this phase are
less closely linked in stratigraphic terms. To the W of
wall 368 a small pit (450) was excavated 0.70m
through the putative ground surface. The pit fill (451)
contained angular rubble and the old ground surface
(441) contained smaller fragments of building material
which seems to relate them to the construction of the
first cathedral. They were sealed by a layer (373/406)
of medium to dark-brown silty loam containing
decayed pieces of sandstone and red-orange clay. This
layer was present throughout the whole trench and
was found to contain 18 sherds of pottery
(SECWGW), 12 of which were from the same vessel
(sf 702, sf 704). Approximately 10m to the E of wall
368 features were encountered which may be contemporary with the early building work. Here, almost
2.5m below the existing floor level, a layer of hard,
compact grey clay with mortar inclusions (453)
overlay a small area of flat stones (464) and a thin

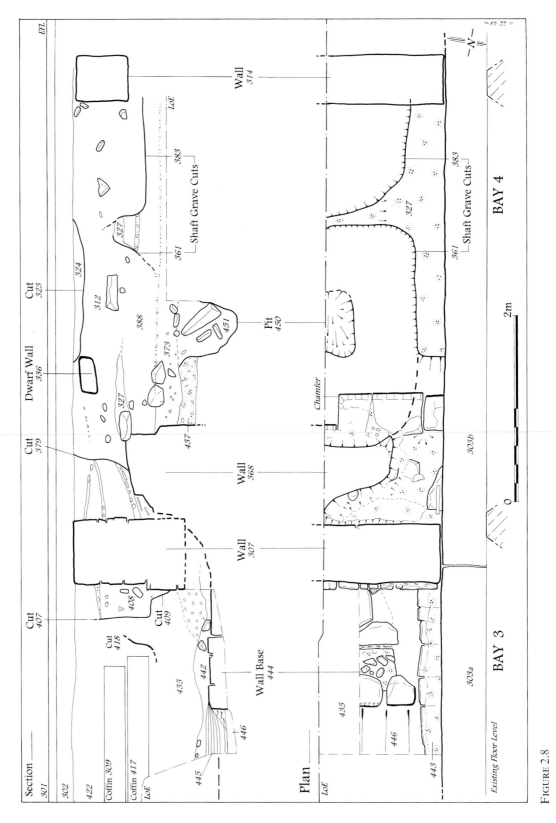

FIGURE 2.8

Detailed plan and section of walls 307, 368 and 444, and the burial lairs in the N nave trench

FIGURE 2.9

View from above of wall 444, which consists of facing stones with a core of white sandstone

FIGURE 2.10

View from E looking at the elevation of post-medieval wall 307. To the right the step in the foundations of 303a is marked by the horizontal scale

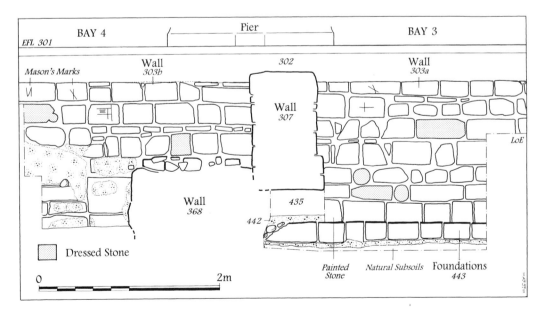

FIGURE 2.11

Elevation of wall 303 in the nave

FIGURE 2.12

View of the full width of 303a (same as 710) revealed after the early 20th-century brick duct was removed

layer (463) of pink and brown clay containing charcoal flecks. None of these features can be readily interpreted as only a small area was available for investigation, but the presence of mortar in layer 453 and the compacted surface suggests it represented the ground level following the initial building work. In addition to these *in situ* features there are architectural elements re-used in the phase-3 building works, which derive from the earlier phase-2 structure. These include a number of half-drums which appear to have been made for cylindrical piers and other masonry used in wall 303a. The half-drums are 0.7m in diameter and may represent free-standing columns or engaged wall shafts (see Section 3.2). The extent to which wall 303a was constructed from re-used stone is unclear, but in addition to the column drums, there are moulding fragments, a painted ashlar block and a number of blocks with masons' marks and signs of earlier use. It seems likely therefore that wall 303a is substantially built of masonry from the earliest church.

Dating evidence

There are no scientific dates or datable finds from the phase-2 structures. Some guidance to age is provided by grave 455 which dates to AD 660–890 and must have been long-forgotten by the time that the buttressed wall 368 was built. The radiocarbon date of grave 462 is less relevant, because the phase-2 built features cannot be stratigraphically linked to it.

The most valuable evidence for dating is provided by the historical record of the consecration of the first cathedral in 1136 (see Section 1.1). It seems likely that this chamfered plinth and buttressed wall are part of this structure. Stratigraphically it is the earliest

masonry building in the sequence and the architectural features, simple though they are, are consistent with a 12th-century date.

Interpretation

The main elements attributed to this phase appear to be part of the W wall of the first cathedral built by Bishop John. The most conspicuous feature of wall 368 is the shallow buttress-like feature. If the central axis of the original cathedral has been retained in the later buildings then the buttress could be one of a pair clasping the NW corner of the cathedral. The absence of a buttress in the S trench suggests, however, that although the later cathedral showed the same orientation, the centreline of the first may have differed.

The use of red sandstone is interesting, since later buildings preferred a cream-coloured stone. The presence of cream sandstone in the core of wall 444 may indicate that contrasting red and cream stone were used for the external walls. Cream sandstone was certainly used in the interior. All of the re-used stone in wall 303, including the half-column drums, was of a cream colour.

Overall the scale and sophistication indicated by the phase-2 building are greater than had been expected for the early 12th-century cathedral. The full implications for the design are explored elsewhere (see Section 1.1; Mentel 1998).

Phase 3: cathedral of Bishop Jocelin (late 12th century)

This phase is represented by substantial but unfinished building works, on the same orientation as the first cathedral (phase 2), but apparently on a much larger scale.

The most closely investigated element was a wall (303a) which ran under the N arcade of the nave and provided a foundation for the later 13th-century piers (Figure 2.11). This wall was well constructed of cream sandstone ashlar incorporating many re-used architectural fragments. It extended from just W of the crossing through the third bay, where it terminated. The corresponding wall (607) on the S side of the nave was of similar construction but extended only through the first bay. These two walls presumably represent the N and S walls of an unfinished nave. Although the S wall was not investigated in detail it is quite clear that it was never finished. Moreover, there is no sign of a return wall on the W side. There is a slight suggestion in the masonry that the W front of this building was intended to occupy the position of the earlier W front (368), because it is just at this point that the wall terminates. The details of this terminus were unfortunately obscured by a later, post-medieval wall (307), but it seems possible that the original W front was still standing during the construction of 303a.

The character of the wall (303a) merits further discussion. The full depth of the wall was examined in the first and third bays on the N side where the excavations were extended below the level required for the new heating ducts. Further observations were made of the full width of the wall (303a = 710) during the watching brief as the old ducting was removed (Figure 2.12). The wall survives to a depth of 1.7m and is 2.8m wide (Figure 2.13). The N, presumably exterior, face was not extensively exposed but appears to have been finely finished with tight jointing. The quality of the masonry in the S wall (607) was not as fine as in the N (303a).

The inner face was much more varied but also exhibited a high level of craftsmanship. The courses are even, the re-used masonry has been skilfully adapted to the coursing and almost none of the yellow mortar was present on the face of the wall (Figure 2.14). Whether this was a face designed to be seen is a point to which we will return.

The wall (303a) appears to have been set into the natural sub-soil in a steeply profiled foundation trench (458) which crossed the excavation trench diagonally (Figures 2.6 and 2.15). This trench cut the stone spread 464 and layer 453, and appears to represent a widening of the construction trench for the foundations at this point. A stepping-out of the foundations (303a) was visible within, and coincided with, the line of the cut. The step in the foundations peters out at the edge of the cut and the foundation trench may have been widened to allow for a strengthening of the foundations at this point. The cut was not fully excavated, nor was the base of the wall reached. Elsewhere the foundation masonry (443) was set close against the bedding trench and, as has been noted earlier, these foundations cut a burial (462). The

foundations (443) step out 0.22m from the wall face and contain the most regular of the stone used on the inner face (Figure 2.16). Although the full stretch of the wall was not exposed, this projecting foundation step appears to follow the gradual slope of the site, dropping some 0.2m in a run of 10m. At the base of this stepped course a yellow mortar (442) lapped on to the face and spread away from the wall (Figures 2.10 and 2.16). The pattern of the mortar-spread suggests a pause in the building work or a seasonal lift.

The material used in wall 303 appears to be largely recycled from the earlier church on the site (Figure 2.11). The fabric included a number of carved and moulded stones, a stone with traces of red paint, several mason's marks and a topmost course which was composed of half-column drums (Figures 2.17–2.20). The half-drums had been placed so that the flat surface was outermost with the curve to the inside of the wall. Even where these had been removed in the past the curving impression was preserved in the mortar surface. There appears to be another course made up of these drums at a lower level in the wall. There can be little doubt that these derive from the first cathedral.

The thick mortar layer (442) at the third bay and at the foot of wall 303 was interpreted as debris from its construction. It was overlain by a layer of brown silt (435) which contained flecks of reddish-orange clay/loam with inclusions of charcoal, bone and mortar. Traces of a layer of mixed dark brownish-grey silt containing fragments of clay, bone, mortar and stone chippings (434), which overlay 435, survived as only a small fragment abutting the foundations of wall 307, since elsewhere it was cut away by later graves.

When the construction work for the wall 303a was finished, the foundation trench (458) was backfilled and the level was rapidly raised by a series of deposits (453, 457, 452, 448, 447, 429, 427, 426, 423) containing varying quantities of clay, rubble, mortar and sand (Figure 2.13). These were explored only on a limited scale and produced no finds, but seem to have effectively buried most of wall 303 and established a ground surface about 1m below the existing floor level. The deeper excavation carried out at the extreme E end of the N trench revealed layer 453, at the base of the excavations, a possible working surface for the construction of foundation 303. This and the succeeding layers appear to represent soil and rubble dumped to raise the floor level. Above 457 was a loosely compacted layer (452) of sandstone and mortar rubble which thinned to the E where it was overlain by, and became indistinguishable from, a compact mortar spread (448). This layer was hard packed and contained some sandstone fragments and was in turn overlain by a layer of rubble (447), which consisted of small sandstone fragments in a matrix of dark-brown sandy silt and mortar. This was overlain by another layer (457), a dark-brown clayey silt which also contained flecks of mortar. This, in turn, was overlain by a thicker (0.32m),

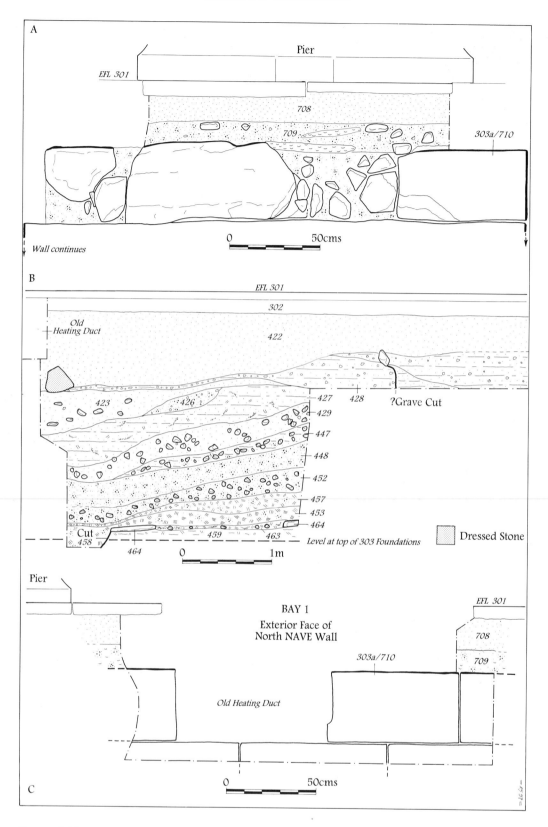

FIGURE 2.13

Detailed elevations (A and C) and section (B) relating to the E end of wall 303a/710

coarser, more stony rubble layer (429) which contained lumps and flecks of yellowy-brown mortar in a light creamy-yellow mortar sand matrix. The final layer (427) was composed of reddish-brown silt containing discreet pockets of yellowy-orange clay and fragments of mortar, sandstone chippings and charcoal. This was overlain by a small discreet dump (426) of yellow mortar and small pebbles.

FIGURE 2.14

View of wall 303a showing reused masonry

FIGURE 2.15

View in to cut 458, the foundation trench for wall 303a, from above

FIGURE 2.16

View of the stepped course foundation (443) for wall 303a

FIGURE 2.17

View of wall 303a, with a reused half column drum clearly visible under the N sign. The white soil (519) beyond the scale is sand, probably waste from the mason's yard

Less extensive soil build-ups relating to this period were also observed in the fourth bay, where layer 373/406 overlay the old ground surface (437) and pit 450 contemporary with the phase-2 W cathedral wall (368).

FIGURE 2.18

Mason's mark on wall 303a

FIGURE 2.19

Mason's mark on wall 303a

FIGURE 2.20

Mason's marks from wall 303a

Finds and dating evidence

There are only two points of reference for the dating of phase-3 developments. First, the grave 462, disturbed by the construction of wall 303, has produced a radiocarbon date in the age range 1047–1280 (see Appendix). On stratigraphic grounds it is more likely to have been associated with the same early cemetery as the other radiocarbon-dated burial (455), than to have been buried inside the first cathedral. The second reference point is provided by the consecration of Jocelin's cathedral in 1197. The presence of reused masonry in the wall 303a makes it plain that this wall was built after John's cathedral had been dismantled to make way for Jocelin's work. While it does not help to refine the chronology, the archaeological evidence provides an indication of how far Jocelin's work had progressed before it was suspended: very little, it would appear. Beyond the consecrated E end work was suspended at a fairly preliminary stage. There are no finds which would provide more precise dating.

Interpretation

The inner face of the N foundation wall (303a) was neatly built considering the variation in the building materials. Such attention to the finish suggests that it was intended to provide more than invisible support. One possibility is that this deep wall formed part of the lower storey of Jocelin's work, a small fragment of which survives in the NW corner of the existing crypt. The expansion of the foundation trench (458) seen in the first bay, can perhaps be explained as the excavation made to accommodate the W wall of a large crypt. Alternately, the depth of the wall 303 may simply have been to provide sound foundations and to support a higher floor level (closer to the modern level), but if so, the quality of the finish is exceptional.

Phase 4: early 13th-century cathedral

The archaeology relating to the cathedral built during the 13th century is the richest of the various phases recognised in this report. In part this is because the building has survived intact to the present day, but it also reflects the great increase in size of the completed building over its predecessors. In order to clarify the events associated with the construction and use of the nave, three phases have been distinguished. The construction of the nave was a drawn out process. Phase 4 describes the initial episode of construction, while phase 5 refers to the completion of the construction following a break of 30–40 years. Evidence relating to the use of the nave, largely for burial, has been placed in phase 6.

On architectural grounds it is believed that the nave was laid out around 1200 as part of the comprehensive rebuilding of the late 12th-century cathedral, which had been damaged by fire shortly after its consecration. Following the laying out of the foundations and lower walls, the nave remained incomplete as attention returned to the E end and it was completed only towards the end of the century (Fawcett 1990a). The walls of the nave were carried up to the height of the windows as part of the laying out process around 1200. This had the consequence of fixing the bay width and aisles position, although to judge from the consistent design, work on the interior did not recommence until the middle of the 13th century.

There is no knowing how high the walls of Jocelyn's incomplete nave ever stood, but in a reduced form they were utilised as the foundations of the aisle arcades of the 13th-century cathedral. The main piers stand comfortably on the broad (2.8m) walls of the unfinished late 12th-century nave. The 12th-century walls (303a, 607) may have been reduced to suit the new floor level, but otherwise they appear to carry the piers without modification (Figures 2.21 and 2.22). The column bases lay outside the excavation areas and were not examined closely, although the watching brief allowed a section near to the base to be recorded. Apart from any modification of these walls, the first work associated with this cathedral seen in the nave was the extension of the central foundations. On the N side the extension (303b) ran some 9m to the middle of the fifth bay, while on the S side the extension (606a) had to be over 18m to reach the same point, because the 12th-century foundation (607) was long enough to support only the easternmost pier. The foundation additions (303b, 606a) were easily distinguished from the earlier structures by their workmanship, their dimensions and their materials. The finish of these purpose-built foundations (303b) was much coarser than seen in the phase-3 walls of Jocelyn's nave. The coursing was much less regular, the exterior face rougher and prone to be covered with mortar. Both the walls incorporated large quantities of re-used masonry, but the mortar could be distinguished by colour. The extension (303b) was clearly seen to terminate in the fifth bay, where a vertical butt joint marked a break in the laying of the foundations.

The sloppiness of the phase-4 builders had a beneficial consequence because during work on the superstructure spilled mortar accumulated against the foundations and allowed later cuts to be clearly recognised. In the third and fourth bays this survived as a solid spread of cream-coloured mortar (327) up to 0.10m thick that covered the full width of the trench and lapped up against the foundation wall (303b). This mortar continued into the fifth bay but was less extensive and had been more disturbed.

Associated with the changes in the fabric of the foundations was a set of features which stretch across the nave at the fourth column. These include a pair of massive squared blocks into which sockets had been roughly cut (0.22m square). These blocks were set in a

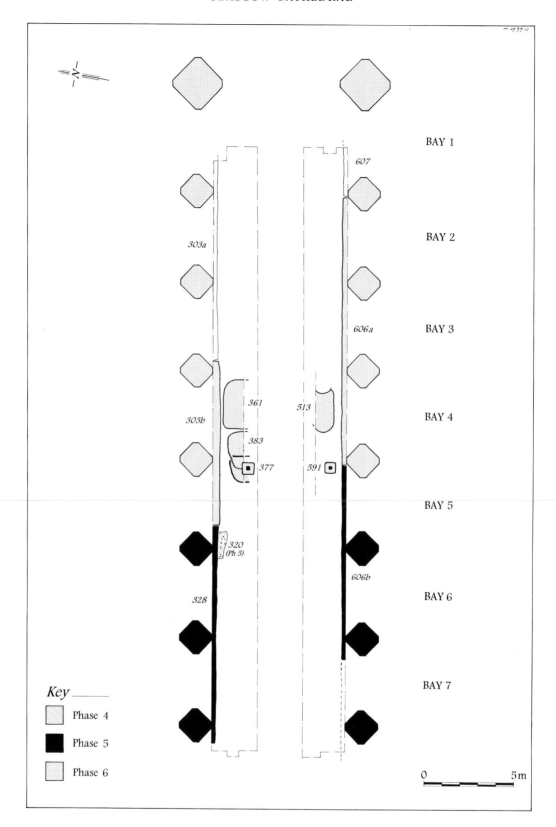

FIGURE 2.21

Plan of major walls and burials of the nave for phases 4 (early 13th century), 5 (mid-13th century) and 6 (13th–17th centuries)

substantial, unmortared rubble foundation (377/591) packed into a broad trench (449) (Figure 2.23). The rubble consisted of white sandstone including the

occasional masonry waster and discarded fragments (see Section 3.2). An exceptional inclusion recovered from the rubble (591) in the S trench was a cross head

FIGURE 2.22

View of wall 303b; chamfered plinth of 368 is visible in the foreground

(sf 174) broken in two, which was probably a discarded sanctuary marker (see Section 3.2; Figure 2.24). In the N trench, the fill (377) was emptied to reveal a ditch (1.6m deep x 1.5m wide) with a flattish bottom, sloping slightly to the E (Figure 2.25). The socketed stones were a close match in size. The N one measured 0.62 x 0.62 x 0.54m, while the S one was 0.58 x 0.54 x 0.48m. The sockets were centred on the upper surface and of similar dimensions (N: 0.22 x 0.22 x 0.18m; S: 0.20 x 0.20 x 0.14m) (Figure 2.26).

The ground surface at this time was below the existing floor level. The depth varied from little more than 0.1m at the extreme W end to as much as 0.8m below the intended final floor level (close to the existing level) in the middle of the nave. The survival of soil layers which would have been contemporary with this initial phase of construction have survived only in a few isolated places between later burials. The mortar spreads (327, etc) show that while work was going on, the foundations stood proud of the interior and sealed slight deposits which had accumulated in and around the unfinished phase-3 nave.

An uneven deposit of compact yellowy-brown mortar and stone rubble (442) overlay the stump of the W wall (368) of the first (phase 2) cathedral, which varied in depth from 0.10–0.90m. This probably represents debris from the demolition of the second (phase 3) cathedral. This was in turn overlain by a layer of brown silt (435) with flecks of reddish-orange clay/loam and inclusions of charcoal, bone and mortar, which may have accumulated during the phase-4 construction.

Once the construction was completed the floor level was raised to approximately the existing level. In the W portion of the nave it is not possible to distinguish any introduced levelling material because of the intensity of the later burial activity. Towards the E end of both the N and S trenches, however, the levelling material could be identified because it consisted of deep (up to 0.8m) deposits of white sand (422, 423, 501). This sand contained small fragments of white sandstone and lumps of mortar. The later burial activity had disturbed this deposit and introduced organic material and numerous disarticulated bones into the sand, but exceptionally a pyramid of clean sand (519) survived almost to the floor level between a number of burial cuts (Figure 2.27). This undisturbed deposit was almost purely sand and stone chippings, which suggests that the levelling material was the waste from dressing the stone used in the 13th-century cathedral and may indicate that the masons' yard was located near to the crossing.

Finds and dating evidence

The most important dating evidence relating to this phase derives from the rubble-filled ditch (449) containing the socketed stones. This was an English cut halfpenny from a short cross penny, issued between 1180–1247. This coin is unlikely to have been lost in Scotland after 1250 (see Section 3.6). If this coin is in its primary context, then it suggests a relatively early date for the work in the nave. The rubble fill of the trench with the socketed stones appears to represent a single event, but such a small coin could have been lost earlier and incorporated with other re-used pieces of rubble, including the cross head and the small amount of rubbish represented by 13 sherds of pottery (SECWGW; sf 716) (see Section 3.7).

The halfpenny was the solitary coin to have been recovered from the nave, while the small number of pot sherds from the ditch (449) represents one of the largest groups of finds from the nave. This typifies the scarcity of finds other than those associated with burial. For instance the mortar spread 327 contained a single sherd of medieval pottery (see Section 3.7).

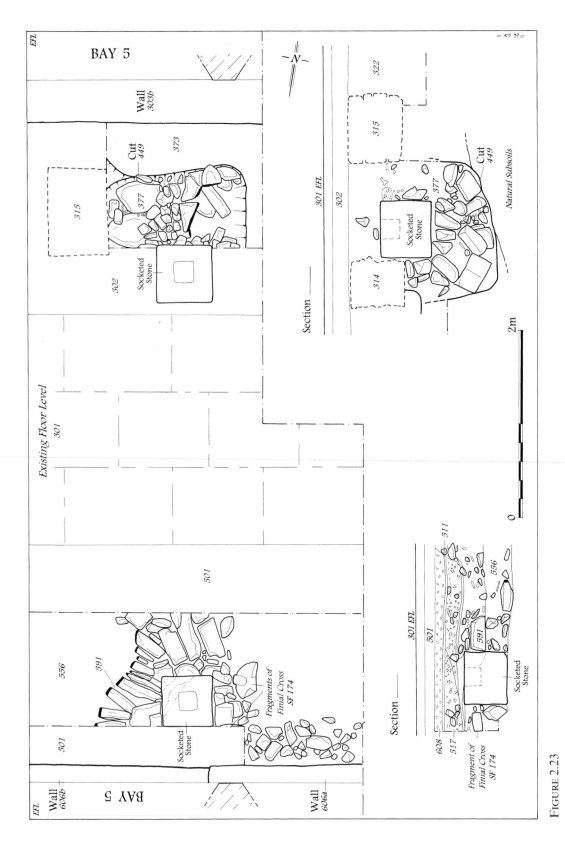

FIGURE 2.23

Plan and section of pits 377 and 591 for the temporary W front of the 13th-century nave

FIGURE 2.24

Fragment of the cross-head as found within the rubble around the S socketed stone in pit 591

FIGURE 2.25

View of a section through pit 377 with socketed stone

These occasional pottery finds provide relatively little help with the dating since they cannot be dated with any more precision than to between the 12th and 15th centuries.

It should be noted that mixed in with the rubble supporting the socketed stones (377/591) were a number of disarticulated bones. These are most likely to derive from the same early cemetery (see phase 1 above) that was disturbed by the earliest construction works. We cannot rule out, however, the possibility that these bones came from graves associated with the cathedral developments of the 12th century.

A feature apparently associated with the break in the building programme was a substantial mortar deposit (320) at the fifth column. This feature was cut through by the later (phase 5) foundation and was only partially observed, but it looks to have been roughly rectangular and aligned with the columns. One possibility is that this provided a support for a buttress, perhaps of timber, which was part of the temporary west front. This feature overlay an earlier grave (367). Unfortunately no corresponding feature was noted on the S side of the nave. Even less certain to be part of this phase was a deposit rich in charcoal and burnt bone found filling a hollow in the natural clay (329) at the W end of the trench. This was sealed by layer 322, but is hard to date with confidence. It could be related to the building work.

The archaeological evidence does not alter the conventional dating based upon the architectural analysis. On balance the view that the architectural details suggest a date in the second half of the 13th century remains the most likely time for the work assigned to this phase (Fawcett 1997, 68–69). What the archaeology does suggest is that there was a pause in construction once the nave was half complete.

Interpretation

The archaeological evidence shows that construction of the nave took place in the two distinct phases. In

FIGURE 2.26

View from above of pit 591 with socketed stone and fragment of cross-head adjacent to the scale

FIGURE 2.27

Small island of white sand (519) surviving amongst later burials in the S nave trench

both the N and S sides of the nave, the phase-4 foundations consist of the modified walls of the previous unfinished nave and purpose-built footings. These extensions along the line established by the earlier walls ran to the fifth bay, where a change in build is marked by butt joints. This change in build represents more than a seasonal break. These stones are carefully positioned to align with the fourth columns of the nave and are supported by a sturdy drystone foundation. It suggests that the nave was about half-complete when work on it was suspended to concentrate on Bondington's expanded E limb. Judging from the massive scale of the rubble founda-tions and the socketed stones this temporary timber facade was a sturdy structure intended to last the

30–40 years required to complete the E limb. The fact that the structures are located below floor level suggests that these features relate to a structure which was erected before the floor was finished. On the basis of the evidence available we cannot rule out the possibility of a choir structure, but the scale and position of the subfloor footings do not particularly support this.

This phase also saw the initial flooring of the nave. Although none of the original paving remained, the subfloor was raised to an appropriate level. If the floor was laid and the proposed temporary W front was weather tight, then the nave may have come into use at this time. The dedication of an altar to St Serf in 1249 (Durkan 1970, 61–62) suggests as much. Indeed

FIGURE 2.28

View of the W end of the foundation wall 328 for the nave piers, revealed after the early 20th-century brick duct was removed

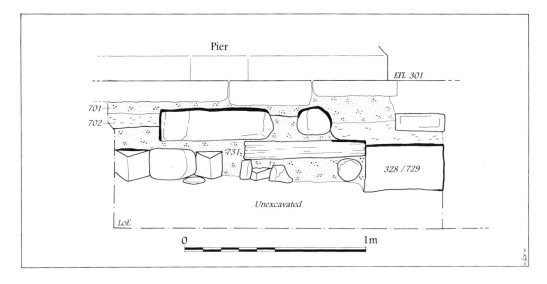

FIGURE 2.29

Detailed section of W end of wall 328

some of the burials (described in phase 6 below) could belong to this initial phase of use.

Phase 5: completion of the laying out of the nave (mid 13th century)

There is relatively little evidence relating to the completion of the nave, apart from the continuation of the foundations for the columns. The westward extensions of the foundations (606b and 328) followed the same alignment but were narrower than their eastern counterparts, had a much less straight face and exhibited a much more irregular and sloppy finish. The mortar was noticeably different too (see Appendix). On the N

side, where the structure was more closely examined, it appears that the foundations were built by digging a trench and filling it with roughly coursed rubble, some of it reused. The line of the foundations was taken very tight to the column bases. At the extreme W end of the N wall (328), the inner face was less than 0.5m from the column base and it terminated just beyond the final column without being tied into the W front (Figures 2.28 and 2.29). This method of construction, consisting of uncoursed rubble apparently roughly thrown up in a trench, is reminiscent of the foundations seen in the crypt (see Section 2.2). The foundations cut through an earlier burial (370), the remains of which were embedded in the mortar of the foundations and therefore could not be recovered.

Apart from the foundations themselves there was little other direct evidence of the work on the W portion of the nave aside from the chance survival of two post settings (567, 569) which presumably held scaffolding. The presence of mortar and white sandstone fragments within the fill of the posthole suggests that they relate to the construction work. Such postholes must have been common features, but presumably most have been removed by later burials. It is also worth noting that the thick build-up of mortar (327) noted against the foundations to the E, which is believed to derive from work on the superstructure, was not observed W of the fourth column. This suggests a change in working practices.

As in the E part of the nave, soil was probably introduced to raise the floor level W of the nave after the foundations had been laid. Unlike the white sand used in phase 4 this infilling was not distinctive (Figure 2.27). The dominant layers (322, 608 and 434) were dark-brown loamy soils containing small fragments of mortar, chipped stone and large quantities of disarticulated bone. Because of the subsequent intense burial activity it is impossible to identify the original character of this material. Indeed there may have been little or no requirement for levelling deposits towards the W end where the natural ground level was close to the floor level. In places where the natural subsoil was close to the surface lumps of clay were present, but elsewhere limited amounts of organic soil were introduced. Naturally this was greatly enriched by the introduction of burials. On both sides of the nave this was bottomed only in the extreme W end where the graves and other features had cut right through it to expose the natural subsoils (329, 520).

Finds and dating evidence

There were few finds which can be attributed to this phase. A number of potsherds were recovered from the layer 322 through which a large number of graves had been cut over several centuries. This heavy disturbance is reflected both in the mixed character of the soil itself and the character of the pottery, which was highly fragmented and derived from a large number of vessels dating from the 12th to the 17th centuries. The dating of this phase is still dependant on the architectural superstructure which has been broadly dated to the late 13th century. Fawcett (1997, 68–69) believes that the nave must have been completed before the disruptions of the Wars of Independence, which in the Glasgow area became pronounced by the end of the 13th century.

Interpretation

Since the events of this phase are all related to the building works, the most pressing question concerns the gap in time between the presumed erection of the

temporary W front during phase 4 and the resumption of works leading to completion. The evidence to evaluate this is slight. On the one hand there is no discernible difference in the architectural scheme between the fourth and fifth bays, which might point to a short break. On the other hand at the subsurface level there are pronounced differences after the resumption of work. The masonry style of foundation is different, as is the mortar. The spillage of mortar from working on the superstructure was also absent W of the fourth bay. These differences strongly suggest that the same masons were not involved. It is an open question how long it would take for building practices to change within a work force such as built the cathedral.

Phase 6: burial activity in the nave (13th–17th centuries)

After the nave was completed, it became a popular place of burial and remained so after the Reformation, even following the re-configuration of the cathedral. The nave was the most heavily used part of the church for burial because space below the crypt floor was restricted and the E arm was carried on vaults which limited possibilities there. Above ground, the nave developed multiple foci for devotional activity as altars were founded at the arcade piers. The location of the earliest attested foundation, made in 1249 to St Serf, is unknown (Durkan 1970, 61–62) but in the later Middle Ages an altar to Serf was probably located at the first or second pier on the N side of the nave. The late medieval popular enthusiasm for the cult of saints, which has been so well documented for England (Duffy 1992), evidently also existed in Scotland (MacQuarrie 1997, 1–14). It is reflected here in, for example, the chantry movement (Fawcett 1994a, 217), in the rise in the endowment of altars at Glasgow (where the well-documented altars predominantly date from the 15th and 16th centuries; Durkan 1970, 59–69) and in the publication of Scotland's first printed book: the great compendium of hagiographical material that is the Aberdeen Breviary (*Breviarum Aberdonense* 1510).

It is not possible to say precisely when the medieval burials began, but the density could easily represent several centuries of interments (Figure 2.30). These burials are heavily intercut and the majority of graves have been subsequently disturbed. Despite the confusing density of graves, clear stages of burial could be distinguished with a degree of confidence on the basis of stratigraphy and rites. For this report five episodes of burial can be distinguished:

a) scattering of graves from a cemetery below the early 12th-century nave, beginning around the 8th century (phase 1),

b) simple medieval graves within the nave (phase 6)

40

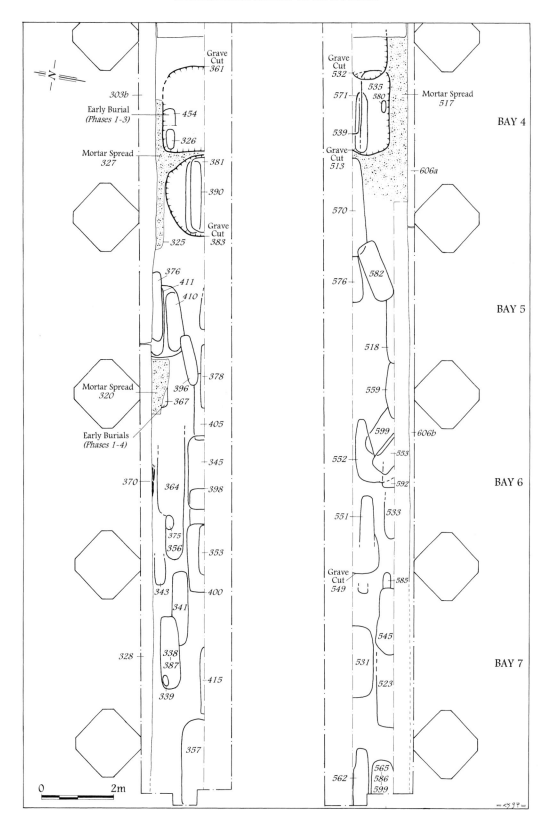

FIGURE 2.30

Schematic plan of the medieval burials in the nave (phase 6)

c) burials in deep lairs within the nave (phases 6–7)

d) early modern graves in coffins some of which were treated with lime (phase 7)

e) 19th-century burials in the crypt, treasury, and possibly the SW tower (phase 8).

This discussion will concentrate on the second and third episodes which probably overlap.

Although the middle three stages (b, c and d) exhibit distinctive burial rites, there are points of similarity between them. They are linked in an evolutionary

41

sense, given that they appear to represent a continuous tradition. Indeed many of the deceased may have been related since burial plots might eventually come to be regarded as the property of families. There is overlap between these three stages of medieval and early modern burial practices. For instance the man (sk 353) who was killed by gun shot was probably buried in the late 17th century, but his grave would have been indistinguishable from medieval burials were it not for the presence of lead shot within his skull (see Figures 4.19 and 4.20). Equally, use of the deep lairs spanned the late medieval to post-medieval transition and features coffins appropriate to both traditions.

Given the recovered evidence it seems as though the early (phase 1) cemetery went out of use or was re-sited after the construction of the first cathedral. The excavated pre-12th century burials were shallow, in some cases within 0.2–0.3m of the presumed ancient ground level. The bone was much less well preserved than in the later medieval burials and there was no sign of coffins. The earliest graves were initially identified where they had been cut into by the cathedral construction work and survived only where the position of the masonry structures or the introduction of the levelling deposits (322, etc) protected them from later grave-diggers. Towards the W end where little or no soil had been introduced any early burials would have been obliterated by later burials. There is little sign of late medieval and early modern burial in the W end of the nave. Burial seems to have continued in the nave after the partition to create the Outer High Kirk was raised in 1647 and may not have ceased until the church was remodelled in 1713 (see phase 7 below). In the 18th and 19th centuries burial was effectively restricted to the three easternmost bays, where they obliterated most traces of the medieval burials, although some important fragments did survive.

The full sequence of burial could not be investigated everywhere in the nave. At the W end, where the density of burial and the depth of over-burden were least, all of the burials were investigated. In the fourth bay exceptional stratigraphic conditions revealed a distinctive group of burials in deep shafts or lairs. These were completely excavated. Elsewhere the burials were investigated only to a depth sufficient for the new heating ducts. These excavations investigated probably about 10–15% of the area which was available for burial in the nave.

Medieval burial sequence

The earliest burials interred in the nave survive in the W end, where they occurred at least three deep. These graves, which were not precisely laid out, were simple, shallow, dug graves in which the body was only occasionally contained in a coffin. They frequently cut one another and on occasion deviate surprisingly far from the axis of the church. As one moves further E

FIGURE 2.31

View of medieval burials at W end of N nave trench

the density of graves increases as does the presence of disarticulated remains. Where the sequence of burial was not completely excavated the quantity of burials is unknown, but the quantities of disarticulated bone give the impression that there were as many burials in the fifth bay. There is no evidence to indicate how soon after construction burial in the nave began, but it continued until the Outer High Kirk was formed in the W bays (Figure 2.31).

Towards the W end the graves cut through the earliest (phase 1) features on the site, the backfilled ditches and hearth (see phase 1 above), into the natural subsoil. Elsewhere they were dug into a layer of material introduced to level the interior of the nave (322). This was a well-mixed, homogenous, dark, organic soil which contained large quantities of disarticulated human bones and occasional fragments of coffins, nails and pottery. In most instances it proved difficult to detect the edges of the graves, because of the similarity between the grave fills and the soil (322) through which most were cut. An equivalent layer (503) was present on the S side of the nave. Locally it was possible to establish relative sequences, but since the only consistent evidence of stratigraphic relationships was provided by intercutting graves it proved

FIGURE 2.32

View of burial 545 (left of the scale) with traces of coffin visible around the legs

impossible to provide a comprehensive sequence for all the burials.

Coffins

The majority of burials which appear in the earliest phases were not placed in coffins. Presumably they were buried in shrouds of some description. A number of small pins were recovered from the nave, which may have fastened such shrouds. Where coffins were present they were usually very poorly preserved and represented by fugitive stains and the occasional nail. The intercutting of the graves ensured that no complete record of a coffin was recovered. There is evidence to suggest that the earliest were simple rectangular or trapezoidal boxes. So few nails were recovered that it seems that these boxes were joined with pegs and that the nails were used only to fasten the lid (Rodwell 1989, 164).

Only a few burials provided much evidence for coffins. Even undisturbed graves such as those of sk 551, sk 545 (Figure 2.32) or sk 562 contained only scant traces of pine-wood and a few nails. The best preserved portion of a coffin was found in grave 332 where the white sand levelling deposit (422/423)

created a freak condition which preserved not only the coffin but also some of the skin (Figure 2.33). Only a small portion of this burial survived disturbance from later graves but enough of the coffin was recovered for it to be identified as having been made from pine wood.

Most of the disarticulated bone was unceremoniously scattered around, but there is some evidence to suggest that when earlier burials were encountered the bones were treated with some reverence. The clearest sign of this was a pit (374) containing disarticulated remains including two skulls. Occasionally elsewhere small piles of bones indicated where disturbed skeletons had been tidied into the corner of a new grave.

Overall it appears that coffins were relatively rare among these early graves. Only 14 out of 64 burials had traces of wood, but nails were recovered from another 16, which could indicate a total of 30 coffins (see Section 3.4). In stratigraphic terms the majority of coffins occurred amongst those graves which are relatively late in the sequence.

Burial postures

There are too few undisturbed graves to allow for a statistically meaningful analysis of burial posture, but some trends are clear. Where the evidence survives the largest number of individuals were buried with their hands laid across their pelvis, with arms either straight or flexed. Given the partial evidence, it is impossible however to be certain about what might have been the dominant rite. Some of the observed variations may have arisen because of differences between shrouded and coffin burial rites. In the case of the remarkably preserved coffin burial (sk 334) in which skin survived around the hands, it looks as though the hands were arranged as in prayer (Figure 2.34). In all other cases it was impossible to tell exactly how the hands had been arranged. In some cases one hand was placed in the lap and the other was laid by the side. For example, in coffin burial sk 364 the right arm was extended with the hand positioned below the pelvis, while the left arm was flexed with the hand resting on the pelvis. The opposite arrangement was seen in sk 545 where the left hand was placed over the pelvis while the right hand was extended, lying by the side.

The arrangement of the arms flexed across the abdomen was an alternative seen in one well-preserved shroud burial (sk 396; Figure 2.35), but it was not especially characteristic of burial without a coffin. Sk 378 had no coffin and its arms were resting by its sides.

Multiple burials

There were two definite instances of multiple burial in a single grave and two possible instances. Post-medieval finds from within the grave fill of both indicate that these were late in the sequence. It was possible to be certain that these were multiple burials only because they had been little disturbed by later graves. It seems doubtful that multiple burials in more

FIGURE 2.33

View of burial 334 showing hands partially mummified in a praying position by local soil conditions. Most of the burial was removed by a post-medieval burial

FIGURE 2.34

Detail of burial 334 showing hands preserved 'in prayer'

disturbed contexts would have been recognised. In grave 337 the bodies of two adults (sk 387 a mature adult male, and sk 338 a mid-adult female) and an infant (sk 339) were stacked one upon another. All appeared to be buried at the same time. No signs of a coffin were noted, suggesting they were all shroud burials. The lowest skeleton (sk 387) had its hands crossed over at the wrist and positioned over the pelvis. Directly over sk 387 was positioned the other adult (sk 338) with the baby (sk 339) placed beside the head. Some infant remains were also located by the right pelvis of this adult. The arms of the adult were flexed to the body with the hands resting over the pelvis. The grave fill (393) produced an iron nail.

In grave 412 the bodies of two men (sk 410, sk 411) were laid out side by side (Figure 2.36). There was no indication of either of the burials having been contained in a coffin and therefore both appear to have been simple shroud burials. The two bodies had been placed elbow-to-elbow, with the left arm of sk 411 folded across its lower chest and the hand on the upper right arm. The right arm of sk 410 was missing having been cut away by a later burial. A single sherd of Scottish medieval redware (sf 706) was found in association with sk 411.

Amongst a number of partially excavated burials at the W end of the S nave trench were two burials (sk 586, sk 590) which appeared to have been placed one

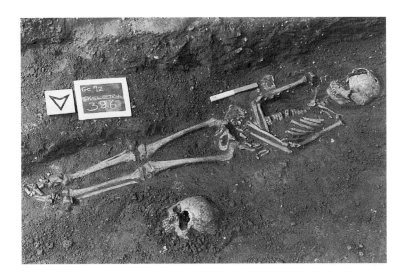

FIGURE 2.35

Burial 396, a typical of shroud burial with arms flexed across abdomen

FIGURE 2.36

Double burial (sk 410 and sk 411)

on top of the other within the same grave cut (566). Only the legs of these graves were examined and no sign of a coffin was noted. A slightly different multiple grave (526) contained a spare skull (sk 573) in the fill

containing a coffin burial (sk 570), along with sherds of pottery (SECWGW and medieval redware; sf 713).

Infants and children

Twenty-three infant and child burials were identified. These were generally well preserved only if they were found sharing an adult grave or if they were somehow protected from later disturbance. In one instance only the upper torso and left arm survived of a baby (sk 318). An otherwise unrecognisable juvenile (sk 326) survived only because it was placed on the hard mortar spread (327) which was avoided by later grave-diggers; elsewhere the body of a juvenile (sk 533) was protected from further damage when it was sealed beneath a post-medieval cross-wall (505). There seemed to be no particular area for children's graves. A further child grave (397) was located near the seventh pier of the N trench; the child's body (sk 398) was typically poorly preserved. Another infant skeleton (sk 580) was mostly swept away by a later burial.

Burials in lairs

A dramatic change in burial rite seems to come late in the medieval sequence, with the creation of precisely located, deep burial plots which contained a number of sequential burials (Figure 2.21). These were most clearly seen in the fourth bay where the graves were cut through a thick layer of mortar (327, etc) which derived from the construction of the nave and served to clearly demarcate the grave cut (Figure 2.37). It was possible to identify these lairs on both sides of the nave (361, 383 and 513). Each proved to contain a series of burials laid down over an extended period of time. In some cases the previous occupant was neatly placed to one side of the cut in other cases only a few bones remain to indicate earlier use (see Section 4.2). Apart from being clearly visible in plan, these burials were deep (up to 1.25m) in comparison with other

FIGURE 2.37

View from the N of burial lairs (361) coming down onto wall 368

graves, which were generally less than 0.5m below floor level. These graves are interpreted as family burial vaults, known from the early 15th century as 'lairs' (Craigie 1931).

The clearest example was a wide straight-sided grave shaft (361) centred in the fourth bay in the N trench (Figure 2.8 and 2.30). Although it contained only one complete burial, the 2m wide cut was much larger than that required for a single coffin. The corners of the cut were rounded and gave the impression of having been re-cut on occasion. Only a few fragments of a single burial (sk 371) remained. It had been disturbed by later activity, which left bone only in the areas of the pelvis and the feet. This may indicate that the lair was being actively tended at the time of the formation of the Outer High Kirk. Thereafter the lair would have been inside the kirk and inaccessible. The latest burials were probably relocated to a new lair. The backfill (346) of the shaft contained finds which support a post-medieval date for this activity including a clay pipe stem, a sherd of pottery (SECWGW; sf 700), a glass fragment (sf 469), a fragment of a leather shoe sole (sf 92) and a small piece of worked shale (sf 699). The most significant object found in the shaft was a bronze seal matrix (sf 96) of 13th- or 14th-century date (see Section 3.5). Unfortunately it was not recovered from a secure context.

In the lair to the W (389) there was a stack of three coffin burials which had been interred on separate occasions. The coffin 391 of the earliest burial (sk 390) was poorly preserved with the coffin floor remaining only in the region of the pelvis and upper legs. Scant remains of the second coffin (382) survived and the body too was poorly preserved because the upper torso (sk 381) had been treated with lime. This post-medieval practice was a common feature of the latest burials in the eastern three bays (see phase 7 below). This grave also contained a flint core (sf 105), possibly

from a flintlock gun. The latest burial placed within the lair also produced evidence of coffin furniture characteristic of the post-medieval period. Also within the fill (350) were two sherds of pottery (SECWGW; sf 701) and a fragment of clay pipe stem (sf 456). The final use of this grave must pre-date the construction of a partition wall (314) of the Outer High Kirk which sealed the lair. This may be dated to the establishment of the Kirk in 1647 or, more likely to the refurbishment in 1713 (Fawcett 1997, 34).

On the S side of the nave an earlier sequence of burials seems to have survived in the lair. In the fourth bay a substantial lair was cut (513) to a depth of 1.24m below the present floor level (Figure 2.38). The primary burials within the lair were of a mature adult woman (sk 571) and an infant (sk 580). A group of disarticulated bones (598) at the base of the cut, probably represent earlier burials disturbed during the digging of the pit. The adult burial (sk 571) was complete. No trace of a coffin was found and the skeleton had been buried with the arms by its sides. An unidentified iron object (sf 565) was found in association with it. The infant burial had been placed by the right leg of the adult. Little remained of the infant with only the skull and a few long bones surviving and the burial may have been disturbed. The topmost skeleton (sk 535), an adult woman, placed within the shaft grave was a well-preserved coffin burial. The feet of this skeleton were flexed outwards and the arms had been laid out straight beneath the body. Fragments of coffin wood and nails remained.

Later than the grave from within the shaft were two others, which were overlain by the wall of the Outer High Kirk. These two graves (sk 525 and sk 539) had been treated with lime and traces of wood and nails were associated with burial 539.

Unfortunately the mortar spread which allowed the shaft graves to be so easily identified was confined to

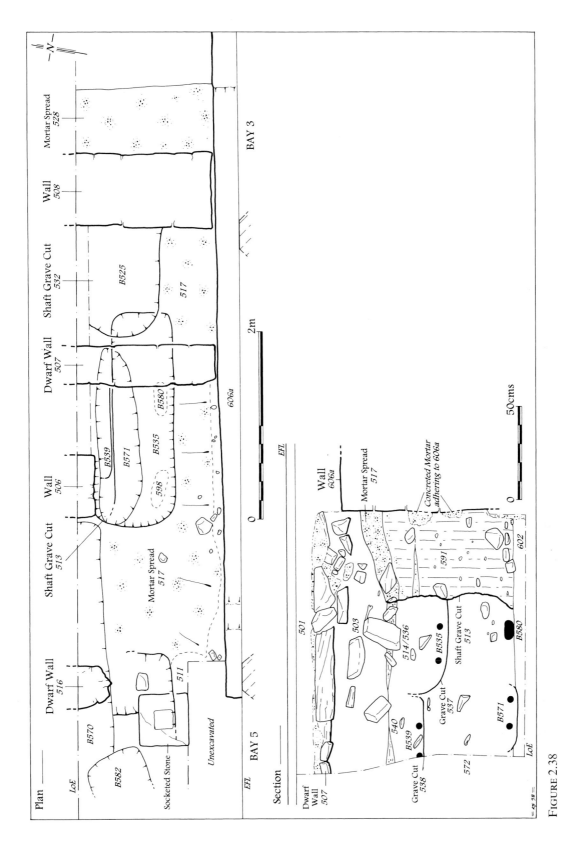

FIGURE 2.38

Detailed plan and section of burials and walls in fourth bay of S nave trench

the fourth bay. Further E the medieval burials had been largely removed by post-medieval burials, but the precise positioning of the later graves suggests that lairs could have existed here. To the W of the fourth bay there was no evidence for the precise re-use of particular burial plots (Figure 2.31).

Finds and dating evidence

Jewellery and other personal items were excluded from the burials placed in the nave. As a result, such dating as suggested by the small finds is largely incidental to the burials, except in the case of the coffins and, perhaps, the seal matrix.

The deposits through which most of the burials were cut (322, 556 etc) contained small quantities of medieval pottery (SECWGW or redwares). These were isolated sherds which showed every indication of having been redeposited. As such these pottery sherds, the earliest of which could date to the 12th century, do not provide secure guide to the beginning of burial activity. Finds from the surrounding material and fill of the graves were rather sparse and suggest that the graves were not kept open for long. The small collection of materials from a layer (556) at the W end of the nave stands out for its density of finds, which include two sherds of Scottish medieval redware (sf 710), a needle (sf 101) and an unidentifiable fragment (sf 487), both of copper alloy, 30 nails, and a small iron hook (sf 516). In the fourth bay the mortar (327) was overlain by a layer (312) of dark brownish-grey silt which contained bones and modern plaster mouldings, but despite this contamination it should be equated with layer 322 elsewhere. This layer (312) contained an assemblage of 64 pottery sherds including SECWGW, medieval redwares and Scottish post-medieval reduced wares (sf 692). Incidental finds of note were extremely rare, so much so that the potsherd rudely shaped into a gaming counter (sf 93) recovered from the fill of a burial (sk 356), together with the bashed bronze ferrule (sf 479) buried with sk 552 are among the most interesting. Without a doubt it is the occasional late potsherd or clay pipe fragment recovered from grave fills that take on the most significance as they allow late-medieval or early-modern burials to be recognised.

The most interesting find from a grave fill was the seal matrix (sf 96) recovered from deep within one of the lairs (361). This seal dates to the 13th or 14th century but cannot be firmly associated with the early use of the lair. The final activity in this lair, the removal of the latest burial(s), can be dated to the late 17th or early 18th centuries on the basis of the pipe and pottery fragments within the fill and the position of the wall of the Outer High Kirk.

The most valuable evidence for pin-pointing the end of the use of the nave for burials is provided by the establishment of the Outer High Kirk in 1647 (Fawcett

1997, 34). This was marked by the erection of wall 307 which ran between the third pillars but did not originally reach the nave ceiling. In 1713 it was raised to the full height of the nave and there are indications that the interior may have been re-modelled at this time. The re-modelling may account for the series of slight partition walls, all of which sealed graves. It seems entirely likely that no further burials were made in the western part of the nave following the refurbishment of the Outer High Kirk in 1713 but, prior to that, burial continued here as in medieval times. In the eastern part of the nave burial continued until the 19th century.

Interpretation

The distribution of medieval graves provides compelling evidence that burial within the nave was closely regulated. Despite the profusion of skeletons, the graves were not located randomly or haphazardly. As far as can be reconstructed, the last three bays on the W provide the best indication of how the graves were arranged in the earliest stage of burial in the nave. Here burials were placed in shallow graves, occasionally in coffins. There is some local deviance from the strict orientation of the building, as in the fifth bay on the N, or the sixth on the S, and there are multiple burials in the same grave. Generally the burials are tightly grouped, suggesting a high degree of control over access to burial space within the cathedral. In the liturgically-charged E end of the nave, there appears to have been a heightened formalisation of the burial patterns, from the 15th century at the latest (see Section 5). This change, to a more formal marking and management of burial places, cannot be detected in the W of the nave. The inter-cutting of graves may be an indication that burials in the W end were less well marked.

A significant shift to more formally defined burial plots seems to be indicated by the introduction of deep lairs, as seen in the fourth bay. The size of these cuts and the evidence of re-use indicates that these lairs were utilised by family groups, a point addressed in the skeletal analysis (see Section 4.2). Given the precision of the periodic excavations in these lairs, it is reasonable to suppose that the lairs were marked on the surface by inscribed slabs. It may be that these lairs should be seen as part of the more active use of the nave from the middle of the 15th century when the altars began to be founded at the columns in the nave. It may well be that the lairs were owned by the families who endowed and maintained the altars. The use of these burial lairs clearly extended into the post-medieval period given the presence of the lime-treated graves within the lairs. The apparent cleaning out of lair 361 suggests that the remains were valued enough to be translated to a new lair once it was revealed that the modification to the interior of the Outer High Kirk would effectively seal the lair.

There is little that is exceptional in the evidence for burial rites. The variations in arm position are unremarkable. The unique discovery of the burial with hands fixed in a praying position may reflect a common rite, but clearly this posture was not universal. Unfortunately the incompleteness of many of the burials makes it impossible to correlate these postures with chronology, age or sex. Similar limitations in the data do not invite attempts to correlate coffins with age or sex, but it does seem that burial in a coffin became more common only gradually throughout the Middle Ages, and primarily so only in post-medieval times.

Phase 7: post-Reformation structures and burials (17th–19th centuries)

In archaeological terms the impact of the Reformation was not immediately visible within the nave. While above ground the altars were being demolished, below ground it is hard to notice a sharp change in the late medieval burial practices (Figure 2.39). In 1647, however, the Outer High Kirk was established in the five westernmost bays of the nave (Fawcett 1997, 34). To create a new space for worship, a partition wall was erected, the foundations of which remain (307/508; Figure 2.40). A significant remodelling took place in 1713, when the wall was raised and the new doorways established (Burgh Records v, 506). The work of 1713 may have also seen the church fitted out for Presbyterian worship and this seems to have finally excluded burial from the area of worship. Burials continued to be made in the E of the nave until the 19th century.

The main wall of the Outer High Kirk was built to tie-in with the third pier from the crossing. This wall is present in an early 19th-century engraving which shows a blank face, except for two doors in each aisle (Figure 2.43). This choice of location impeded the excavation as the third pier is more or less where the wall of the early 12th-cathedral lies (368, 444, 589) and is where the foundations of the late 12th century (303a) bond into those of the 13th century (303b; Figure 2.41). Considering the final height of the wall, the foundations (307) seem remarkably light, only 1.2m deep and 0.70m wide, stepping out to 0.80m. The masonry was randomly coursed of irregular stone blocks bonded with pale yellow brown lime mortar. The W face was noticeably better finished on the W side. The N side of the foundation had been built over the early 12th-century wall (368) but was not bonded to it and was separated by a soil layer (435). A vertical-sided construction trench (407, 409, 577) cut through the layer 422 and several burials. After construction, the trench was backfilled (408, 380, 578) with sandy soil containing rubble, mortar, and disarticulated human bone as well as a few sherds of medieval and post-medieval pottery (sf 705) and a clay pipe fragment.

The excavations revealed a series of light-weight foundation walls running N–S across the interior (Figure 2.39). These walls could be contemporary with the main partition (307) judging from the similarity of the mortars used in the various walls. All of these insubstantial walls (314/516, 319, 321, 336/507, 505, 506) rested however upon graves, some of which seem to indicate that burial continued on until the end of the 17th century. The grave of the man who had been killed by gun shot (sk 353) probably dates to the later 17th century (see Section 3.9) and the grave 348 with well-preserved coffin furniture dates to this period or the early 18th century. The removal of some of the inhumations from the lairs may mark the end of burial in this area (see phase 6 burial discussion above).

The narrowest wall (336/507) was only 0.46m wide, but was one of the most consistently built of these little walls (Figure 2.42). It ran parallel to the main eastern wall of the Kirk and may have provided a narrow (1.5m) corridor or vestibule, access to which was via the doors visible in the early 19th-century engraving (Figure 2.43). Reconstructing the interior of the church is much more speculative as there are no surviving descriptions or images. It appears that the Outer High Kirk had galleries of some sort by 1649 (Fawcett 1997, 34) and the aforementioned engraving, dated 1822, shows a stair leading to the door in the S aisle above ground level. Presumably this led to the gallery. The burial evidence, however, suggests the continuation of interment here was not inhibited.

From the arrangement of the footings, there are two possible variations in the layout of the galleried interior. Presbyterian church design exhibits a preference for altering the Catholic orientation and shifting the liturgical focus to the S and occasionally to the N (Hay 1957, 42–43). If a plan with galleries on three sides is assumed, then it is only a question of whether the third gallery is on the N or the S with the communion table and pulpit opposite. The evidence is ambiguous, but on balance points to a central liturgical space in the fifth and sixth bays with a focus to the N. The centrally focused plan is a common theme of post-Reformation Scottish architecture. In this case the preference for a S-sided pulpit may have been overridden by the fact that the traditional entrance to the nave was from the S.

Walls which may have supported the E and W galleries can be identified with some confidence. Wall 314/516 ran N–S between the fourth piers. This roughly faced rubble wall was five courses deep (0.54m) and 0.43–0.48m wide. On the S side it did not quite reach the S pier foundations (606). Its counterpart to the W (505) also ran N–S, aligned just to catch the E side of the sixth columns. It was of similar scale and build and also stopped just short of the S pier foundation (606), but it was not observed in the N excavation trench. This absence is readily explained by the slightness of these footings, which could easily have been removed when the fittings of the Outer High

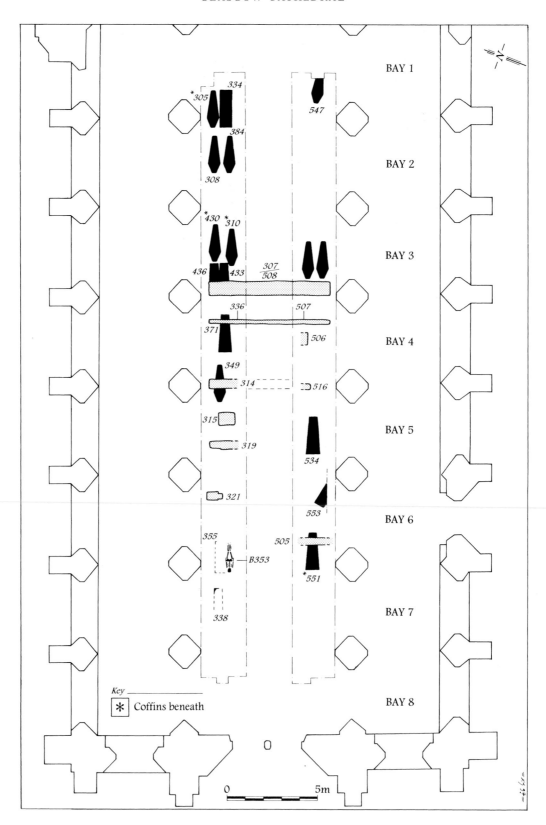

FIGURE 2.39

Schematic plan of post-medieval burials and modification to the nave (phase 7)

Kirk were removed in the 19th century. These walls could have served as sleepers for a raised timber floor, but perhaps more supporting walls would be expected if this were the case.

Three pieces of masonry in the fifth and sixth bays in the N trench would seem to support the case for believing that the liturgical focus was on the N side. Two short stretches of foundation wall (319 and 321)

50

FIGURE 2.40

View from above of the walls from the post-Reformation remodelling of the nave

FIGURE 2.41

View of wall 307 built upon wall 368 below and butted against wall 303 on the left

which ran N–S on either side of the fifth column may have supported a liturgical structure, alternately they could have carried a gallery. Although in the E arm of the cathedral the galleries were sited in the aisles, at some other converted churches galleries were located within the main space. Both of these walls are even slighter than the others argued to be gallery supports (314/516, 505). The former were only 2–3 courses deep and roughly built. Wall 319 was less substantial, being only 0.40m wide, but wall 321 was similarly insubstantial, with a width range of 0.39–0.48m. These seem scarcely suited to supporting a gallery, however, together these slight walls would frame the focal point of the ideal Presbyterian plan, the place that in the 17th century would be occupied by communal communion tables (Hay 1957, 63–65).

Easily the most substantial post-Reformation feature was a sturdy stone platform (315) on the N side between the fourth and fifth columns (Figure 2.44). Its rough but level surface (1 x 0.6m) was supported by a depth of almost 1m. The platform was joined to wall 319 by a band of hard compact mortar (365) containing lumps of sandstone. This feature may have served as the footings for a pulpit.

No ready explanation can be provided for a short (0.20m) stub of a wall (506) observed in the S trench (Figure 2.42). It was two courses thick, roughly faced and 0.66m wide. It was probably contemporary with these other walls but that is all that can be said with any degree of certainty.

There were other fugitive features which clearly relate to the use of the Outer High Kirk or its demolition. In the S trench W of the fourth column, a hard and compact layer of creamy light-yellow sand and mortar (517) was overlain by a thin black band of charcoal and ash (511). This seems to represent *in situ* burning since the mortar layer (517) was scorched red.

FIGURE 2.42

View from above of walls 508 and 507 overlying burial lair 513 in S nave trench

The black, burnt layer (511) immediately underlay a layer of hard packed orange clay (608) which was present only in a localised spread. On the basis of such slim evidence it is hard to be certain, but this might indicate the site of a stove.

The flooring for the new Kirk was flagstone, perhaps re-using the medieval paving. There is little indication in the way of artefacts that the flags were lifted, except where necessary for the construction of the various walls, but the refurbishment probably did involve re-laying the floors. The subfloor deposits were loose layers, often quite sandy towards the E (302, 322, 501). Further west, layer 503 was a compact dark brown organic soil containing mortar and rounded stones and chips of decayed sandstone. The layer extended over most of the W end of the trench and ran under layer 501 up to the wall 307. These broad homogenous layers contained small pockets of loose mortar (504) and a dump of stones (502).

Burials

Despite the construction of the Outer High Kirk, burials were regularly made in the nave until the end of the 17th century and thereafter on a more restricted basis. From the 17th century onwards all are in coffins of the classic 'single break' type, a number of which were very well preserved because the bodies had been treated with lime (see Section 3.4). This process, which was presumably intended to deter grave-robbing, turns the skeletons into a soft powder, but prevents the timber from decaying completely.

At least two graves can be identified within the space of the Outer High Kirk. One is of a young male (sk 353) who was killed, perhaps executed, by musket shot of later 17th-century or, less probably, 16th-century

date. Burial within churches was officially discouraged after the Reformation. The presence of this grave within the Outer High Kirk marks this man out as exceptional despite this apparently ignominious death. The other contains a coffin (348), the decoration of which can be dated on stylistic grounds to the late 17th century at the earliest (see Section 3.4).

To the E of the Outer High Kirk burial continued unabated until the 19th century, when access to the lairs was gradually restricted. The burials in this area were made in tight rows which presumably filled the E part of the nave. They tended to be buried at least 0.5m below floor level and were excavated only if they were in the space allotted for the heating duct or if deeper structures were being excavated. Six of these limed burials (sk 305, sk 308, sk 310, sk 334, sk 384, sk 430) were excavated, but they were only the final undisturbed graves in an area of dense burial. Large quantities of disarticulated bone and fragments of coffin fittings attest to these earlier burials.

Finds and dating evidence

Pottery recovered from features relating to this phase was predominantly medieval, although some post-medieval wares were present. The layers (312, 322) that the cross walls have been built over contain post-medieval pottery and indeed one of the walls itself (321) contained a sherd of Scottish post-medieval reduced ware. The style of the coffins and fittings used in the final phase of inhumation identified by the excavation indicates a date of around 1700, but burial in this area to the E of the Outer High Kirk seems to have continued through the 18th and into the 19th century: the historical record shows that burials were

FIGURE 2.43

Engraving of the interior of the nave from the crossing by William Brown in 1822, showing the E wall of the Outer High Kirk (Durkan 1970, 64). Note the various doors and the original form of the nave ceiling

made in the Oswald lairs in the crossing as late as 1871 (SRO, MW.1.287).

There can be no doubts surrounding association of finds with sk 353. The skull of a young male contained three balls of lead shot (sf 97) which had entered the head from the front. Another ball was found resting on the clavicle. The balls cannot be precisely dated, though are probably 17th or, less likely, 16th century (see Section 3.9). Although some nails were present, no coffin outline was noted in this grave, suggesting that burial in shrouds continued until interment ceased in this part of the nave.

Interpretation

The preferred reconstruction of the interior of the Outer High Kirk is as follows: galleries on the E, W and S sides with the S one being set in the aisle; a vestibule or linking corridor running the length of the E side underneath the gallery; the E and W galleries linked into the existing bay structure running across the fourth and seventh bays thus creating a central liturgical space in the fifth and sixth aisles (Figure 2.45). It seems likely that the N aisle was isolated by filling in the arcading to create a 'backstage' area where the session clerk and minister could have some accommodation. The focus of the worship was in the N side of this space, where minor masonry foundations indicate the position of the principal liturgical structures, such as the pulpit and communion table.

Phase 8: modern refurbishment (1835–present)

A slight indication of the sober interior finish of the Kirk is provided by the discovery of a few fragments

FIGURE 2.44

View of stone platform 315, possible footings for a pulpit

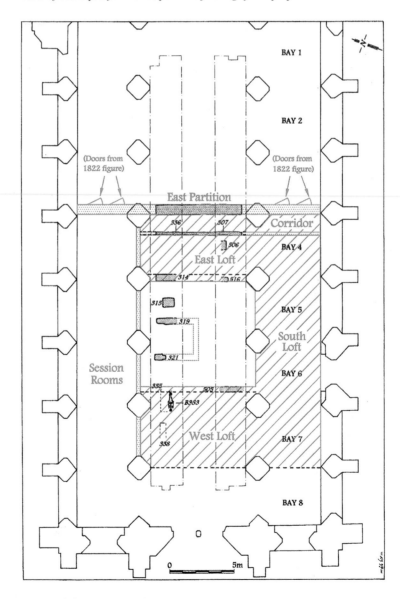

FIGURE 2.45

*Conjectural reconstruction of the floor plan of the Outer High Kirk
c1713*

of ornamental plaster. These mouldings from a wall or ceiling fittings exhibit simple ogee profiles and white paint only (sf 81, sf 89, sf 94). They may have formed part of the Outer High Kirk although they come from a 19th-century demolition context.

Another feature relating to the remodelling was a shallow pit (313) which cut the fill of the lower pit and wall (336). It measured 2.02 x 0.82m and was only 0.17m deep and flat-bottomed. The scoop had been dug against walls 303 and 307, and cut the western construction trench of wall 307. The fill (316) was a medium brown silt mixed with various dumps of ash and cinders.

The slate slab floor rested on the highly mixed soils in the E end, but in the damp NW that had been raised on brick pillars, presumably to promote drying.

The final major event prior to these excavations was the installation of heating ducts in the aisles and across the E and W sides of the nave in 1916.

2.2   THE CRYPT
by S T Driscoll

Two trenches were dug in the crypt, both running N–S across the central area between the aisles (Figure 1.7), through the complex array of columns supporting the vaulting of the E end and adjacent to two of the most sacred spaces of the cathedral: the supposed site of Tomb of St Kentigern and the Lady Chapel. The E trench was located just to the W of the Lady Chapel and the W trench was located immediately to the W of the plinth marking the location of the tomb of St Kentigern. The size and run of the trenches here, as elsewhere, was determined by requirements of the heating ducts. The planned depth was 1.1m below the floor slabs, although in many places the archaeological deposits were exhausted before this level. The notional width was 1.2m, but in practice it was much more variable, extending to 4.1m in one place because of the run of floor slabs and the position of graves.

Crypt E trench

In both trenches (Figure 2.46) the natural subsoil appeared as a compact, coarse glacial sand, which had evidently been exposed and sculpted to fulfill the architectural requirements of the ambitious eastern arm begun about 1240. The site was so thoroughly terraced into the slope that no features or deposits which pre-date this construction survived.

Phase 4: early 13th-century cathedral

In the E trench the natural sands (125) had been largely excavated away to accommodate three massive foundations running E–W, which occupied most of the available area (Figure 2.47). The N (109) and S (106) foundations carried the main aisle piers which in turn support the piers of the choir arcades and thus support the entire E end to its full height. The central foundation (108) carried the piers that support the vaulting and the choir floor rather than the full weight of the cathedral superstructure.

As is to be expected, both N and S foundations were substantial structures. Although exposed only to a depth of about 1m, presumably they extend for some considerable depth. The width of the foundations was not consistent and the line taken wavered considerably: the N (109) measured 2.6m in width, while the S (106) was 3.4m.

Stonemasons from Historic Scotland cut slots in the foundations for the ducts by hand and this controlled demolition allowed the structure of the wall to be observed and for the recovery of individual stones with a minimum of damage. Even before the cutting of the slots it was clear that the foundations were made largely, probably entirely, from stone recovered from the earlier cathedral. This included carved architectural features such as piers and jamb fragments, caps and bases, and simple blocks of dressed masonry with plastered and painted surfaces (Figure 2.48; see Sections 3.2 and 3.3). The foundations were bonded with a hard, pale brown lime mortar (107) similar to that seen in the vaulting supporting the choir (see Section 3.9). The masonry was only roughly coursed and little effort had been made to dress or trim the more irregular of the stones. It appears that the mortar was applied in a very liquid state by pouring it in and around the white sandstone. The cutting of the slots for the ducting demonstrated that the foundations retained their structural integrity and that the mortar remained firm and resilient.

The central foundation (108) was broader than the other two, measuring 3.7m at its widest, tapering to 3.3m at the W side of the trench. The method of construction was similar to that of the two flanking foundations and re-used architectural masonry was also incorporated into it. The full depth of the footings was not determined, but because this foundation carries the smaller piers supporting the crypt vaulting, they may not be as deep as those intended to carry the full height of the cathedral.

The northern foundation (109) fits so tightly in its construction trench that no cut was visible. The cut of the construction trench (128) for the southern foundation (106) was visible as a 0.22m gap filled by an organic brown silty sand containing lumps of brown clay (136) and capped with building debris. The primary fill was quite clean with only occasional flecks of mortar and was excavated to a depth of 0.7m at which point it became too narrow to continue. The foundations continued down below this point. The upper (0.25m) fill (129) was mainly of mortar, stone chippings and some painted plaster. The central

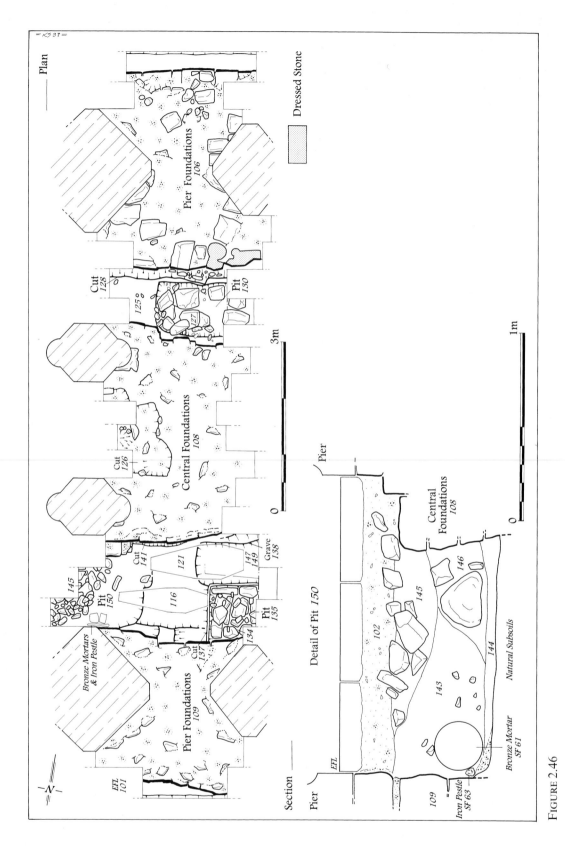

FIGURE 2.46

Plan and section of crypt E trench. The architectural sculpture marked 'dressed stone' was left in situ

FIGURE 2.47

View from the S of the three massive foundations in the crypt E trench. Architectural fragments are visible in the make-up of the foundations in the foreground

FIGURE 2.48

Fragment of painted masonry (sf 114) in situ in foundation wall 106

foundation had a construction trench (141) visible on its N side, which, at only 0.12m wide, was very narrow.

In the E trench the foundations consumed almost the entire space within the excavation, but there were a few other features present, which relate either to the construction or medieval usage. Between the S and central foundations a rectangular pit (130) had been cut into the natural sands and pebbles (125). The neatly cut pit extended beyond the western trench edge and its vertical sides bottomed out to a flat base after 0.92m. The primary fill included a few disarticulated human bones (132) within a mid-brown sandy loam (131) which also contained fragments of mortar and thin lenses of sand. The upper fill (127) consisted of angular stone blocks. Neither the form or the contents of this pit provide much information about function. It clearly post-dates the laying out of the foundations, but is probably best explained as the setting of a structure used in the construction.

The crypt W trench was of a similar size and orientation to the E trench (Figure 2.49). It was located immediately to the W of the square platform marking the location of the tomb of St Kentigern. As in the E trench, the N and S foundations (224 = 106, 245 = 108) dominated the excavated area. There was no trace of a central foundation however. The scale and structure of foundations (224) and (245) corresponded in every respect to the foundations seen to the E.

There were no traces of the natural A and B soil horizons, which suggest that the area was stripped of soil before the construction began. A thin layer (219) of dark organic soil overlaying the natural sand subsoil (228) probably represents a trampled deposit contemporary with the construction. This trample layer (219) survived only in a few patches: elsewhere it had been removed by graves (for example, 205, 208, 216, 217). The only other feature which might relate to the construction period was a small (0.40m in diameter), discreet circular deposit of mortar (243) which may be filling a shallow (0.06–0.08m deep) post setting.

The excavation exposed the W side of the platform supporting the square array of columns known as St Kentigern's Tomb (Figure 2.50). As exposed, the platform appeared to be a fairly slight construction. Below the dressed stone surface only a single foundation course (251), some 0.3m deep was visible. This foundation was roughly built of coarsely dressed stones bedded in light-brown mortar which extended only a little beyond the platform of the tomb. As far as could be seen, the tomb foundations appeared to rest directly on the natural sand subsoil, but it is possible, and seems likely, that more substantial foundations are present but were not exposed by our excavations. What is also clear is that there were no other earlier foundations in the area. This is an important observation because, as will be discussed, claims have been advanced for the presence of foundations of an apse

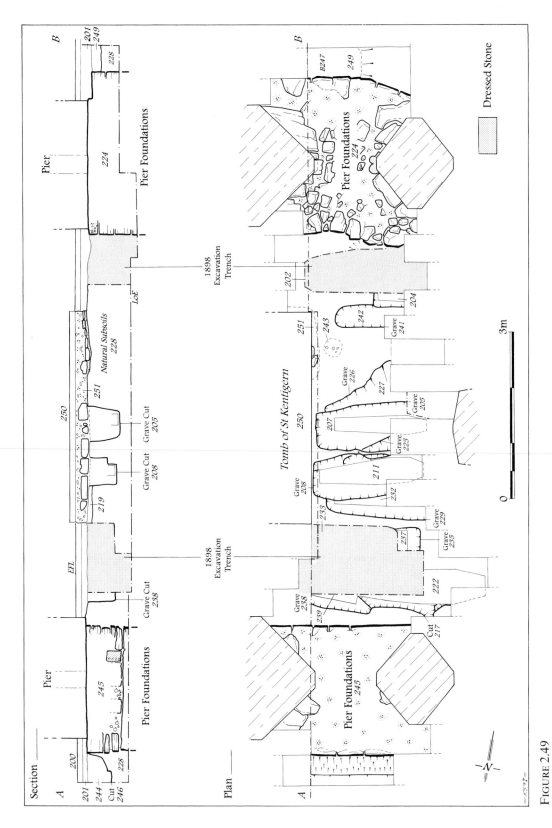

FIGURE 2.49

Plan and section of crypt W trench

FIGURE 2.50

View of crypt W trench, from the NW. The tomb of St Kentigern is behind the protective hoarding. The partially re-excavated trench originally dug by MacGregor Chalmers can be distinguished from the various 19th-century graves by its greater depth

which enclosed the site of the saint's tomb (Chalmers 1905).

Burials

It has been noted that there was no central foundation in the area to the W of St Kentigern's tomb. One reason for this may have been to permit burial near to the saint's grave. There are two badly disturbed graves which may represent medieval burials. The better preserved (sk 227) was located centrally with respect to the tomb, but was oriented SW–NE. The simple grave cut (226) contained no coffin and the fill was indistinguishable from the surrounding sand. The skeleton (sk 227) was that of a female which survived in good condition except where it had been cut away by a 19th-century burial (205). The lack of a coffin and the clean nature of the fill suggest that this was a medieval burial.

Another apparently medieval grave (241) was located slightly to the S. It also produced no trace of a

coffin and the fill was quite clean. The skeleton (sk 242) was in a fragile condition and only the bones of one foot survived. A third grave (225) survived only as a cut with a few disarticulated bones. No sign of a coffin was present and its orientation was similar to the grave to the S (226). This burial was probably medieval.

Dating evidence

In the E trench, apart from the human bone, all of the finds associated with this phase derive from construction work. These include fragments of the earlier cathedrals which were incorporated into the foundations. These are discussed in detail below (see Sections 3.2 and 3.3). The human bone most probably derives from earlier graves disturbed by the construction.

Apart from the form of the stratigraphically early burials there is no evidence to date the two graves seen to the W of St Kentigern's tomb. The absence of coffins or other finds from either grave and the poor preservation of the bone in one of the burials point to a medieval date.

Interpretation

The foundations that dominate the E trench give some insight into the primary stages of the construction of the E arm. The complete absence of any trace of A or B soil horizons or any earlier feature indicates that the building plot was landscaped prior to construction. Following the creation of a level stance, large, slightly irregular trenches were dug for the foundations which were built tightly into the trenches. The irregular dimensions and the coarse finish of the foundations provide an interesting contrast to the above-ground precision. There was also a contrast between the roughly finished central foundation in the E trench and the tidy work around the tomb of St Kentigern.

Given that there is no evidence for the translation of St Kentigern's bones (Duncan 1998), it must be presumed that the existing four-piered tomb-shrine was raised over the same tomb that was venerated in Jocelin's and John's cathedrals. The tomb-shrine and the crypt vaulting have attracted serious attention for some time (Watson 1901, 118–24), but the full architectural significance of this *quasi ciborium* has only recently been articulated (Wilson 1998, 57). The vaulting design of the crypt focuses an exceptional degree of attention on the tomb, so it is not surprising that around the saint's tomb work was undertaken with a high degree of care. Thinking back to the sequence of building, it seems altogether likely that this stone canopy was the first element of Bondington's eastern arm to be erected.

There was little evidence for medieval burial around the tomb. This may in part be accounted for by the disturbances of later post-Reformation burials and the MacGregor Chalmers excavations (1905). Conditions encountered in the nave would suggest that regular burial would have generated considerable quantities of disarticulated bones, but there were none that could not be linked to the post-Reformation graves. The conclusion to be drawn is that throughout the Middle Ages burial in close proximity to the saint was reserved for the most remarkable of individuals, presumably distinguished clerics. Over the centuries there seem to have been very few who measured up. Certainly there is a significant distinction between the density of burial in the nave and that indicated for the crypt, especially near to the tomb.

The stone fitted with a drain found to the W of the western trench on the centre line of the cathedral has been interpreted as the site of a font by the excavator (Gordon 1980). This area to the W of the tomb was liturgically important and it is more likely that there was an altar or chapel here, which Durkan (1970) suggests eventually became the parish altar used by the Glasgow Barony (ie rural) parish. This too would have militated against burial in the area except for significant individuals. The fact that one of these burials was of a woman, perhaps suggests that these burials, if medieval, were relatively late.

The absence of any evidence for earlier structural remains around the site of the tomb and the indication that the ground had been substantially reshaped prior to the construction of the E arm in the 1240s have important implications for the understanding of the construction and design of the cathedral. Firstly, it seems quite unlikely that the body of the saint remained undisturbed during the construction work. It is reasonable to expect that a temporary translation of the relics took place, even if they were returned to the original location. Quite possibly the position of the tomb could have been relocated to satisfy architectural requirements, but in any case, the traditional view that the position of the 13th-century cathedral on the steep slope was determined by the presence of the saint's tomb needs to be critically re-evaluated. Certainly there are other factors which were brought into play including the concern to bring light into the crypt and the position of the Bishop's Castle which effectively prevented construction much further W.

Phase 7: post-Reformation structures and burials (17th–19th centuries)

There was no evidence of any medieval activity in the E trench. The paucity of medieval finds suggests that once the floor had been laid in the 13th century the slabs were not raised again until the 19th century. The exception was the burial of a hoard of ecclesiastical metalwork, which may well mark the Reformation (see Section 3.5).

The hoard was contained in a pit (150) located adjacent to the northern aisle column in what would have been the NW corner of the Lady Chapel. The flat-bottomed pit, which occupied all the space between two columns, was 0.55m deep and contained two bronze mortars and an iron pestle (Figures 2.46, 2.51 and 2.52). Its western end fell just into the E trench, which is to say outside the Lady Chapel, and extended an unknown distance to the E into the Lady Chapel. The empty mortars were laid on their side and placed hard against the N foundations, as was the pestle which became stuck to the masonry as it corroded. They rested in a compacted layer of silty sand (144). Various fills of the pit could be discerned: a dark grey sandy silt with large stones (146) and the finer deposit of dark grey silty sand (143), containing the mortars themselves. The pit was capped with compacted rubble (145). Despite this complexity, it appears that the digging and filling of the pit was a single event. There is every reason to believe that the pit was dug specifically for the mortars, but since the full extent of the pit was not examined, there may be other liturgical objects awaiting discovery. There were no finds which might have helped to pin down the date of deposition, so it is presumed that it was done around 1560, the time of the Reformation, when measures were undertaken to protect the precious treasures of the cathedral.

In the northern half of the central area of the E trench, the compacted sand layer (228) lay directly under (201) the mixed soil and mortar layer which filled the whole central area between the foundations, and provided bedding for the floor slabs.

Burials

There is incidental evidence to suggest that burial in the crypt was relatively commonplace from the 18th century onwards. There were many artefacts in the layer of trampled soil containing mortar, chipped stone and coal (105) immediately below the floor slabs. Most numerous were nails and shroud pins, but most telling were four 17th-century coins spanning a period from the 1640s to c1695 (sf 37–39, sf 42; see Section 3.6). The implications of this are considered below.

The earliest firm evidence of post-medieval burial in the crypt, consists of the battered traces of a coffin grave between the central and N foundations (Figure 2.46). This grave (138) was cut into the natural compacted sand and was sealed by a mortar spread (140) containing charcoal, which was itself cut by a later grave (137) and by a rubble filled pit (135). Grave (138) contained evidence for a badly disturbed wooden coffin, preserved as a faint soil stain and isolated fragments of wood and nails. Only the lower half of the skeleton (149), with traces of coffin (148), fell within the excavation and it was substantially

FIGURE 2.51

First view of the bronze hoard. The end of the pestle can be seen to the left of the inscribed mortar

FIGURE 2.52

The bronze hoard in situ *after the post-medieval burials had been cleared from the crypt E trench*

disturbed by a later grave (137) which had been placed in the same plot. No trace of a coffin was seen for this second grave (sk 147), the lower portion of which had in turn been disturbed by a later grave (116).

To the N of grave (138) was a rectangular pit (135) which may also have been a grave, although it contained no human remains. It was dug against the N foundations and clipped the cut of the neighbouring grave (138) to the S. This vertical-sided and flat-bottomed pit (0.94m wide x 0.50m deep) extended beyond the trench to the E. The fill of the pit consisted of tightly packed masonry rubble and loose mortar (134). Both the second burial in the grave to the S (149) and the later grave to the E (121) avoided this

intractable material. Apart from its location and flat-bottomed profile there was no indication of the function of the pit. In the absence of other explanations it seems likely that it was a grave which had to be filled in to stabilise the paving, when the floor was relaid in 1843. The pit was sealed by the trampled layer (105), upon which the modern paving stones were bedded.

The earliest post-medieval grave (229) in this area had been largely removed by grave (208) (Figure 2.49). The traces of wood present within the fill (230) suggest the presence of a coffin, but little of the skeleton (232), possibly female, was recovered. Only traces of wood and 20 iron nails (sf 624) were recovered from the fill suggesting a simpler coffin, which may indicate an earlier grave, perhaps late medieval or post-Reformation.

A small rectangular depression (126) was observed cut into the upper surface of the central foundation (108). This probably represents an attempt to level the surface of the foundation prior to the laying of the present floor. Contained within the depression was a single sherd of 18th- to 19th-century brown-glazed red earthenware.

Finds and dating evidence

The outstanding finds dating to this period are the bronze mortars, which, although made in the 13th and 14th century, are probably best understood as liturgical objects which were buried for protection at the time of the Reformation (see Section 3.5). There were no finds accompanying the mortars that would provide an indication of the date of deposition, but it was certainly before the burials, and probably before the intensification in activity represented by the numerous coin finds of the 17th century. It must be admitted that the mortars could equally have been deposited at any time following their manufacture in the 14th century.

The fills of the latest graves (117, 122) in the E trench, near the findspot of the mortars, contained shroud pins, but were otherwise identical to the mixed layer (111, 113) seen between the central and N foundations and which was cut by all the graves. This subfloor deposit represents the accumulation of material going back to the construction of the cathedral. It includes small quantities of pottery and other small finds: four sherds of SECWGW (12th to 14th century), and three sherds of 19th-century white earthenware (sf 283), a single 18th- to 19th-century sherd of brown-glazed red earthenware (sf 302), two clay tobacco pipe bowl fragments and a copper-alloy button (sf 56). The stratigraphically analogous layer of medium brown silt (110) between the central and southern foundations tells a similar story. It contained three sherds of pottery (SECWGW; sf 206, 255), a number of copper-alloy objects including a watch key (sf 45), a small bell (sf 46) and a glass boot-button (sf 44). More tellingly this layer also contained a 1742 halfpenny of George II (sf 43).

In the crypt there are a number finds of coins dating from the 17th century onwards. In the layers of trampled soil immediately below the floor slabs there were many artefacts, including coins. In layer (105), around the find spot of the bronze mortars, nails and shroud pins were common and the mixed pottery assemblage also points to prolonged activity: three sherds of pre-1820 tin-glazed pottery and a number of sherds of brown and white earthenware (sf 105), four sherds of pottery wasters or kiln furniture and four clay pipe stem fragments. Most telling were four coins minted between the 1640s and 1695 (see Section 3.6). A similar story is suggested by the finds from a thin column of soil (114) preserved S of the southern foundations by the early 20th-century heating duct. It contained two coins, one of which was a Charles I or II turner dated to 1640–63, the other was an Elizabeth I sixpence (1574–78). Both coins were worn and had probably been in circulation for some time prior to deposition. In the W trench (201), three 17th-century coins were discovered in the uppermost soil layer (201): two 1695–96 turners of William II and a worn bawbee. Like the layer below the slabs in the E trench, this layer contained a mix of pottery from various dates, but with a concentration of coins indicating activity in the late 17th century.

Burials in the crypt were never as dense as in the nave and although there are a few traces of medieval burials near to the tomb of St Kentigern, most of the graves date to post-Reformation times. The best preserved graves were, not surprisingly, the latest, and dated to the middle of the 19th century. There is a possibility that some of the earlier burials, which have all been heavily disturbed by later graves, date to the 17th or 18th century, but on balance the historical evidence argues against burial prior to the departure of the Barony congregation in 1798.

Interpretation

The burial of the bronze mortars cannot be precisely dated, but may be associated with the disruption in the late 1550s which culminated in Archbishop Beaton's departure for Paris, taking the cathedral treasures with him for safe-keeping. The mortars would have been too heavy to travel with and may have been buried at this time with the intention of recovery at a later date.

Apart from the ten coins recovered from the crypt, only one other coin was found during the rest of the excavations. Given that burial in the nave continued after the 17th century but that no 17th-century coins were found in the nave, it seems unlikely that this large number of coins is related to burial rites. An alternative explanation is that these represent losses when the lower church was used for worship. Perhaps a chest for the storage of alms was located in this area and these finds represent coins which had slipped between the cracks in the paving. Similar concentrations of coins have been noted in medieval Swedish churches, most of which were floored in timber (Klackenberg 1992, 335). The existing crypt flooring is a very tight fitting heavy flagging (in places 0.2m thick), which was renewed in 1843. We may presume that prior to the refurbishment the medieval flooring had become worn and cracked to the extent that coins could be easily lost.

In the late 16th century, following the Reformation, the crypt became a place of worship for the newly formed Barony parish. It remained in service as a church until 1801, when it was transformed into a burial ground (Stones 1970, 146). This involved

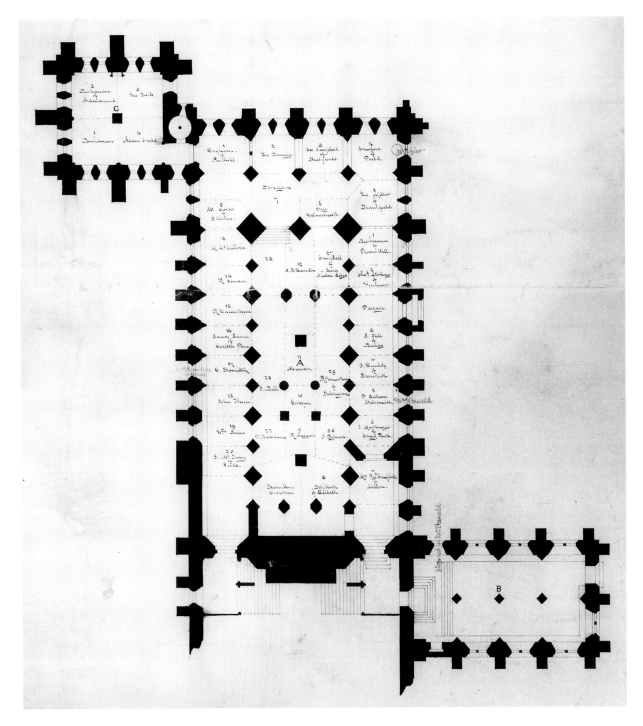

FIGURE 2.53

Plan of burial lairs in the crypt demarcated by iron railings made between 1857–64. Reproduced by kind permission of the National Archives of Scotland (NAS RHP6503/37)

introducing a small amount of earth and erecting railings to partition the space into lairs (Figure 2.53). The earliest surviving inscriptions in the crypt floor date to the 1810s, but since the soil present at that date effectively discouraged burial below the floor we may suspect that these stones are not in their original position. A letter of 1837 from the minister, William Black, makes the case for retaining this earth which was 'about two feet of depth':

the only cause of its being put in was to have sufficient depth of earth above the coffins to prevent a nauseous effluvia from the Bodies from being felt by persons visiting the Cemetery, the removing of that portion of earth now, would harrow up the feelings of persons who have their friends interred there...
(SRO, CR4/144).

Despite the prospect of hurt feelings, in 1843 HM Office of Woods and Forests instructed that the

FIGURE 2.54

View of 19th-century burials 116 (on the left) and 121 (on the right)

accumulated earth be removed and the floor be repaved at its original level (SRO, MW.1.188, Part III). Only after the floor was repaved could the practice of burial below the floor recommence. The graveslab fragment (sf 136) bearing the date 1693 (see Section 3.9) was probably placed under the floor during this tidying operation.

The use of the cathedral as a place of burial was increasingly discouraged during the later 19th century and latterly required the permission of HM Board of Works. The latest evidence for burial in the crypt, as indicated by inscriptions, can be dated to 1875 and 1878.

Phase 8: modern refurbishment (1835–present)

Burials

The two best preserved burials in this area (116, 121) (Figure 2.54) were significantly later than the graves previously discussed in the E trench. Grave (116) preserved substantial portions of stamped metal plates depicting winged cherubim and other features of mid-19th-century coffin furniture (119) (see Section 3.4).

A single mother-of-pearl button, probably for fastening the shroud (sf 48), was found with the skeleton (118). Grave (121) was located slightly SW of grave (116) and avoided the edge of the stone-filled pit (135). This grave overlay and had caused the removal of the lower half of skeleton (147). The coffin (124) (Figure 2.55) for this grave also had stamped decorative plates and evidence that it had been covered in velvet, probably black in colour. The fill of these late graves (117, 122) consisted of a grey-black organic soil with coal and mortar similar to the layers through which they cut (111, 113). In addition to the occasional pot sherd these fills contained shroud pins.

Because there was no central foundation in the western trench it was possible to accommodate a number of graves in close proximity to St Kentigern's tomb. Most of these burials were contained in well-preserved, ornate coffins which date from the mid- to late 19th century.

In the W trench the best preserved burials were a late pair which appear to be approximately coeval judging from the coffin furniture. Grave (205) contained a coffin (212) and a well-preserved skeleton of a woman (sk 207) who was buried wearing a pair of gold hoop earrings. She appears to have been the only burial to be accompanied by jewellery. The grave fill (206) contained disarticulated human bones (210), fragments of wood, tin coffin-decoration (sf 717), handles (sf 70) and velvet (from the covering of the coffin) and pottery fragments (sf 681).

The coffin (213) in grave (208) to the N was similar to that in (205). The well-preserved skeleton (211) of an immature female, aged about fifteen years, had been buried in a shroud fastened with pins over the sternum, with two interlocking bronze rings. The grave fill (209) was similar to the fill (206) of grave (205) and contained pottery sherds which ranged from SECWGW (sf 682) through to modern white earthenware (sf 431), a fragment of clay pipe stem, and a copper-alloy ring (sf 57). Fills (204), (206) and (209) contained shroud pins.

FIGURE 2.55

View from the back of in situ furnishings on coffin 124

A number of graves were also present to the NW of the tomb, which were badly damaged by the archaeological excavations of 1898. Three closely packed, but probably not intercutting, graves were damaged by the N trench of these investigations. Grave (235) was almost completely removed; only the skull of skeleton (237) survived, while only the corner of the coffin in grave (238) was present. The best-preserved grave (217) was stratigraphically later than grave (238) and was probably the latest grave in this area. The bottom half of grave (217) had been cut away by the 1898 trench, but substantial parts of the coffin (223) with its decoration of embossed iron and fabric covering survived. The burial was most notable for the sophisticated early denture made from real teeth mounted on gold pins set into hippopotamus ivory (see Section 4.2). Judging from the inscription to the W of the saint's tomb, these burials may be identified as: 'Robert Fulton Alexander | Susan Anderson | and | their children'. A nearby inscription, immediately SW of the tomb commemorates: 'John Ryburn | Born 19th January 1766 | Died 30 November 1844', who may be identified with grave (204).

Two infant skeletons (sk 247, sk 248) and disarticulated adult bones (sk 252) were uncovered S of foundation (224). The skeletons were laid one over the other. The upper infant (sk 247) died at around six years while the lower was no older than two. They lay immediately next to an inscription reading: 'The burying place | of the late | James Mackensie Esquire | of Craig Park | where four of his children are interred | James MacKensie died 13th June 1838'.

Other archaeological investigations

The last major event to be observed in the crypt was an archaeological excavation undertaken by architect Peter MacGregor Chalmers in 1898 to investigate the area around the site of St Kentigern's tomb (Chalmers 1905). His theory was that the E end of the late 12th-century cathedral terminated in an apse which enclosed the site of the saint's tomb as indicated by the configuration of the crypt vaulting. To test his idea MacGregor Chalmers laid out trenches along the N and S sides of St Kentigern's tomb. These were thin slots, neatly dug, straight-sided and generally less than 1m wide. Both trenches cut through the later burials, and carried on beyond 1.5m, the depth at which our investigations stopped. In the N trench it looks as if the excavation continued for a considerable depth. Decayed traces of substantial wooden shoring (221) remained in situ in the N trench (216). The profiles of the exposed soils, showed that these trenches had been dug through undisturbed natural subsoils. The backfill gave a very clear idea of what MacGregor Chalmers discovered, which is helpful since his report contains no account of the excavation. At the lowest levels (220) the backfill was predominantly a pink-brown

clay containing the occasional sherd of post-medieval pottery. This shows that MacGregor Chalmers had his trenches dug right through the natural sands and into clean boulder clay. This gave way to a mixed layer of clay and lighter soils (214) which contained further post-medieval finds of pottery and clay pipe fragments, together with the battered remains of the coffins and disarticulated human bones (215), which had been disturbed by the excavations. What was completely absent from the excavations was any sign of masonry either in situ or as demolished, robbed-out remains. The southern MacGregor Chalmers trench (202) had no shoring and looked less ambitious, but it too was dug down to the clay and its fill (203) contained disturbed human bones along with various post-medieval sherds and other finds, but no sign of building remains.

The cathedral foundations and all the dug features were sealed by a very mixed-up layer (105=201) which served as the bedding material for the floor slabs. The majority of coin finds from the crypt (7 out of 10) derive from this top layer. It also contained a full range of pottery from the medieval period onwards, as well as the occasional button or clay pipe fragment. The implications of these coins have been discussed above.

The north and south extremities of our excavation were defined by the brick heating ducts which were installed in 1914–16, which probably led to the discovery of the famous painted voussoir.

Summary

Kentigern's four-posted tomb-shrine appears to have been built on shallow foundations which rest directly on the natural compacted glacial sands. If an earlier structure or old ground surface survive, then all traces of it are contained within the confines of this 13th-century structure. Evidence for the antiquity of this location was not discovered but it seems certain that from the 1130s, and probably long before, this was the spot venerated as the burial place of the saint.

In charting burial activity there is some evidence for medieval and perhaps for 17th-century graves, but not on the same level of intensity as in the nave. Burial here must have been much more restricted. This changed dramatically in the early 19th century, with the departure of the Barony congregation. Even after the refurbishment of 1843 the space continued to be used for a series of opulent burials. By the late 19th century burial within the church was getting increasingly difficult and these coffins were as distinctive as was their place of burial.

2.3 THE CHOIR
by S T Driscoll

A single 1.4m wide trench was excavated behind the present communion table and W of the columns which divide the choir from the ambulatory (Figure 1.7). It was excavated to the upper surface of the vaulting which forms the extrados of the Lady Chapel vault, immediately below. Because the excavation was conducted entirely within the space above the vaulting there were no features which pre-date the construction of the eastern arm of the cathedral in the early 13th century.

Phase 4: early 13th-century cathedral

Upon the removal of the material infilling the void between the vaulting and the floor, the roughly finished upper surface of through-stones were seen to be set in a pale brown mortar (Figure 2.56). The upper surface of stones which formed the peak of the vault, showed clear signs of having been trimmed to allow the existing floor to be fitted (Figure 2.57). It is not certain when this might have taken place, but it was clear from the form of the neighbouring stones that this stonework originally protruded above the original floor level, which can be determined from the level of the pier bases in the choir. Since the uppermost stones originally protruded above the floor level it must be assumed that they were hidden beneath a platform for the high altar or a shrine to St Kentigern.

The excavations revealed evidence which relates to the construction of the upper levels of the choir. An area of rough flagging (005) was set directly on the vaulting through stones to the W of the central pier (Figure 2.58). The irregular flagstones were set in mortar and formed an uneven surface some distance below the final finished floor level. The flagstones appear to represent a temporary working surface.

The flagstones were overlain by a rubble layer which had been dumped to support the floor. This rubble (002) was a loose deposit of mortar, stone, tile and architectural rubble. Some of this material clearly relates to the original 13th-century building campaign, but it is mixed with later post-medieval material. The clearly medieval material includes fragments of moulded stones, some of which were unweathered and have no adhering mortar (Figure 2.59). They appear to have been discarded because they were broken or botched during their manufacture (see Section 3.2). The deposition of this seems to have taken place as part of the original construction process.

Phase 7: post-Reformation modifications (17th–19th centuries)

The trimming of the vaulting, mentioned above, may be reasonably supposed to have been done when the choir was being reconfigured for Protestant worship. Amongst the rubble infilling above the vaults was stonework which derives from demolition, the stones showing signs of wear and having been mortared in

place. Some of the smaller moulded stones appear to be of the same size and treatment as the work identified as the base of the shrine of St Kentigern (see Section 3.2). Whether this particular identification is correct cannot be determined, but the fine scale of the mouldings suggest that they came from a screen or other lightly constructed structure.

Phase 8: modern refurbishment (1835–present)

Amongst the rubble infill was evidence of a third deposition (after the original medieval and the putative Reformation era deposits) which relates to the 19th-century restoration work. The debris which can be specifically assigned to this work consists of fragments of carved plaster, mostly undecorated regular rectangular blocks, some of which show signs of having been carved with a knife or chisel. A few more finely worked pieces were clearly used to replace broken elements of the stiff-leaf arcade capitals (Figure 3.46) which, presumably, had been damaged when galleries were installed in the aisles.

Apart from the existing floor, the final phase of activity was the construction of a timber floor the supporting structure for which consisted of a joist system built of brick and timber (003) set into the infilling rubble and mortar. The joist supports were low walls built of large bricks (0.32 x 0.15 x 0.10m), which ran N–S at approximately 1.3m intervals. Four wooden joists survived within the excavated trench, arranged in two pairs running E–W upon the brick walls. No trace of actual flooring survived.

2.4 THE TREASURY (SESSION ROOM)
by S T Driscoll

Minor excavations were undertaken in the former treasury (now the session room) to allow for the installation of new electrical services and control panel (Figure 1.7). These excavations extended across the N stair to the crypt, but none of the trenches were of any great depth since they were simply to accommodate the electrical services. Limited evidence of medieval structures was encountered, but most of the discoveries date from post-medieval times, when the space no longer served as the cathedral treasury and had been transformed into a burial aisle (Figure 2.60).

Phase 4: early 13th-century cathedral

The main structural feature encountered within the trench was a buttress (672), which projected from the N wall of the crypt in to the SW corner of the room (Figure 2.61). It was associated with a stone scatter (671).

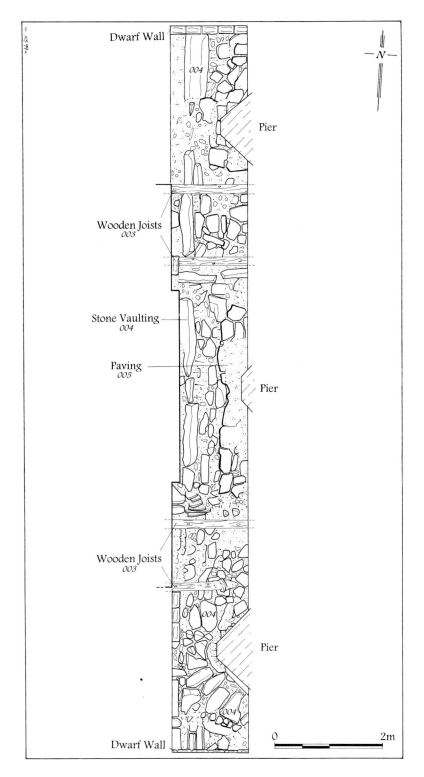

Dwarf Wall

004

Pier

Wooden Joists
003

Stone Vaulting
004

Paving
005

Pier

Wooden Joists
003

004

Pier

004

004

Dwarf Wall

0   2m

—N—

FIGURE 2.56

Plan of choir showing extrados of crypt vaulting and timber floor joists

The stone buttress (672) had been incorporated into the W wall of the treasury building, from which it projected (Figure 2.62). The trench was excavated to a depth of 0.6m only, which was not deep enough to reveal the foundations or a construction trench. The only possibly contemporary deposit was a small patch of pinky-orange mortar (661) in the corner formed by the buttress and the W wall.

FIGURE 2.57

View of extrados of crypt vaulting exposed in choir trench

FIGURE 2.58

Infilling of flagstones (005) above crypt vaulting in the choir trench

Interpretation

The sequence of building represented by the buttress and the treasury wall show that the treasury building was not a primary feature of the cathedral design. The evidence suggests that this northern projection was added as a two-storied structure during the course of the mid 13th-century building campaign (Fawcett 1997; Durkan 1970; Stones 1970). Unfortunately the mere presence of this buttress, long recognised, does little to help resolve the question surrounding the dating of the treasury building.

Phase 7: post-Reformation structures and burials (17th–19th centuries)

The predominant layer below the modern concrete flooring was a well packed, dark, organic soil (651), which filled the whole trench to the full excavated depth level of 0.60m. This layer had clearly been much disturbed in the recent past as indicated by the presence of post-medieval earthenware and clay pipe fragments. The cause of the disturbance was the use of the space for burial, which was evident from several intact graves and a disarticulated skull and pelvis (sk

FIGURE 2.59

13th–14th century moulded stones and 19th-century plasterwork recovered from the choir trench

658) found within layer 651, as were fragmented memorial stones (Figure 2.63).

There are signs that the subfloor deposits were built up from time to time, presumably to support a sagging floor. The presence of small scatterings of stone (659) overlying a layer of loose greyish-brown sand (660) in the SW portion of the excavated area is one instance. Another more substantial stone setting (671) consisting of a jumbled arrangement of five stones set in mortar was seen immediately inside the threshold of the treasury. This seems to have served as levelling material.

Burials

Portions of five burials were examined in the trench. One of these (664) lay below the required depth of 0.60m and was not excavated, but could be seen to be contained in a coffin. Two burials in coffins were arranged one (656) on top of the other (653) at the N end of the trench, close to the original position of the Rennie memorial. The remaining two burials (665, 668) were situated at the S end of the trench, but only the top end of the burials fell within the trench. Again these burials were within coffins, the wood of which was well preserved as were other perishable materials such as the shroud and hair. These partially examined burials were those of an infant (668), in an appropriately tiny coffin, and an adult (667), of which only the head and shoulders were exposed.

From the state of preservation it appears that all these burials date to the 19th century and it may be reasonably presumed that they are members of the Rennie family who were commemorated in a memorial stone mounted on the W wall. This limestone panel had been severely eroded and in places the inscription was illegible or faint (indicated in square brackets), but enough survived for it to be reconstructed as follows:

[David R]en[nie] [Glasgow] | Died. . ..A[ged]. . . | . . .[B]lack, his step-daughter, . . . | . . .and are here in[terred] | . . .and of. . . | . . .ennie, his second son. . . . . . . .9. . . . | . . . ennie, his daughter, who died. . . | . . .[inter]red at St John's, N[ewfoundland] | . . .[h]is son, placed at this stone. . . . | . . .of the. . . . | . . .ennie who died in London. . . | . . .[a]ged . . ..years.

Other fragments of a white marble memorial stone, probably also originally wall mounted, were recovered from the subfloor rubble (651). The slab (sf 334) was broken into a large number of quite small fragments, some bearing only a letter or two. Only portions of the text can be reconstructed (see Section 3.9). It could be an additional memorial erected by the Rennies or could have come from elsewhere in the churchyard.

The transformation of the treasury into a burial aisle took place in the early 19th century when the crypt and the chapter house were also transformed into burial places. The treasury, described as a 'dripping aisle' because of its leaky roof, was in a poor state of preservation by the time the programme of restoration reached this part of the cathedral. However, prior to its decline we may presume that it contained some of the more exclusive lairs within the cathedral.

2.5 THE WESTERN TOWERS
by J H McBrien

In the Spring of 1988 an 11–week excavation was carried out by the Scottish Urban Archaeological Trust at the W front of the cathedral in advance of landscaping operations associated with the redevelopment of the Cathedral Precinct (McBrien 1989).

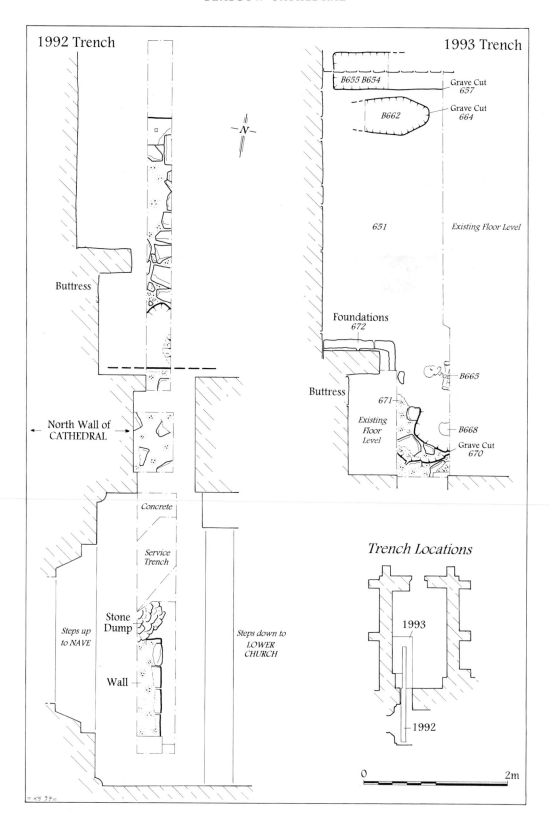

FIGURE 2.60

Plan of trenches in the treasury or session room

The principal purpose of the excavation was to recover information about the towers which flanked the W doors of the cathedral until their demolition in the 19th century. In the post-Reformation period these towers housed the Consistory Court and the Officials' Court (Durkan 1986a), but there was no conclusive information about the date of their construction or their subsequent structural history. The most accurate

FIGURE 2.61

View of buttress 672 embedded in W wall of treasury

architectural information about these towers is contained in a set of measured drawings of the cathedral (Figure 2.64) produced shortly before their demolition (Collie 1835). Limited excavation had taken place on the site of the taller NW tower in 1973 (Talbot 1975), but the results of this work were largely inconclusive. The excavator then felt that more extensive excavation was desirable.

The area available for excavation was limited by the position of known burials and by the need to keep clear the access routes to the northern side of the cathedral and to the ceremonial W door. Excavation towards the foundations of the standing walls and buttresses of the cathedral was restricted by the need to avoid disturbing a modern drainage gully and electricity cables.

Two areas were laid out at the beginning of March 1988; the first being a southern extension to the 1973 in the N tower trench, but including a planned overlap of approximately 1m so that the previous results could be reassessed in the light of new information (Figures 1.7 and 2.65). The second area was laid out to include as much of the area of the SW tower as was possible within the above constraints.

The initial excavation of post-demolition deposits was severely hampered by the presence of large quantities of disturbed human skeletal remains deposited in the second half of the 19th century. These were not examined but were carefully removed and collected for reburial. Later in the excavation, work on the basal deposits' deepest features had to be halted for safety reasons when the local water-table was reached. It was

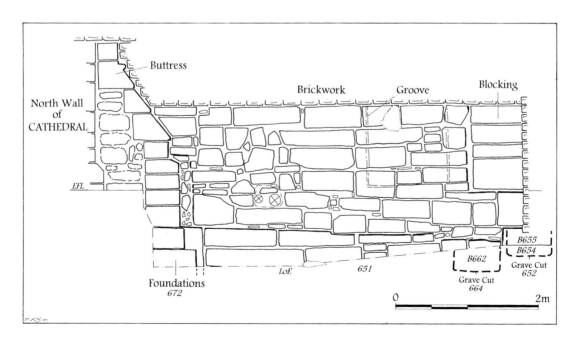

FIGURE 2.62

Elevation of W wall of the treasury

FIGURE 2.63

Grave cuts appearing within 651 at the right end of the trench in the treasury

not felt, however, that significant deposits remained unexcavated because of the paucity of artefacts in the excavated portions of the fills, and because the stratigraphic relationships had been established.

The excavation revealed two burials which predated the SW tower and a rubbish pit which pre-dated the construction of the NW tower. The NW tower appears to have been constructed in the early 14th century and the SW tower sometime later in the 15th century. Following the demolition of the towers in the 19th century a number of drains, ossuaries and utility trenches were dug on the site of the SW tower.

The NW tower

Phase 5: completion of the laying out of the nave (mid 13th century)

The earliest deposits uncovered were pits and structural features associated with the building of the tower (Figure 2.65). The oldest feature identified was a pit (1130) dug into the natural boulder clay. The homogenous nature of its dark brown clay/loam fill suggested that this may have been a rubbish pit. Cutting the fill of this pit were construction trenches (1121, 1137) for the mortared rubble foundation of the tower's S wall (1118) and for a large drain built of mortared sandstone sides and massive cap-stones (1100). All of this masonry was presumed to be locally sourced yellow sandstone. When uncovered, this drain was still carrying excess groundwater away to the northern side of the cathedral. It was clear from the common fill of the construction trenches, a grey-yellow sandy gravel with frequent cobbles and some

mortar, that the walls and drain had been built at the same time.

Phase 6: use of towers (13th–17th centuries)

A number of pits (1128, 1132, 1090) which post-date the building operations were dug between the tower walls and drain. The fills of pits 1128 and 1132 suggested that these too were rubbish pits.

Finds recovered from the pit fills included food refuse in the form of animal bones from pit 1132. Pit 1128 produced small fragments of what was probably window glass and lead offcuts. The glass was in a fragile condition and upon excavation these small flat pieces disintegrated. There were several fragments of lead strips, 18–100mm in length and one fragment of H-profile window came. The rubbish pits contained sherds of pottery including SECWGW and Scottish medieval redwares, which would be consistent with a date in the 13th–14th centuries.

The most northerly pit (1090) fell only partly within the area of excavation, and its full size and shape remain unknown. The fill (1070) of this feature was unlike the others in that it was composed of relatively clean re-deposited clay without the artefacts present elsewhere. It is possible that this was the southern edge of a grave cut post-dating the tower.

In the angle formed by the walls and apparently respecting them, an irregular layer of grey-yellow mortar (1061), similar to the wall mortar, sealed the pits and foundation trench fills. This layer thinned and became more compact as it spread northwards. Where

FIGURE 2.64

Western elevation of Glasgow Cathedral made shortly before the demolition of the towers (Collie 1835, plate XVII)

their position it seems likely that they were associated with access to the drain for cleaning or repair during the period of use of the tower.

Phase 7: post-Reformation activity (17th–19th centuries)

A layer of fine dark grey silt (1060) up to 0.07m deep had accumulated over the mortar floor. Lying directly on top of this was a thin but uniform spread of slate fragments (1058). The slate spread was in turn covered with a mixed clay deposit (1057), the upper surface of which was very compact and contained a high proportion of stone, hand-made brick and mortar fragments. This mixed mortar deposit is interpreted as a repair to a decaying structure. Part of the problems in interpretation experienced by the 1973 excavation were because they halted at this surface and never examined the pre-demolition levels. The southern and western edges of these mortar repairs were damaged immediately after the removal of the tower in 1848, by a robber trench (1046) dug to remove the better quality stones. This trench was backfilled with crushed mortar and sandstone fragments (1045).

At about the same time as the stone robbing, a trench (1116) was cut along the course of the large drain, to the depth of the bottom of the cap-stones, presumably to allow the drain to be cleaned out. This was then backfilled (1112) and material (1009) brought from elsewhere in the graveyard to landscape the site of the tower. This material contained large quantities of disarticulated human skeletal remains.

Phase 8: modern (1835–present)

In recent times the W front of the cathedral was landscaped. A drainage gully was built against the wall and soil was imported to the site to provide the base for a path and a lawn. A narrow trench (1011) next to the drainage gully contained a high voltage electric cable to power the cathedral floodlights.

Dating and interpretation

The relationship between the W end of the nave and the tower could not be investigated because electricity cables and the rebuilt 19th-century buttresses intervened. The foundations for the nave, however, may have been laid c1200 and Fawcett (1997, 68–69) suggests that the ceremonial W doors were complete in the middle of the 13th century, and that the great W window is essentially of late 13th-century date. In the absence of direct evidence it appears that the nave was constructed before the tower foundations were laid out; although the tower appears to have been

the mortar was not present as a distinct layer, fragments were found pressed into the deposits immediately below. It is possible that this was the ground floor surface of the tower, compacted and worn away in the centre of the room. The absence of any tile fragments or stone flagging suggests that the original flooring, which was bedded in the mortar, was removed at some date prior to their demolition, probably around the time of the Reformation.

Cutting through this surface was a series of small rectangular-ended slots (1102, 1103, 1107, 1109) on either side of the large drain. Unfortunately, later features removed the material which lay between the slots making their interpretation uncertain, but from

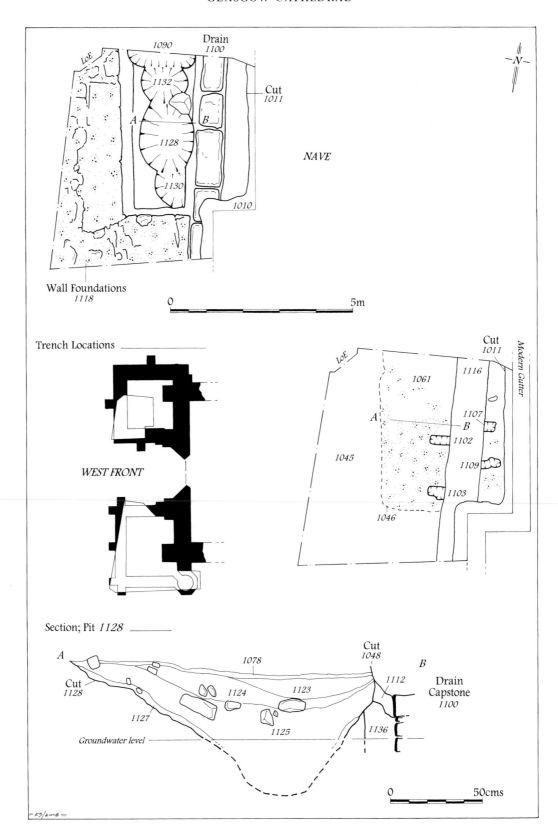

FIGURE 2.65

Trench location (excavation areas shown as blank), plans and section in NW tower

constructed prior to the completion of the N aisle of the nave, sometime in the later 13th century. The absence of glazing in the western window of the aisle was noted during the demolition of the towers (Eyre-Todd 1898, 277) and this suggests that the tower was started before the completion of the W front.

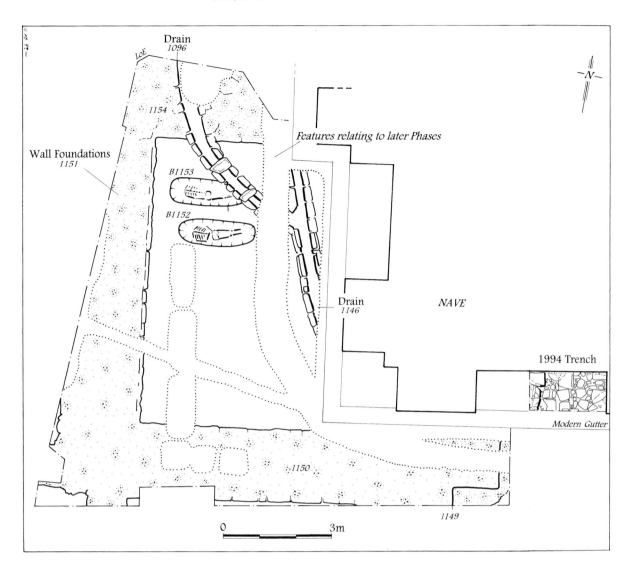

FIGURE 2.66

Plan of burials and drains in the SW tower

FIGURE 2.67

View of drain running through N wall of SW tower

The hard mortar surface at which the excavation of the NW tower stopped in 1973 has been shown to be an early modern repair to a decaying structure. The large drain (1100) had been uncovered on at least two earlier occasions since the tower's demolition, but has now been shown to have been constructed at the same time as the tower foundations.

The SW tower

Phases 1–3: pre-construction burials (end of 12th century)

The earliest features encountered in the area of the S tower were two shallow depressions (1152, 1153) in the clay subsoil, containing fragmentary inhumations (Figure 2.66). Levelling of the site in the past had caused the removal of the skull and frontal portion of the ribs and pelvis in both cases, and various other bones from each (see Section 4.3). Only the lowest-lying fragments survived. The position of the surviving remains suggested that each body had been wrapped in a shroud and buried in an extended supine position with feet to the E. In one instance the arms had been crossed over the abdomen. There was no evidence for coffins or grave goods.

Phase 5: completion of the laying out of the nave (mid 13th century)

These burials were truncated during the construction of the tower, when the area was levelled and construction trenches were dug for the tower wall foundations (1150, 1151, 1154). The tower site has a pronounced downwards slope from the SW. The shallowest of the sandstone rubble foundations were found near the cathedral W doors. Here the level of the foundations was approximately 0.25m below the level of the threshold of the W doors. Excavation elsewhere showed that the foundations extended approximately 0.30m below this level. At the tower's SE corner, however, where the slope of the hill was steepest, the foundations had been carried to below the 0.9m depth of the excavation.

A sandstone slab-built culvert (1146) lay in the E half of the trench and ran towards the SE corner (Figure 2.67). A spur (1096) of this culvert ran through the N wall of the tower. The W side of the drain showed three courses of surviving masonry which continued with running bonds into the stonework of the tower, clearly indicating that the culverts had been built at the same time as the N wall foundations.

Finds recovered from the construction trench fills of the drain 1142 and the wall 1154 included two sherds of green-glazed Scottish medieval redware pottery probably produced before the middle of the 15th century. Modern artefacts, including a clay pipe, were recovered from the silted up drain itself. No artefacts were recovered from these fills that were identifiably later than the 18th century. This drain had silted-up completely and had partially collapsed by the time of the tower's demolition.

A scarcement was built into the western wall foundation (1151). It was marked by a straight line near the interior edges along which was carved a simple ledge on the upward protruding stones (Figure 2.68). A friable layer of mortary sand (1019, 1025) approximately 0.04m deep lay within the tower and overlay the scarcement. From this level the more precise masonry of the tower's walls carried upwards.

The mortary sand that had been laid in the tower did not appear to have been a firm floor surface, but may represent levelling material for a laid surface. Although no evidence of the floor surface itself was recovered it is likely that, as in the case of the NW tower, it was paved in stone and removed around the time of the Reformation.

At the SE corner of the tower it was seen that the buttresses which clasped the corner of the tower were embedded in later masonry (1149). This masonry consisted of irregular rubble, but only a small part of this rubble mortar spread fell within the area of excavation. It seems likely that this construction served as the foundation for an octagonal stair tower which was added sometime in the later Middle Ages or post-medieval period (Eyre-Todd 1898, 280). The form of the tower is shown clearly in Collie's plan of 1835.

During the removal of heating ducts in May 1994 a small trench (2.5 x 1.1m) was excavated to the E of the 1988 trench. This revealed a spread of irregular stones in mortar and a large chamfered sandstone block (Figure 2.66). The relationship between this and the stair tower or buttress was not determined, however, as the excavation was halted at a depth of 0.40m and the small area excavated thwarted any attempt at interpretation.

Phase 8: modern (1835–present)

The tower was demolished to ground level in 1846. Thin lenses of demolition debris and landscaping deposits were recovered overlying the N wall foundations (Figure 2.69). Cut through these deposits was the construction trench for a large sandstone slab-built drain (1087) which ran S and then E, cutting through the earlier collapsed drain (1096) and the SE corner foundations (1150). This drain was cemented in place and lined with a bituminous substance. The fill of the construction trench (1088) for this drain contained disturbed human remains and mid 19th-century pottery sherds. It was clear that this was a late attempt to improve the drainage of the area in front of the W doors.

FIGURE 2.68

View of scarcement in the W wall foundation of the SW tower

The cap-stones of the late drain were exposed by a trench (1062) dug for the construction of the modern drainage gully of the cathedral. Also dating to the modern era was an irregular ossuary or re-burial pit (1148) dug through the remains of the tower's N wall. This contained moderate amounts of human bones which were collected for re-burial without analysis.

Further modern landscaping work was carried out using material (1005) which contained quantities of fragmented human remains. A series of seven regularly shaped ossuary pits (1022–1028) were dug through this material. These pits varied in size, but were arranged in an L-shaped pattern. Three of the pits (1023, 1027, 1028) were dug directly on top of the foundations, which suggests that the foundations were not visible at the time the pits were excavated. Because of the difficulty in digging through the masonry it appears that these pits were abandoned at a shallow depth and a series of deeper pits dug (1022, 1024, 1025, 1026). Each was found to be carefully packed with disarticulated human remains (Figure 2.70), the majority of which were skulls and long bones. One could speculate that these bones represent the clearing out of lairs in the tower during the demolition process.

It was noted during their collection that several of the skulls had been cut for autopsy or anatomical study (see Chapter 4).

The exterior face of the western wall foundation was partially removed for the construction of a clay-lined burial plot which was provided with a ceramic drain (1017). This drain was laid towards the SE corner of the cathedral, where it was inserted into the slab-built drain (1087). The electricity cable trench (1012) ran beside the present drainage gully as it did in the northern area.

Dating and interpretation

The archaeological evidence recovered from the southern tower reveals that, like the northern tower, it was a later addition to the W front. The narrower and shallower foundations suggest a later medieval date. The recovery of 15th-century pottery from the construction trenches provides a *terminus post quem* and suggest that this tower cannot have been built before the second half of the 15th century. Documentary sources indicate that this was a period when the

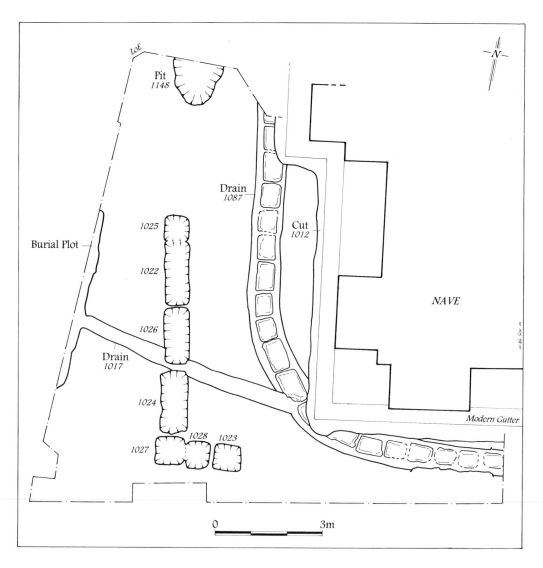

FIGURE 2.69

Plan of modern features, including ossuary pits, in the SW tower

FIGURE 2.70

Detailed view of ossuary pit 1025 in SW tower

cathedral was short of space for administrative and other purposes (Durkan 1986b). By the beginning of the 16th century, however, the documentary sources suggest less pressing need for space indicating that the problem had been solved. These observations lend weight to archaeological arguments in favour of a late 15th-century date for the southern tower.

The two earlier inhumations found may be judged to be Christian burials from their position and alignment. Their location outside the W doors possibly indicates relatively high status, perhaps as clergy, but that they were buried after the construction of the nave and thus probably date to the 14th century or later.

Discussion

Unfortunately a number of finds recovered from this excavation were unavailable for further study and a full catalogue does not exist. These missing finds included pottery and the possible 14th-century window glass. Therefore the dating of the construction is based upon preliminary assessments of the artefacts made in the interim report.

The excavation was successful in revealing a clear structural sequence for each of the western towers and in answering the problems of interpretation posed by the 1973 excavation. In addition, there was sufficient dating evidence to propose a chronology for the construction of the towers.

Modern work on the history and architecture of the cathedral (Stones 1970; Fawcett 1990a) has shown that the 13th century was a period which saw many different attempts being made to add to the fabric of the cathedral, some of which were postponed soon after commencement, only to be completed or adapted at a later date.

The relationship of the tower foundations to the nave shows that work on the NW tower was begun sometime after the nave was laid out. The material recovered from the rubbish pits, which post-date the foundations, is of late 13th–early 14th century date. This combined with the architectural and historical evidence suggest a date of the later 13th century for the tower foundations. The historical evidence for the origins of the tower reinforce this view.

The deposits inside the NW tower indicate a considerable period of use, decay and repair. A trampled and worn mortar surface, itself not likely to be original, was overlain by silty debris and evidence of subsequent modification and repair, perhaps after the Reformation. Evidence for ad hoc repairs in the early modern period was also present and serve to underline the cathedral's good fortune in a period when other great churches in Scotland were simply allowed to fall into ruin.

Work on the SW tower does not appear to have begun until the later 14th or early 15th century. The area was levelled before construction could begin, disturbing two earlier burials. The pottery recovered from the construction trenches for the tower is Scottish medieval redware, a type not believed to have been produced after the mid 15th century. This differs from the SECWGW and Scottish medieval redwares recovered from the NW tower which are consistent with a 13th–14th century date.

The modification or demolition of the original buttress at the SE corner of the tower indicates that the SE stair was a later addition, perhaps dating to the 17th century. This was suggested in the 19th century when the architectural merits of the towers were discussed prior to their demolition. The apparent late date of the stair was taken as evidence of a late date for the tower itself. The original foundation arrangement at this corner certainly bears little comparison with the pre-demolition plan drawn by Collie in 1835.

The slab-built drain (1087) through the southern tower certainly post-dates the tower's demolition in 1846, but copies the manner of construction of the drain in the northern tower quite faithfully. It is probable that this was inserted in the remains of the tower after the demolition of the northern tower in 1848 revealed the still-working medieval drain of similar design. The imitation of the early drain is a great compliment to the medieval masons who designed and built it.

The excavations demonstrate that the western towers of Glasgow Cathedral were not part of the original plans for the nave. The northern tower may date to the early 14th century, although its foundations were perhaps laid near the end of the 13th century. The southern tower seems to have been built in the later 15th century in order to increase the usable space within the cathedral and was evidently never completed. Both towers were adapted to the needs of later ages and were allowed to fall into the state of disrepair. Their poor condition contributed to the view that the towers were of inferior workmanship to the rest of the cathedral, which led to their removal.

2.6 EXCAVATIONS FOR SERVICES TO THE NE OF THE CATHEDRAL
by L Johnstone

The installation of closed-circuit TV and telephone cables both within the graveyard and along Wishart Street provided an opportunity to monitor the archaeology in these areas in 1996–97.

Trench 1

Trench 1 was in the NE of the graveyard. The trench extended NW from the graveyard wall, round the chapter house and then SW to an electrical junction box on the N side of the crypt (Figure 1.7). The trench was approximately 0.3m in width but varied in depth.

Below the topsoil was a layer of silty loam and sand, which was extremely mixed from the repeated process of grave-digging. Disarticulated human bones were recovered from this context. These were not analysed and were reburied when the trench was backfilled.

Two sandstone blocks were uncovered running across the trench at right angles to it. It is believed that these stones mark the division of burial lairs. Other areas of trench 1 had been disturbed by modern activity. This was evidenced by the presence of fairly recently disturbed soil and fragments of plastic and electric cables.

Trench 2

This is simply a continuation of trench 1, outside the churchyard. The topsoil covered a mixed sandy loam containing an occasional disarticulated human bone. An articulated skeleton (sk 2003) was located below the sloped ground to the E of the graveyard wall at a depth of 0.7m below the topsoil. It was excavated and is described below (see Section 4.4). The grave fill was of a light yellow/brown sandy clay (2005) which had frequent inclusions of sandstone fragments. Below the topsoil, the soil matrix contained large quantities of disarticulated bone, including a mixture of animal and human bone, a fragmented adult skull and a complete infant skull. This assemblage of bones, unusual for such a small area (1.5 x 2.2m), probably represents post-medieval tidying up of the graveyard.

Unfortunately, due to a failure in the notification procedure, work was commenced on this trench without archaeological supervision. In consequence, at least one other *in situ* burial is thought to have been destroyed.

Discussion

The graveyard wall has lain on its present line from at least the mid-18th century when a memorial to Mr Patrick McKinnon, who died in 1757, was built into the E boundary wall. The burials beyond this wall probably date to an earlier period when the graveyard was more extensive.

3

THE FINDS AND ENVIRONMENT

3.1 INTRODUCTION
by S T Driscoll

All of the artefacts recovered during these excavations date from the 12th century or later. Most are related directly to the construction and modification of the cathedral fabric and its use as a burial place.

Among the most important finds were the architectural fragments recovered in the foundations where they had been reused to support the existing building. The architectural sculpture mostly belongs to the late 12th-century campaign, while the wall-painting and decorated architectural fragments date exclusively to the later 12th century. Because of their rarity the wall-paintings have been subject to both detailed stylistic study and scientific analysis. Sadly there are neither sufficient architectural fragments nor wall-paintings to allow full understanding of the late 12th-century cathedral.

Finds of medieval metalwork were rare, but several important discoveries were made. Most exceptional was the hoard of two bronze mortars with an iron pestle which were buried in the crypt. Not only are such large mortars a rare survival from the 13th or 14th century, but uniquely one has the name of a 13th-century bishop prominently cast into it. The other notable medieval find is a personal seal from the 13th or 14th century found in a grave in the nave.

Large quantities of post-medieval coffin fittings were recovered. The majority of these come from residual contexts, but there were also a significant number of intact or partially intact coffins. In a few remarkable cases local ground conditions had led to the preservation of the wood. Because post-medieval coffins have rarely been studied in Scotland, this

seemed an important opportunity to present a relatively well-dated assemblage.

The excavation also produced several curiosities. A clutch of musket balls was recovered from a burial (sk 353), some of which were found inside the traumatised skull. One individual buried in the middle of the 19th century had a set of false teeth made from human teeth, gold and hippopotamus ivory.

3.2 ARCHITECTURAL STONEWORK
by S T Driscoll, G Ericsson and R Fawcett

Sixty-seven stones with architectural carving or other decoration were recovered during the excavations, including 18 with well-preserved 12th-century painting (see Section 3.3). There were a great many more worked stones and fragments of stones, originally from the 12th-century buildings, which are not discussed in any detail here. Most of these were plain ashlar. The high level of finish throughout gives the impression that both 12th-century cathedrals were executed to a high standard. The largest number of the architectural stones were discovered in the crypt, where they had been reused in the existing foundations. Since these foundations were laid in the 13th century, the majority necessarily derive from the two 12th-century building programmes. The first cathedral, undertaken by John, the first bishop, was consecrated in 1136. The second, conducted by Bishop Jocelin reached a level of completeness sufficient to allow it to be consecrated in 1197. The bulk of the stone used was a locally derived white sandstone, probably from quarries north of the present George Square in central Glasgow (Lawson 1990, 22–24). Some pinker stone was present in the first cathedral, but in the second and third the stone is uniformly white. The excavated material

81

compliments an existing collection of architectural stone previously discovered in undocumented circumstances, some of which is currently on display in the cathedral crypt. In the following text catalogued fragments are preceded by 'c'.

Phase 2: cathedral of Bishop John (early 12th century)

Apart from the wall with the chamfered plinth and buttress (368) discovered in the nave, which is interpreted as the W front of the first cathedral, there are few architectural fragments that certainly derive from the early 12th century. The most securely-dated fragments are a series of half-column drums built into a wall footing (303) interpreted as the N wall of the nave of the late 12th-century cathedral (Figure 2.14). Only four drums were visible in the top course of the wall footing (303) during the excavations, but mortar scars on the top of the wall marked the position of others. The proportions of some of the stones in the wall suggested that at least one more course of that wall was built from similar column drums. Moreover, during the mid 19th-century restoration work it was recorded in the *Scotch Reformers Gazette* for 29 July 1843 that:

> ...a number of half-column blocks, two and a half feet in diameter, were dug out fresh and sharply cut as if from the hands of the mason, ...we have no doubt that these Old Saxon Columns formed part of some ancient church. Many of the blocks which interfered with the operations... are now lying outside the cathedral for the purpose of being removed.

There are two additional fragments of engaged shafts (c 2, c 3) from around small openings such as a door or window, which probably derive from the first cathedral. The plain, round-sectioned, free-standing shaft (c 4) also seems to belong to this building phase.

The half-column drums suggest either that there was an aisled part of the church or that there was a crypt. The use of half-columns has 11th-century French antecedents. For example, they appear in the nave arcading of Bernay Abbey (built in 1030–60) and in Auxerre Cathedral where the half-column drums are used in clustered piers supporting the crypt vaulting (built c1023). The motif was also well established in England by the mid 11th century. Examples of half-column drums flanking the chancel arch are to be seen in St Nicholas's church at Worth, Sussex, and St Mary's church at Stow, Lincolnshire, while their use in nave arcading is a feature at Great Paxton, Cambridgeshire (Fernie 1983). Possibly the most important comparison is with the giant order at Jedburgh Abbey (Thurlby 1995) which Rainer Mentel (1998) has recently suggested was modelled on John's cathedral at Glasgow (Jedburgh was also a joint project of David I and John). If nothing else, this comparison helps convey the style and scale of the first cathedral (as in Figure 1.4)

The evidence indicates that the first cathedral was built of finely dressed sandstone ashlar. There is a suggestion that it was built with contrasting lighter interior and darker exterior stone, but the difference could be due to weathering. If, however, the pinker hue of the chamfered plinth was deliberate the exterior may have been polychrome, as at Kirkwall. The half-column drums suggest the presence of either an aisle arcading, possibly with a gallery level, or a substantial chancel opening. The large quantity of half-columns which appear to have been built into the later nave wall (303), perhaps suggest that they were used in a nave with arcades. These half-column drums are of plain round section and it seems likely, judging from the two nook-shaft fragments with angle roll-mouldings, that the rest of the interior had a similarly restrained Romanesque appearance. There is no evidence for stone vaulting in the first cathedral.

Phase 3: cathedral of Bishop Jocelin (late 12th century)

Prior to the excavations, the second cathedral was known only from the upstanding fabric surviving in the SW compartment of the crypt. This small portion of walling with its engaged column, wall bench and slightly unusual quadripartite vaulting are much discussed (Radford and Stones 1964; Fawcett 1990a). The column in particular attracted attention, because its decorative features were significantly earlier than the rest of the crypt. The keeled shaft stands in a water-holding base and is crowned by an early stiff-leaf capital with a quirked square abacus. The short shaft supports a single, half-diagonal vaulting rib. A few other loose pieces of masonry are also known from this phase including a water-holding base for an engaged keeled shaft with spurs at the angles, which is on display in the cathedral. Perhaps the most discussed single element of Jocelin's cathedral is the window voussoir painted with a palmette design, which has been ascribed on art historical grounds to both the early and late 12th-century campaigns (Cameron 1986; Radford and Stones 1964, respectively). Subsequent scientific analysis of the paint, however, clearly links the voussoir with late 12th-century painting scheme (see Section 3.3). This brightly painted voussoir hinted that the interior of the second cathedral was highly decorated. During the excavation wall footings for an incomplete nave were uncovered underpinning the eastern piers of the existing nave. These well-made wall footings incorporated earlier masonry including the half-column drums mentioned above. Although incomplete, the depth of the nave foundations suggests that the eastern arm featured a substantial crypt extending well into the space now occupied by the nave.

The excavations produced a large body of architectural material which fills a great many gaps in our understanding of the interior appearance of the late

12th-century building. These include evidence for figurative and abstract paintings in selected areas, which is considered in detail below (see Section 3.3). An even greater number of unpainted carved and shaped architectural stones were recovered. These include a range of capitals, pier fragments, door or window jambs and arches, vaulting ribs, and voussoirs, greatly expanding the range of decoration known from this structure.

The architectural fragments derive from a variety of settings. For instance the volute and corinthianesque capitals appear on nook shafts of doorways or windows (c 6, c 7, c 50), while the water-leaf capitals are from wall or vaulting shafts (c 8). Water-leaf capitals appear in northern Britain from the second half of the 12th century, for example the Galilee Chapel of Durham cathedral built between 1153–95 (Halsey 1980). At Jedburgh Abbey variation in capital choice marks out building campaigns of slightly different date: the nave capitals are all of water-leaf type, while those in the earlier presbytery mix water-leaf and crocket capitals (Fawcett 1994b; Simpson 1965). The range of material recovered from Glasgow supports the notion that a sequence of building campaigns were undertaken in the late 12th century.

All the shafts which can be identified with the late 12th-century cathedral were keeled, except for those associated with smaller openings. Most of the shaft fragments are from walls, similar to the surviving *in situ* wall shaft, but there is also evidence for compound piers. The keeled shafts are a conspicuous feature of the N nave wall of Holyrood Abbey (Fawcett 1994b), while in the Galilee Chapel at Durham even the nook-shafts of the W wall are keeled (Pevsner 1983).

The rib vaulting fragments (c 32–35) are also all keeled and may be compared with the vault in the SW compartment of the crypt. The limited evidence of intersections suggests that the vaulting was of quadripartite type, with four sections divided by ribs springing from the corners of the bay (Cocke *et al* 1996).

Keeling is also seen on some of the string course fragments. Two keeled fragments (c 21, c 22) probably come from the upper element of an external base course or from a string course forming a major horizontal articulation of the building, such as from the junction of a pilaster or apse buttress. One example of a variant external string course was recovered (c 20), which featured top and bottom chamfers on a rectangular core and was also probably the upper element of a base course. A lighter string course represented by three examples (c 23, 24, c 31) probably formed part of an interior horizontal articulation. Apart from the string courses, the only exterior decorative feature recovered was an unusual round cross-head (c 5), probably from a free-standing cross.

Most of the voussoirs appear to have come from windows rather than arches or doorways and are plain, although one voussoir bears a single incised

chevron on its soffit (c 11). The chevron pattern was a common motif seen in major northern churches from the early 12th century, for example at Dunfermline Abbey (1138), Durham Cathedral (1120) and Jedburgh Abbey (1138) (Cruden 1986; Fawcett 1994b, 2; McWilliam 1978; Thurlby 1994). In Durham Cathedral the chevron patterns are more complex and found mainly on arch voussoirs (Pevsner 1983), but at Dalmeny parish church there are chevron voussoirs similar to the one from Glasgow (McWilliam 1978).

The basic repertoire of keeled features is also present among the painted stone material. Probably most common was the use of white lime-wash, sometimes with red masonry lining as seen on both ribs and wall stones (c 35). Some of the vaulting ribs were painted with abstract designs. Brightly coloured abstract designs were also used to pick out structural elements such as voussoirs, vaulting ribs and plain wallstones (c 8, c 26, c 28, c 29, c 30, c 33, c 34). Related to this paint-enhanced decoration was an example of a wall shaft painted to look like porphyry (c 27). These decorative structural features probably helped to frame and mark out those portions of the cathedral where figurative scenes have been painted on the wall (c 36–44) since there are many identical unpainted stones.

The cathedral consecrated in 1197 was never finished, but even so it does appear to have been designed to be substantially larger and more complex than its predecessor. It is impossible to say how much of the E end was completed by 1197, but enough of it survives to indicate that the SW chamber of the later crypt was originally intended as part of a crypt. The deep foundation of the incomplete nave indicates that the main level of the nave was on a higher level than the crypt, probably not far off that of the present nave. It has been presumed that this crypt featured a square E end, but there are a few string course fragments which may have come from the buttress of a curving structure such as an apse. Whatever its intended form, some of the interior was decorated with well-executed foliage capitals and other carved detail and highlighted with painted walls, vaults and openings. The size of the voussoirs implies large window and door openings. It is possible that the crossing was formed using keeled compound piers. This church was at least partly stone-vaulted to a simple quadripartite design with keeled ribs.

Phases 4–5: early to mid 13th-century cathedral

A certain amount of the architectural material recovered post-dates the consecration of 1197 and may relate to an incomplete phase of work begun before the existing eastern arm in the 1240s. There are a number of voussoirs (c 11–16), which could date to the 13th century and might also be for the structure that followed the E end of 1197. These fragments give

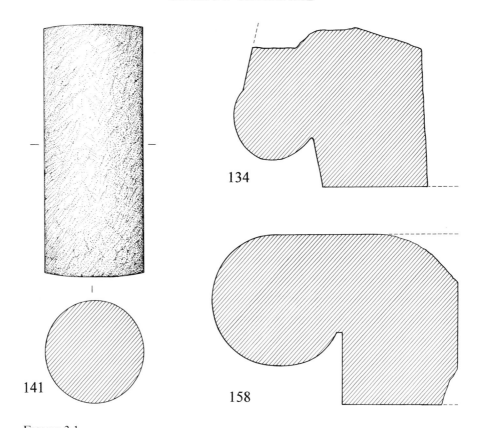

134

141

158

FIGURE 3.1

Early 12th-century architectural fragments (sf 134, sf 158 and sf 141) at 1:8

no real clue as to the design of this early 13th-century E end.

The bulk of the 13th-century material was recovered from below the floor in the E of the choir and is of relatively small scale. This seems likely to relate to internal screen partitions or structures associated with the high altar and the feretory shrine of St Kentigern, which Fawcett (1996, 62) suggests stood to the E of the High Altar.

Catalogue of carved architectural material

The bulk of the material in the architectural stonework catalogue was recovered from the crypt where it had been built into the foundations. These stones were removed from the foundations with care by skilled masons working with hand tools as the slots for the heating ducts were cut. They were not removed under direct archaeological supervision so it was not possible to record the precise location of the stones as they were released from the foundations. Unless otherwise noted the stones have come from either of the crypt trenches (CE/W).

The catalogue is organised into three chronological periods which correspond to the main historically recorded building campaigns: (1) the early 12th century, (2) the late 12th century, and (3) 13th century and later. Within each period the stones are grouped by broad architectural function. In addition to the stones catalogued here, large numbers of dressed architectural fragments were recovered from the crypt foundations. The total quantity of stone taken to the Historic Scotland Stone Conservation centre for cleaning and further study filled about 20 (2 x 2m) wooden pallets. Unless they were carved or otherwise decorated they have not been noted.

In the following, each entry is headed by a catalogue number, an indication of the area (and phase) in which the item was found, and its small finds number (sf).

Early 12th century

1 NN (4) sf 303a (not illustrated)
Half-column drums from a wall shaft, possibly associated with an arcade arching or a chancel arch. Parallels include Durham Cathedral crypt, St John the Baptist's church, Northamptonshire, and Monymusk parish church. Originally part of the 1136 cathedral. An early 12th-century date is certain as they were re-used in the N nave wall of the later 12th-century cathedral. 700mm diameter, 300mm thick.

2 CE/W (4) sf 134 (Figure 3.1)
An engaged shaft, with a three-quarter roll set back from one face. Could have formed part of the jamb of a doorway or window of more than one order. Possibly early 12th century. 430 x 320 x 190mm.

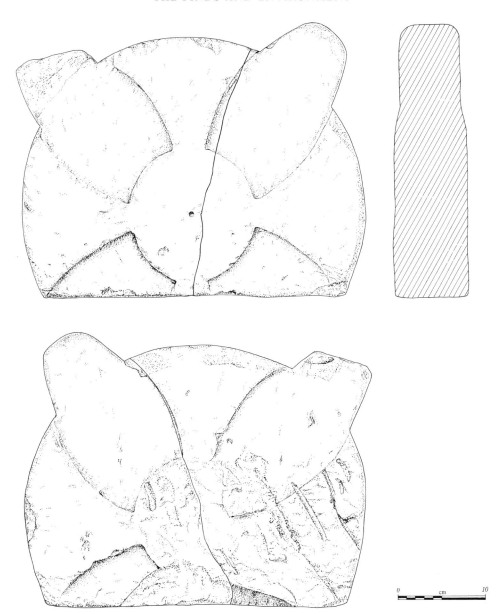

FIGURE 3.2

Late 12th-century disc-headed cross (sf 174)

FIGURE 3.3

Late 12th-century Corinthianesque capital (sf 127)

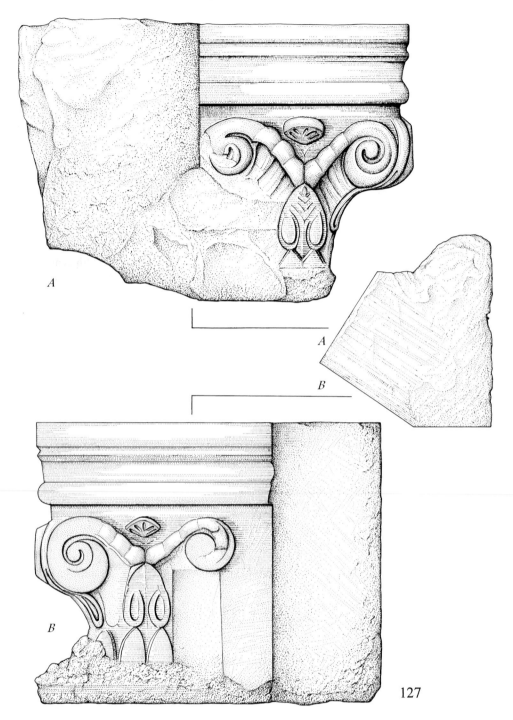

127

FIGURE 3.4

Late 12th-century Corinthianesque capital (sf 127), 1:4 except top view 1:8

3 CE/W (4) sf 158 (Figure 3.1)
Fragment of an engaged shaft which possibly formed part of
the jamb of a doorway or window of more than one order.
Similar to fragment 2. Possibly early 12th century. 540 x 380
x 120mm.

4 CE/W (4) sf 141 (Figure 3.1)
Section of a disengaged shaft, possibly from a window or
door jamb. Date uncertain, but possibly early 12th century.
530 x 220mm.

Late 12th century

Cross-head
K Forsyth

5 NS (4) sf 174 (Figures 3.2 and 5.2)
Two fragments of a disc-headed cross of cream sandstone
decorated on both sides with the remains of the same
pattern: a 'cross-of-arcs'. One side defaced. The cross arms
have curved ends and taper sharply in compass-drawn
curves to a central disc. There is a central compass-point at
the crossing. The curving arms define lentoid recesses which

project beyond the outer rim of the cross-arms. Apart from the noted damage, the piece is in crisp condition and exhibits little sign of weathering. From context 591. 174a: 290 x 220 x 80mm; 174b: 280 x 190 x 80mm.

Cross forms are notoriously difficult to date. The circular cross with sharply tapering arms and central disc is a shape known from Merovingian Gaul (Cramp 1984), and was popular in the Romanesque period. The Romanesque cross-head from St Machar's Cathedral, Aberdeen (Cameron 1989, pl XV), has the same basic shape as the Glasgow cross-head but is much more elaborate and executed in a highly visible open-work manner. Cross forms closely comparable to the Glasgow cross are incised on to two Welsh stones: one from St Dogmael's, Pembrokeshire, dated by Nash-Williams to the 9th century (Nash-Williams 1950, no 388, 213, pl xx), and one from Cae'r hen Eglwys, Laleston, Glamorganshire, which he dates to the 11th–12th century (Nash-Williams 1950, no 203, 133, pl lxii). These, however, are the same cross shape but a different type of monument.

Disc-headed crosses of closely similar form are known from Northumbria: at Heddon-on-the-Wall (Cramp 1984, 241, pl 237, 1341–43) and Monkwearmouth (the matching pair nos 28 and 29; Cramp 1984, 133–134, pl 116, 619–620). A cross from Birtley is also similar in shape to the Glasgow cross, though lacks a central disc (no 4; Cramp 1984, 237, pl 234, 1325–27). Although one of the Monkwearmouth pair of crosses appears to be bedded into the 7th-century fabric of the church, on balance it appears likely that all four date to the 11th century. Elsewhere in Northumbria there are related crosses with splayed arms, rounded ends and central disc, which differ only in having straight rather than curved arms: Birtley 3 (Cramp 1984, 237, pl 232, 1314); Chollerton 2 (Cramp 1984, 239, pl 234, 1331, pl 236, 1335); Warden 5 (Cramp 1984, 248, pl 255, 1391–93); Woodhorn 3–4 (Cramp 1984, 249–250, pl 257, 1401, pl 258, 1403–04, pl 259, 1405). These are all likely to date to the 11th century, indeed, in Cramp's view, the 'head with tapering arms supported by a round centre seems typical of the [Saxo-Norman] overlap period' (1984, 242). Although the plainness of the Glasgow cross-face and its unusual projecting lobes make it difficult to date, the Northumbrian comparanda thus suggest a possible date from the mid–late 11th century and into the 12th century.

The Monkwearmouth crosses are unique in the Northumbrian group in being supported on little stems but this is a feature seen on a cross from St Kentigern's church at Hoddom which is also comparable to the Glasgow stone. The Hoddom piece consists of two fragments, either of the same stone, or of a matched pair, carved on both faces with the same cross design: an equal-armed cross on a narrow stem, having straight-ended arms which taper sharply to a circular centre, its perimeter defined by a groove which forms a shallow roll moulding (Hoddom 27 and 29; Craig 1991, 32–33, fig 15; maximum width 380mm). The overall shape of the stone is square, far easier to execute than the circular form at Glasgow. A cross of this same type was recorded at Hoddom in 1915 on an oblong slab now lost (RCAHMS 1920, 104, fig 7).

The Monkwearmouth crosses are thought to be 'consecration or dedication crosses' (Cramp 1984, 134) and the Heddon stone, which like the one from Glasgow is carved on both faces, is believed to have served as a gable finial (Cramp 1984, 241). The projecting elements on the Glasgow cross are reminiscent of the finial treatments seen in the representations of churches on Irish High Crosses and on shrines thought to be skeumorphs of timber structures (Leask 1977, 46–47).

Alternatively, the Glasgow cross may have marked a grave. It is similar to the headstones surviving at Old Sarum (RCHME 1980, 21), although it is twice as large as those surviving *in situ* at St Blane's, Bute. A further possibility is that the cross marked a significant place in the ecclesiastical precinct, although it is much plainer than the Falkirk parish church cross-head which Cameron believes to be a sanctuary cross (1989, 63; RCAHMS 1963, 151, pl 34). The Glasgow cross has been discovered not far from what would have been the entrance to the 12th-century cathedral, in a secondary position along with miscellaneous building rubble. The fine condition of the relatively lightly modelled cross-head is consistent with having stood for only about a century. Its broken state indicates that it had become obsolete by the start of the 13th century, which makes it more likely to have marked the sanctuary than a grave.

Columns: caps and bases

6 CE/W (4) sf 127 (Figures 3.3 and 3.4)
A Corinthianesque capital, evidently from a nook shaft, possibly forming part of a doorway or window of more than one order. The close derivation of this capital from classical prototypes is illustrated by the rich details of the acanthus leaves from which angle volutes develop and the lower order of leaves around the bell of the capital. The fleurons between the volutes show a similar close derivation, though these are placed on the main body of the cap rather than on the abacus. The deep abacus has a quirked top slab above a cavetto and roll. The abacus is of related type to that of capital 7 below. Late 12th century. Similar capitals were used at Dunfermline Abbey, Holyrood Abbey, Jedburgh Abbey, St Andrews Cathedral and St Brides church, Douglas. 367 x 408 x 295mm.

7 CE/W (4) sf 155 (Figure 3.5)
A volute/crocket capital, obviously from a nook shaft, that possibly forms part of a doorway or window of more than one order. On the two cardinal axes, the bell of the capital has an incised line with a circular hollow at its base. This creates simple leaves, similar to those found on the water-leaf type. At the angles the leaves develop outwards into more complex forms. On the principal diagonal axis the volute is of ultimately classical inspiration, but at the other surviving corner it is a foliate crocket. The deep abacus has a quirked top slab above a chamfer and roll. This abacus is of a related type to that of capital 6 above, though less finely carved. Such capitals are inspired by Corinthian capitals of classical antiquity and were widely used in the 12th century. A similar volute/crocket capital on display in the cathedral has crockets formed from folded-over foliage at the angles where the large leaves which decorate the capital project outwards. Similar capitals survive in place at Jedburgh Abbey. Late 12th century. 560 x 300 x 260mm.

8 CE/W (4) sf 154 (Figures 3.6 and 3.7)
Fragment of a water-leaf capital. There were three sides to this capital and it was attached to a wall face, suggesting that it came from a feature such as a wall or vaulting shaft. Little remains of the decoration on two sides except the uppermost parts of two fleshy leaves that spread across each face. On the right side it can be seen that the upturned corners of the

FIGURE 3.5

Late 12th-century volute/crocket capital (sf 155), 1:4 except top view 1:8

leaves terminated in a flat trefoil. The vertical upper section of the heavy abacus is separated from a chamfered lower section by a quirk. Dated to the late 12th century. 540 x 440 x 210mm.

9 CE/W (4) sf 157 (Figure 3.8)
Fragment of a keeled shaft, presumably from either a wall shaft or from a pier of clustered-shaft type. Similarities are found within the painted elements: 26 appears to be of the same type of shaft, without tail, while 27 is a related but not identical form. Late 12th or early 13th century. 690 x 380 x 180mm.

10 CE (4) sf 106 (Figures 2.47 and 2.48)
Base from an opening of two orders of paired columns. This stone was not disturbed and not recorded in detail. Dimensions (from photograph, approximate): 400 x 180mm x not measured.

Openings and arches

11 CE/W (4) sf 128 (Figure 3.8)
An arch voussoir from an arched opening of more than one order from a doorway, window or arcade arch. A keeled roll at the angle is flanked to each side by a quadrant hollow and a sunk roll of differing forms. There is a single incised

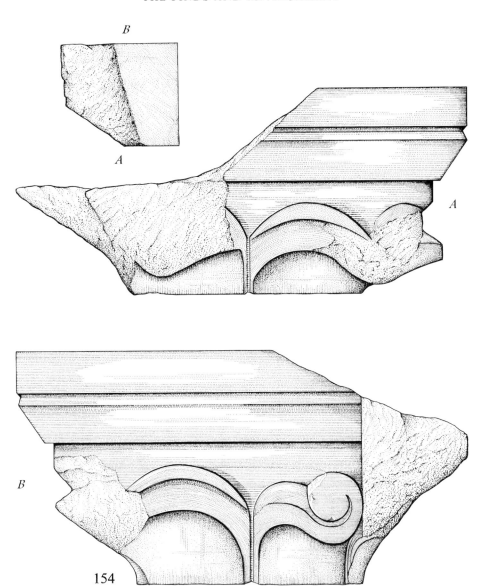

FIGURE 3.6

Late 12th-century waterleaf capital (sf 154), 1:4 except top view 1:16

FIGURE 3.7

Late 12th-century waterleaf capital (sf 154)

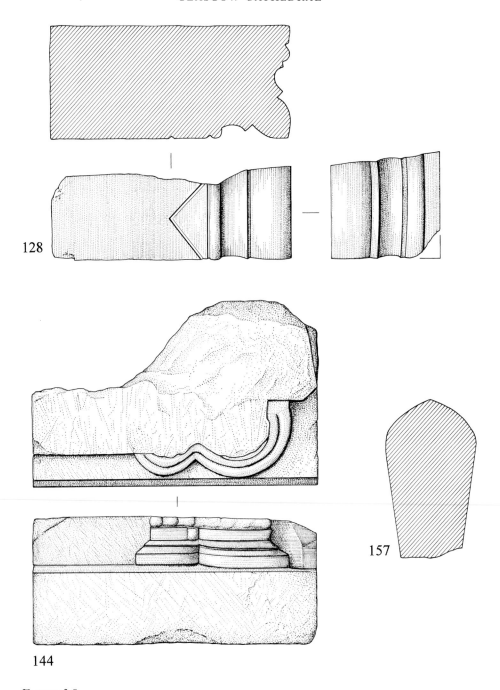

FIGURE 3.8

*Late 12th-century architectural fragments (sf 128, sf 144 and sf 157), all 1:8 except sf 157
1:16*

chevron on the curved soffit face, and traces of painted
(colour) decoration. Comparable treatments are found at
Dunfermline Abbey, Durham Cathedral and Jedburgh
Abbey. Late 12th or early 13th century. 535 x 240 x 220mm.

12 CE/W (4) sf 140 (Figure 3.9)
An arch voussoir possibly from a window rear-arch or, less
likely, from a doorway. A keeled roll projecting from a
straight face is flanked on one side by a half-round hollow
and a quirk, on the other side by a right-angled inset. Carved
from the same formation as jamb stone 14 and voussoir 15,
and related in scale to the base 13. Parallels at Durham

Cathedral, Dunfermline Abbey and Jedburgh Abbey. Late
12th or early 13th century. 370 x 330 x 260mm.

13 CE/W (4) sf 144 (Figure 3.8)
The base stone from a jamb moulding. The base itself is of
two joined parts with a three-quarter curved section at the
salient angle and a smaller adjacent half-round curved
section. The top member of the base is a full roll, followed
by a segmental hollow and with a minimal segmental curve
ending in a short vertical face for the lowest element. The
base rests on a top-chamfered rectangular block. The
supported mouldings evidently consisted of a three-quarter

90

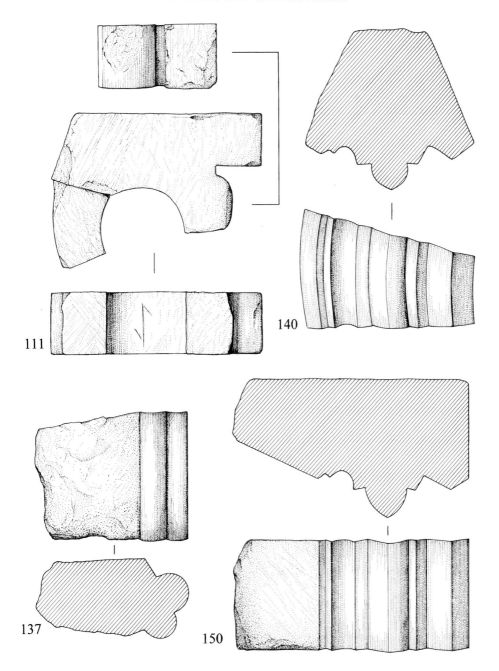

FIGURE 3.9

Late 12th-century architectural fragments (sf 111, sf 137, sf 140 and sf 150), all 1:8

roll at the angle, separated from the right flank of the stone, where two faces meet at an obtuse angle. This may indicate that the stone is more likely to be from a nook shaft of a window than a nook shaft of a doorway. This stone is related in scale to voussoirs 12 and 15, and jamb stone 14. Late 12th or early 13th century. 630 x 370 x 220mm.

14 CE/W (4) sf 150 (Figure 3.9)
A jamb stone, possibly from a window rear-arch or, less likely, from a doorway. A keeled roll projecting from a straight face is flanked on one side by a half-round hollow and a quirk, and on the other side by a right-angled inset. A vertical keel. It is from the same formation as voussoirs 12 and 15, and is related in scale to the base 13. It is from the late 12th or early 13th century. 540 x 240 x 210mm.

15 CE/W (4) sf 153 (not illustrated)
An arch voussoir, possibly from a window rear-arch or, less likely, from a doorway. A keeled roll projecting from a straight face is flanked on one side by a half-round hollow and a quirk, and on the other side by a right-angled inset. It is from the same formation as voussoir 12 and jamb stone 14, and is related in scale to the base 13. Late 12th or early 13th century. 470 x 370 x 210mm.

16 CE/W (4) sf 137 (Figure 3.9)
A stone of uncertain function, probably a voussoir of a window or door, but possibly a jamb stone. It features a conjoined angled pair of three-quarter rolls set asymmetrically at one end. Date uncertain but probably late 12th or early 13th century. 350 x 280 x 170mm.

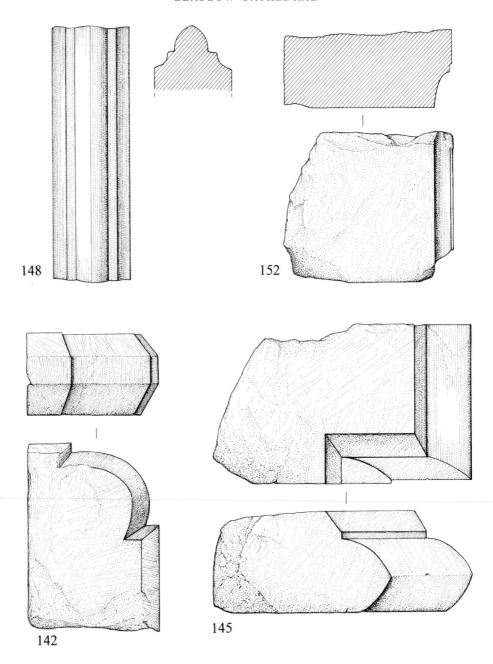

FIGURE 3.10

Late 12th-century architectural fragments (sf 142, sf 145, sf 148 and sf 152), all 1:8

17 N (4) sf 111a and b (Figure 3.9)

A stone of uncertain function, which has been broken in two, possibly before completion. The main feature of this rectangular block is a half-round hollow. To one side of the hollow the face of the stone is set back beyond a quadrant roll. Within the hollow there is an incised mark in the form of a vertical line with diagonally set shorter lines to top right and bottom left; it may have been a mason's mark or a position mark. This stone may have been intended to have formed part of the jamb of a window or doorway, within which a disengaged shaft was set. It bears no trace of mortar or other evidence that it was ever used. Its context, within a dump of unmortared rubble running midway across the nave, suggest that this was discarded before completion. The date is uncertain but possibly late 12th or early 13th century.

From context 377. Dimensions 111a: 204 x 140 x 112mm, and b: 473 x 252 x 136mm.

18 CE/W (4) sf 156 (not illustrated)
Voussoir fragment. 350 x 270 x 230mm.

Vaulting ribs

19 CE/W (4) sf 139 (not illustrated)
Section of vaulting rib, with a central keeled member flanked symmetrically on each side by a roll developing without break into a half-round hollow. This a common form which is found on several painted ribs (32, 34 and 35) some of which have tails and some have not. This form is similar to material on display in the cathedral and to the upstanding masonry on the SW corner of the crypt, which is attributed

92

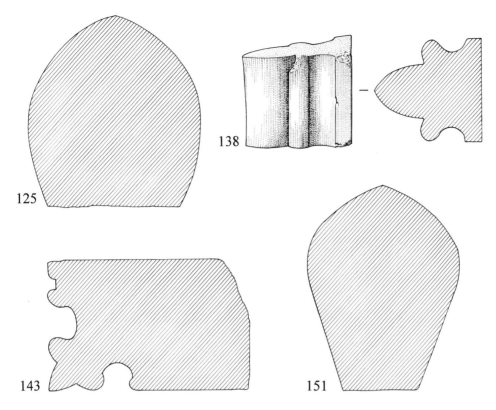

138

125

143

151

FIGURE 3.11

Late 12th-century architectural fragments (sf 125, sf 138, sf 143 and sf 151), all 1:8

to Jocelin and dated to *c*1197. On display is a four-armed intersection of ribs from the crown of a square vault. This loose intersection has a rougher finish and broader keels than those in the surviving rectangular quadripartite vault. Also on display is a diagonal vaulting rib with a similar profile. This is a common rib-form and parallels exist at Arbroath Abbey, Durham Cathedral, Jedburgh Abbey, St Magnus's Cathedral, Sweetheart Abbey and York Minster. Late 12th or early 13th century. 240 x 230 x 190mm.

Other elements

20 CE/W (4) sf 142 (Figure 3.10)
A section of string course with top and bottom chamfers to a rectangular core. It obviously originated from a salient angle with a three-quarter roll set in at the angle. It is possibly from the upper element of an external base course or from the string course forming part of the horizontal articulation of the building. 12th or early 13th century. 400 x 290 x 140mm.

21 CE/W (4) sf 145 (Figure 3.10)
Section of a string course with a keeled roll flanked on one side by a chamfer. Possibly from the upper element of an external base course or from a string course forming part of the horizontal articulation of the building. The combination of an external angle and a re-entrant angle suggests this stone came from the junction of a pilaster buttress or similar feature with the main face of the wall. It is difficult to be certain on the limited available evidence, but the fact that the faces appear not to have been cut precisely at 90 degrees to each other could suggest the possibility that this stone came from a curved section of walling. Possibly part of

buttresses for an apse. In form it is closely related to string course section 22. Late 12th or early 13th century. 600 x 370 x 220mm.

22 CE/W (4) sf 171 (not illustrated)
A section of a string course with a keeled roll, flanked on one side by a chamfer. It is possibly from the upper element of an external base course or from a string course forming part of the buildings horizontal articulation. The combination of an external angle and a re-entrant angle suggests this stone came from the junction of a pilaster buttress or similar feature with the main face of the wall. Late 12th or early 13th century. 540 x 460 x 220mm.

23 CE/W (4) sf 148 (Figure 3.10)
A possible section of a string course composed of a keeled roll projecting from a straight face and flanked by quadrant hollows. Late 12th or early 13th century. 540 x 480 x 180mm.

24 CE/W (4) sf 152 (Figure 3.10)
Mutilated section of string course, capital abacus or other horizontal moulding, composed of a vertical face separated from a quadrant hollow by a slight intake. It is only dressed on one side, probably a string course. 12th century. 330 x 320 x 180mm.

25 CE/W (4) sf 167 (not illustrated)
A damaged but roughly dressed block of stone, with an arrow-shaped mark (perhaps a position mark) incised on one face. Date uncertain. 235 x 300 x 160mm.

Painted structural elements: columns

26 CE/W (4) sf 125 (Plate 1 and Figure 3.11)
A section of a keeled shaft, presumably from either a wall shaft or a pier of the clustered-shaft type. 392 x 371 x 312mm.

27 CE/W (4) sf 151 (Figure 3.11)
Section of a keeled shaft, presumably from either a wall shaft or from a pier of clustered-shaft type. Painted to imitate porphyry. Similar form to shafts 26 and 9. 460 x 350 x 290mm.

Painted structural elements: openings and arches

28 CE/W (4) sf 119 (Plate 2)
Voussoir from a splayed opening, probably a window or door. Architecturally plain but painted with small white dots on blue. 292 x 256 x 314mm.

29 CE/W (4) sf 135 (Plates 3 and 4)
An arch voussoir painted with a shield above draperies. The splay of the voussoir suggests that it may be from the same opening as 28. 400 x 270 x 250mm.

30 CE/W (4) sf 132 (Plate 5)
A voussoir possibly from a window or doorway with painted decoration. 390 x 240 x 230mm.

31 CE/W (4) sf 143 (Figure 3.11)
An arch voussoir from an opening of more than one order (possibly a doorway, window or arcade arch). The principal feature is a triplet of rolls, the leading one being keeled, which is separated from convex or ogee-shaped outer curves by hollows or irregular profile. Parallels are Durham Cathedral, Dunfermline Abbey and Jedburgh Abbey. It bears traces of paint. 440 x 280 x180mm.

Painted structural elements: vaulting ribs

32 CE/W (4) sf 120 (Plates 6 and 7)
Section of a vaulting rib, with a central keeled member flanked symmetrically on each side by a roll developing without break into a half-round hollow. This form is represented in an unpainted form as well (see 19, 23, 34). The entire visible surface is covered with a lozenge pattern in black, white and red. 364 x 231 x 262mm.

33 CE/W (4) sf 130 (Plate 8)
A section of a vaulting rib, badly damaged but possibly of the same section as 32. Painted decoration in an abstract pattern in red and black. 290 x 265 x 230mm.

34 CE/W (4) sf 133 (not illustrated)
A section of a vaulting rib of the same section as 32. It bears traces of a lime wash. 290 x 210 x 170mm.

35 CE/W (4) sf 138 (Figure 3.11)
A section of a vaulting rib of the same section as 32. It bears traces of whitewash. 230 x 210 x 195mm.

Painted structural elements: wall stones

36 CE/W (4) sf 81 (Plate 9)
Painted stone depicting part of a torso with right arm raised. 550 x 260 x 270mm.

37 CE/W (4) sf 129 (Plate 10)
Painted stone with imitation drapery in red and yellows. 332 x 285 x 250mm.

38 CE/W (4) sf 86 (Plate 11)
Painted stone showing part of a face and cross. Damaged during its recovery. 490 x 490 x 480mm.

39 CE/W (4) sf 114 (Plate 12)
Painted stone with imitation drapery in different shades of red, white, brown and black. 370 x 312 x 368mm.

40 CE/W (4) sf 115 (Plate 13)
Fragment of a painted stone. 346 x 315 x 158mm.

41 CE/W (4) sf 116 (Plate 14)
Fragment of a painted stone. 241 x 272 x 79mm.

42 CE/W (4) sf 118 (Plate 15)
Painted stone depicting a wing against a starry background. 470 x 268 x 381mm.

43 CE/W (4) sf 122 (Plate 16)
Painted stone depicting diagonal sweeping lines. 279 x 279 x 214mm.

44 CE/W (4) sf 123 and sf 124 (not illustrated)
Painted stone, featuring a v-shaped pattern in red and black. 123: 449 x 452 x 263mm, and 124: 351 x 221 x 312mm.

13th century

45 CE/W (4) sf 165 (not illustrated)
An arch voussoir with two different sized orders of chamfer, separated by a right-angled re-entrant. Date uncertain, but probably early 13th century. 390 x 250 x 240mm.

46 CE/W (4) sf 147 (Figure 3.12)
Section of what appears to have been a string course composed of a conjoined three-quarter roll and crescent-shaped element. Early 13th century. 540 x 420 x 170mm.

47 CH (4) sf 6 (not illustrated)
Fragment of double filet roll moulding with traces of mortar. This is from a relatively light-weight structure such as a screen. It shares a number of stylistic details with the sculpted stone structure thought to have served as the base of St Kentigern's shrine (Fawcett 1997, 62) which is on display in the cathedral. Perhaps it is more likely that this comes from a screen or railing in the area around the shrine or high altar. Similar in form to 47 and 48. From context 002. 230 x 120 x 90mm.

48 CH (4) sf 13 (Figure 3.12)
Double filet roll moulding. ?13th–14th century. 114 x 94 x 102mm.

49 CH (4) sf 15 (not illustrated)
Fragment of single filet roll moulding. ?13th–14th century. 182 x 125 x 92mm.

50 CH (4) sf 18 (Figure 3.12)
Fragment of single filet roll. ?13th–14th century. 214 x 153 x 118mm.

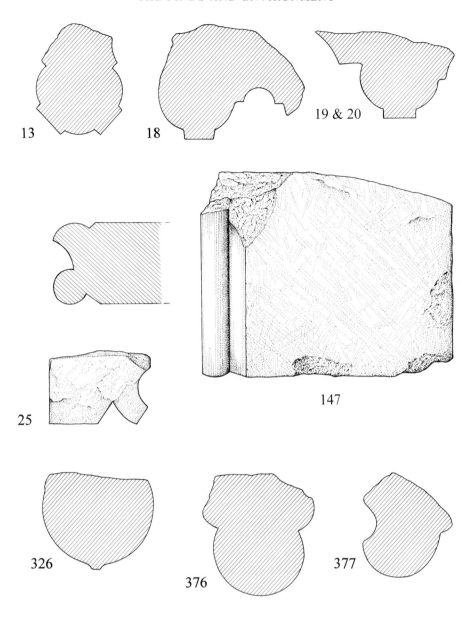

FIGURE 3.12

13th-century architectural fragments (sf 13, sf 18, sf 19–20, sf 25, sf 147, sf 326, sf 376, sf 377), all 1:4 except sf 147 1:8

51 CH (4) sf 19 and sf 20 (Figure 3.12)
Two joining fragments of a single filet roll and concave moulding. ?13th–14th century. 19: 148 x 90 x 59mm; 20: 148 x 87 x 96mm.

52 CH (4) sf 23 (not illustrated)
Fragment of single filet roll engaged column. ?13th–14th century. 330 x 150 x 105mm.

53 NS (5) sf 326 (Figure 3.12)
Fragment of single filet roll moulding. ?13th–14th century. 120 x 95mm.

54 NS (4) sf 376 (Figure 3.12)
Fragment of single roll moulding. ?13th–14th century. 130 x 110 x 60mm.

55 NS (4) sf 377 (Figure 3.12)
Fragment of moulded stone. ?13th–14th century. 130 x 90 x 70mm.

The following small fragments were recovered from the choir vaulting (002), many of them are relatively small and undiagnostic and are simply listed. In addition to these moulded stones there were other fragments of dressed masonry blocks. From their find-spot they are likely to date from the 13th century or later.

56 CH (4) sf 2. Fragment of capital with traces of white paint. 117 x 79 x 80mm.

57 CH (4) sf 17. Fragment of moulding. 120 x 770 x 540mm.

58 CH (4) sf 7. Fragment of half-roll moulding for door/window. 168 x 83 x 120mm.

59 CH (4) sf 8. Fragment of simple roll from column base or moulding. 130 x 100 x 55mm.

60 CH (4) sf 9. Chip of simple concave moulding. 78 x 30 x 74mm.

61 CH (4) sf 10. Chip of edge roll moulding. 45 x 15 x 15mm.

62 CH (4) sf 11. Fragment of roll moulding. 75 x 62 x 41mm.

63 CH (4) sf 12. Chip of simple roll moulding. 149 x 84 x 53mm.

64 CH (4) sf 21. Fragment of half-roll moulding. 93 x 86 x 54mm.

65 CH (4) sf 14. Fragment of moulding. 186 x 49 x 63mm.

66 CH (4) sf 22. Fragment of simple roll moulding. 100 x 90 x 70mm.

67 CH (4) sf 27. Block with scroll moulding.

68 CH(4) sf 25 (Figure 3.12). Two fragments of moulding for window arch. 218 x 110 x 75mm.

Masons' marks

Incised geometric marks were noted on remarkably few of the architectural fragments listed above. The masonry rebuilt into the N nave wall of the second cathedral (phase 3) exhibited however a large number of marks (Figures 2.18 and 2.19), which have been recorded as rubbings (Figure 2.20). Some of these may be positioning marks, others may be legitimate masons' marks. No special study of these marks has been undertaken, partially because, surprisingly, there has been no comprehensive study of the cathedral's masons' marks to date. Masons' marks were observed on loosed blocks of plainly dressed stones from residual contexts (NS 502, CH 002) typified by sf 111 (Figure 3.9) and sf 172. The most spectacular display of mason's marks was on the S side of the N foundation of the phase 3 nave. This wall (303) was built almost entirely from re-used masonry so the marks could as easily date to the early or late 12th century (Figures 2.14, 2.18–2.20).

69 CE/W (4) sf 172
Dressed block with mason's mark. 310 x 390 x 275mm.

3.3 LATE 12TH-CENTURY ARCHITECTURAL POLYCHROMY
by D Park and H Howard

Many of the 12th-century architectural fragments excavated from the crypt in 1992–93 bear remains of painting. Of extremely high quality, this painting, which includes figural as well as decorative elements,

is a particularly remarkable discovery since virtually no other early wall-painting survives in Scotland. Moreover, the fragments had been reused as building material only about half a century after they were painted, and are therefore in exceptional condition. Overall, they represent the most important discovery of late Romanesque painting in Britain since the 12th-century scheme in the Holy Sepulchre Chapel of Winchester Cathedral was uncovered in the 1960s.

A detailed art-historical study of the polychromy has already been produced by Park (1998), though scientific examination of the fragments was undertaken subsequently by Howard (1998). The present report comprises a summary of the art-historical findings, a more detailed section on the scientific examination and, finally, conclusions regarding the light now thrown by this examination on the dating and significance of the paintings.

Art-historical analysis

Some 18 fragments of stonework retain painted decoration, and are of various types including sections of flat wall surface, a voussoir with painting on two faces, and part of a shaft and another of a vaulting rib. The purely ornamental elements in the painting include a three-dimensional lozenge pattern on the fragment of a vaulting rib, decorating either side of the central keeled member (sf 120) (Plates 6 and 7); 'marbling' in red and other colours on the fragment of a keeled shaft (sf 125) (Plate 1); several fragments of imitation draperies on sections of flat wall surface (sf 114, sf 124, sf 129) (Plates 10 and 12); and one example of red masonry pattern, painted on a thin plaster ground (sf 132) (Plate 5). Of four figural fragments, one shows the tip of a wing set beneath a horizontal border against a background decorated with stars (sf 118) (Plate 15). Another shows a male face in profile, with what appears to be a small cross (of which the top is lost) behind his head (sf 86) (Plate 11). On the main face of the voussoir is a long pointed shield, over what seem to be the draperies of a reclining figure (sf 135) (Plate 3). Finally, there is the fragment of a torso with the right arm raised, and with the cloak of the figure swinging in front of the body rather than hanging loose behind (sf 81) (Plate 9).

The paintings are on a fairly small scale: from the head and torso, the figures can be reconstructed as originally approximately half life-size. In Romanesque wall-painting the most common layout comprises one or two horizontal tiers of subject matter above an ornamental dado. Fictive draperies are the most favoured type of dado ornament, and the fragments of such decoration from Glasgow (of which the largest is approximately 25cm high) seem likely to have served this function. All the fragments of late 12th-century architectural stonework, both painted and unpainted, were found as re-used material in the mid 13th-century rebuilding of the crypt, which replaced a Romanesque crypt originally built by Bishop John but remodelled by Bishop Jocelin at the end of the 12th century (see Section 2.1). Consequently, there can be little doubt that the fragments belonged to a scheme in that part of the church. Since the focus of the crypt was St Kentigern's tomb, and since the painted fragments were excavated from the bays to the east of the tomb, there must be a strong possibility that the scheme was directly associated with the veneration of the saint. Romanesque crypts were commonly painted with cycles of the saints whose relics were kept there. A further indication that this may have been the case at Glasgow is provided by the predominately red decoration of the shaft (sf 125) (Plate 1), which imitates not marble as such, but the flecked appearance of porphyry, a material associated with tombs and shrines from antiquity onward. Unfortunately, however, the figural fragments are too slight to be identified with any St Kentigern subjects. For instance, although he is said to have set up several crosses, these were large standing crosses, and not the type which seems to be represented behind the male head (sf 86) (Plate 11).

In attempting to date the fragments as precisely as possible, there is unfortunately almost no early wall-painting in Scotland with which they can be compared. The only other significant early remains are those of c1200 at Dryburgh Abbey (Redman 1997). The chapter house, in particular, retains one of the most complete surviving decorative schemes of its period in Britain, including varied foliage designs, fictive arcading, and ornamented string courses and window embrasures. None of this decoration is particularly close to the Glasgow painting, however, and indeed, as one would expect in a Premonstratensian context, it is altogether much simpler.

The decorative painting at Glasgow points clearly to a late 12th-century date. For example, the masonry pattern (sf 132) (Plate 5) is of a type, characterised by thin double red lines, which became standard from the late 12th century onwards. Although the shaft (sf 125) (Plate 1) imitates porphyry rather than Purbeck or other such 'marbles', it nevertheless conforms to the taste for fictive marbling in the period around 1200, seen at Worcester Cathedral and elsewhere. The drapery fragments also indicate a late 12th-century date; the roughly rectangular but tapering section in the centre of one fragment (sf 129) (Plate 10) is formed by the swags hanging down on either side and is closely paralleled in the lower part of the draperies in the Galilee Chapel paintings of c1180 in Durham Cathedral (for the latter see Park 1991). Finally, the lozenge pattern on the vaulting rib (sf 120) (Plates 6 and 7), which gives an angular effect to the curved central member, is typical in its three dimensionality of late 12th-century architectural ornament, such as the chevron and lozenge designs on the west portal of Jedburgh Abbey (Garton 1987, 73–74, pls 5, 7, 10, 17)

The figure style also clearly points to this period. For example, the head (sf 86) (Plate 11) is much more naturalistic and classicising than early- or mid-Romanesque heads, such as those in the initial of the Kelso Charter (1159). It may be compared, rather, with late 12th-century examples such as those in the 'Morgan Leaf' (c1170) (New York, Pierpont Morgan Library, M.619; Kauffmann 1975, no 84), in the flicked-up eyebrow, the shape of the eye itself, the tiny ear, and the layering of the hair. Northern painting and sculpture of the period is marked by the transition from the clinging curvilinear damp fold style seen, for example, in the Copenhagen Psalter (c1170), to the much more classicising Transitional style typified by the Durham Life of St Cuthbert (c1195), with its relatively naturalistic draperies. Fragments of figure-sculpture from Bridlington and Jedburgh, of c1170–80 and c1180 respectively (Thurlby 1981), show an intermediate stage, with the flat panels of clinging curvilinear now surrounded by multiple folds, and a similar 'multifold' style appears in the arm of the Glasgow torso fragment (sf 81) (Plate 9). Also entirely typical of late Romanesque and Transitional painting is the very strong black outline of this figure. If a dating of c1190 is indicated by the style of the painted fragments, it is confirmed by the other pieces of architectural stonework found in the same archaeological context, including sections of string course and a base stone from a jamb moulding, and capitals of volute, Corinthianesque and water-leaf form.

The discovery of the recently excavated fragments necessitates reassessment of the painted stone discovered in 1914–16 reused in the 13th-century vault of the crypt (Plate 17). Painted on two faces, it must have been the voussoir of a window or doorway; the outer face is decorated with a palmette forming a heart-shaped motif, in what would originally have been a continuous band of such ornament. In the past, this fragment (hereafter referred to as 'the 1916 fragment') has been dated to the late 12th century and the building campaign of Bishop Jocelin, though more recently it has been argued on stylistic grounds that it dates from the second quarter of the 12th century, and was therefore associated with Bishop John's cathedral, dedicated though not necessarily completed in 1136. In support of this argument, the palmette design has been compared with examples of the first half and middle of the century. Simple versions of palmettes within heart-shaped frames appear, however, in the painting of c1200 in the chapter house of Dryburgh Abbey, while the use of continuous bands of foliage forming heart-shaped motifs continues well into the 13th century. It is in fact evident from the style of the voussoir painting (notably, the strange curved lines on the soffit, which are closely paralleled on one of the recently excavated fragments) (sf 122) (Plate 16), as well as from its predominantly green, red and black palette, that it belongs to the same late 12th-century scheme as the newly discovered material.

In conclusion, therefore, all the painted fragments are attributable to Bishop Jocelin's building campaign in the late 12th century. Stylistically, they can be compared with painting and sculpture of the period in northern England, and it may well be that the painter or workshop derived from south of the border. It is possible that St Kentigern was the subject of the paintings, and given that no other medieval cycle devoted to St Kentigern exists, it is a tantalising thought that perhaps 95% of the Glasgow material still awaits excavation.

Scientific examination

Methods of examination

Examination of the fragments was undertaken in April 1998. Following a detailed inspection in normal, raking and UV light, and at low magnification, a small number of samples was taken to identify the original materials and to determine their method of application.

The samples were mounted as polished cross-sections (in polyester embedding resin), and as dispersions. They were examined with an optical microscope at 170–2500x magnification in incident, transmitted and UV light, and photomicrographs were taken at between 500 and 2500x. Microchemical tests were undertaken to identify some metallic ions and functional groups, and histochemical tests to indicate whether oils and proteins were present. A scanning electron microscope (SEM), used with energy-dispersive X-ray (EDX) analysis which provides elemental analysis, was employed to confirm the identifications made with polarised light microscopy (PLM). Identification of organic materials and additional confirmation of inorganic components were undertaken using Fourier Transform Infra-red (FTIR) micro-spectroscopy.

Plaster constituents and application

The painting was typically executed on a coarse lime-based render applied in a single layer (varying in thickness from 4–10mm) over the tooled calciferous sandstone support (Plate 18). In one case (sf 118b) it is evident that a thin slurry of lime was applied to the stone surface, which would have acted both as a sealant and as a chemical key assisting adherence of the plaster. While constituents of the plaster appear to be similar in all the fragments examined, its application and surface texture vary considerably.

The aggregate consists principally of angular and subangular quartz, feldspar, calcareous inclusions, charcoal, green earth, and particles rich in red and yellow iron oxides. In several cases, fibre (possibly chopped straw) is also evident, or voids which once contained fibrous material (sf 130 and sf 135). The fibre was probably added to increase the mechanical strength of the plaster, and may also have functioned as a mechanical buffer by absorbing moisture during its setting. The aggregate is generally well graded, ensuring close packing of the particles, although the inclusions are sometimes as large as $8mm^3$. Microscopic examination of thin-sections indicated a ratio of aggregate to lime binder of approximately 2:1. Although the plaster layer of the fragment painted with masonry pattern (sf 132) is exceptionally thin (approx 1–2mm) the aggregate employed is similar to that of the other fragments.

A single layer of plaster was normally employed, though in two instances (sf 120: the vaulting rib decorated with lozenge pattern, Plate 19; and sf 124: a fragment painted with draperies) two layers of plaster are evident. On the rib, the lower layer is approximately 1mm thick with striations across the surface, and this thickness and surface texture is closely comparable to the plaster of the masonry pattern fragment (sf 132). On sf 124 the lower plaster layer appears to be approximately 3–4mm thick, and traces of red paint appear at the interface with the upper layer. Red paint also appears on the lower layer on the rib (Plate 19), and comprises two different red pigments, vermilion and red earth, applied over a lime ground approximately 100µm thick. The possible significance of these remains is discussed below.

In many of the fragments the plaster surface has been carefully smoothed, so that the aggregate is neatly aligned beneath the paint surface. In others the plaster has a more undulating topography and a rougher surface texture, with some aggregate particles penetrating the paint layer and causing preferential loss in these areas (Plate 20). The varying smoothness of the plaster surface naturally results in differences in surface texture of the overlying paint layer, and it is possible that those fragments with a rougher surface (such as sf 123) were designed to be viewed from a greater distance.

Several fragments show evidence of polishing of the plaster surface. Thus, on sf 118b the uppermost portion of the plaster layer (approx 1mm thick) is compacted and slightly pink in colour. A cross-section of a sample from this fragment shows that a mixture of carbon black and lime white was polished into the surface, and a red paint layer (vermilion) then applied directly over this. Sf 116 has a similarly polished surface, and a thin-section clearly shows the presence of a compacted vermilion layer over lime drawn to the surface (75µm) by the polishing (Plate 21). A thin-section from a fragment painted with draperies (sf 124) shows that red earth was polished into the surface to a depth of 80µm, with the black and white paint layers applied subsequently appearing quite separate and distinct.

In other fragments inclusions of red and yellow iron oxide-rich material are concentrated in the upper

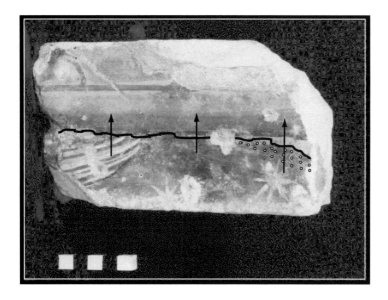

FIGURE 3.13

Diagram of the plaster join on the fragment painted with a wing (sf 118). The shaded area at right indicates where pressure was applied to taper the edge of the freshly applied plaster. Copyright Courtauld Institute

portion of the plaster layer. In one sample from the shield fragment (sf 135), for example, these coloured particles occur in the top 300μm of the layer. A few red particles are evident in the upper portion of the plaster of the 1916 fragment, while yellow inclusions predominate in the plaster of a fragment painted with draperies (sf 114). These variations in the colour of the plaster surface were almost certainly deliberate, and may have been intended to react optically with the paint layers above. A similar technique occurs in the paintings of *c*1175 in the Holy Sepulchre Chapel of Winchester Cathedral, where the greatest concentration of charcoal particles is in plaster beneath areas painted predominantly blue. It seems likely that this charcoal was incorporated to reduce the light scatter from the white substrate, thus increasing the intensity of the blue areas (Howard 1995, 93).

On several fragments a lime ground can be observed over the plaster, applied in preparation for the painting. Such grounds are apparent on the wing and shield fragments (sf 118 and sf 135), on the 1916 fragment, and on the lower plaster layer of the lozenge-decorated rib. On the 1916 fragment the ground is approximately 60μm thick, and applied over a single layer of plaster whose surface is penetrated in places by the aggregate (Plate 22).

Plaster joins are evident in three instances: the fragment painted with a wing (sf 118), the shaft with fictive porphyry (sf 125), and the 1916 fragment. On the first the join is clearly visible at the junction of the border and the tip of the wing (Figure 3.13). Tool marks in the surface indicate where pressure was applied in order to taper the edge of the freshly applied plaster over the set plaster of the layer below. From the position of the wing it is probable that the join was aligned horizontally, and therefore that the sequence of plastering progressed from the top of the wall down. By contrast, the plaster join on the 'porphyry' fragment (sf 125) runs vertically down the arris of the shaft. The top 50mm of the join is quite distinct, though it becomes less clear further down suggesting that the plaster was applied wet over wet. The join on the 1916 fragment is also rather indistinct, though examination in raking light confirmed the presence of overlapping plaster layers on the smaller painted face. Here the tool marks in the slightly undulating plaster run perpendicular to the join.

Evidence from other sites suggests that plaster was typically applied in broad horizontal bands in the Romanesque period (see Rickerby 1990; Howard 1992; Cather and Howard 1994). In the late 12th-century paintings at Winchester, however, and in the scheme of *c*1100 at Hardham, Sussex, smaller patches were used, roughly conforming to borders, scenes or figure groups (Howard 1995; Sawdy *et al* 1998). Unfortunately, there is insufficient evidence at Glasgow to interpret the plastering pattern in any detail.

Preparatory techniques

There is no evidence of setting out with snapped lines or incision, nor in general of preparatory drawing. The only possible evidence of the latter is provided by the traces of red paint on the lower layer of plaster on the rib (sf 120; Plate 19) and on sf 124, which may be the remains of *sinopie* (the preparatory drawings of a fresco). Such preliminary drawings on a lower plaster layer (typically in red earth, and used in paintings executed at least partly in fresco) are very rare in English medieval wall-painting, with the only known examples dating from the Romanesque period. The most notable are in the late 12th-century paintings at Winchester, where vermilion combined with red iron oxide has been identified (Howard 1995, 94). The presence of both pigments on the rib at Glasgow may therefore be significant in this context, though another possibility is that the red paint may survive from a simple decorative scheme executed before the more complex figurative scheme. If so, little time can have intervened, since the keeled rib itself is of late 12th-century date.

Pigments and their application

The palette of the paintings is rich and varied, comprising vermilion (HgS), red lake (on a calcium carbonate substrate), red lead (Pb_3O_4), red earth (Fe_2O_3), yellow earth ($FeO.OH$), green earth ($K[Al,Fe^{III}].(Fe^{II}, Mg)].(AlSi_3,Si_4)O_{10} (OH)_2$), lime white ($CaCO_3$. $Ca(OH)_2$), and charcoal black (C).

The presence of red lake is of particular interest. This organic colorant occurs on the shield fragment (sf 135), while a trace also survives over a layer of green earth on sf 130. In Romanesque wall-painting in England, red lake has only been identified in the late 12th-century paintings at Winchester, though it occurs as early as c800 in the Carolingian scheme at Müstair, Switzerland (Mairinger and Schreiner 1986, 195–196). Its early use was typically as part of an opaque paint layer, and at Winchester it was combined with calcium carbonate to produce a pale pink colour for draperies (Howard 1995, 96). In the shield fragment at Glasgow, however, it appears to be bound in an organic medium, and it was employed as a glaze to saturate and enrich the layer of vermilion (combined with lime white) below (Plate 23). This sophisticated use of the pigment as a glaze is known elsewhere in Britain only from the Gothic period.

Red lead is also rather unusual in Romanesque wall-painting, though it was employed for details in the late 12th-century scheme at Winchester (Howard 1995, 96). At Glasgow, it survives only in one small area of the shield (sf 135), where it was applied over a lime white ground (Plate 24). Traces of the pigment combined with charcoal black and lime white also appear in the underlying layers. Since red lead is unstable in alkaline conditions, an organic binding medium is likely to have been employed. The surviving pigment is in exceptional condition, exhibiting no sign of darkening or lightening, which further suggests that it was ground in an organic material before application.

FTIR analysis of the green earth pigment employed at Glasgow indicated the presence of celadonite. A few particles of green earth were also detected in the plaster itself, where it occurs as aggregate with other materials such as quartz, feldspar, and red and yellow earths. Such aggregate would typically have been obtained locally, and one possible source for the green earth is Ailsa Craig at the entrance to the Firth of Clyde. Ailsa Craig is rich in glauconite-celadonite and other accessory minerals (Harrison 1987, 2, 5 and 15; Craig 1991, 479–480). The pigment was used in various ways in the painting: for decorative linear details, as on the lozenge-decorated rib and the 1916 fragments (Plate 22); for modelling in the flesh areas (sf 86) (Plate 11); and perhaps also over a grey ground (sf 130). In English Romanesque wall-painting, the use of this pigment for shadows in flesh painting has been confirmed only in the late 12th-century scheme at Winchester, where it is among a number of features reflecting Byzantine influence (Park 1983; Howard 1995, 96). The pigment also occurs at Norwich Cathedral in the paintings of c1190, where its subtle yellow-green colour is juxtaposed with the more intense colour of 'salt green' (Howard and Gasol 1996, 20–21).

No mineral blue pigment has been identified in the Glasgow fragments. However, a blue appearance resulting from the optical effect of combining charcoal black and lime white occurs in some instances. This 'false blue' was employed, for example, in the torso fragment, where white and black were combined with a small quantity of vermilion to produce a pale purple colour (sf 81) (Plate 25). The combination of charcoal black and lime white was an expedient method of imitating the more expensive mineral blues, and is common in the Romanesque period. It is prominent, for example, in the 'Lewes Group' wall-paintings of c1100 in Sussex, where it was used for the fictive marbling and draperies at dado level (Howard 1990). It also occurs in late 12th-century fragments of painting excavated from Sherborne Abbey, where the colour is enhanced by its juxtaposition with warm red and yellow earth pigments (Howard and Park, forthcoming).

It is, however, surprising that no mineral blue occurs at Glasgow, particularly since other expensive pigments such as red lake were employed. The mineral blue almost universally employed in major Romanesque schemes was natural ultramarine, as in the late 12th-century paintings at Winchester and Norwich, as well as those in the Galilee Chapel of Durham Cathedral (Howard 1988). In order to enrich its effect by the reduction of light scatter, ultramarine was often applied over a grey or black ground, and this was initially considered the explanation for the black backgrounds of some of the Glasgow fragments. Samples taken from the white dots painted over this ground on sf 86, sf 119 and sf 135 (beneath which any original blue should have survived) showed however that none was present. Instead, they suggested that the ground may have been intended to appear a dark purple colour, since the paint layer consists of charcoal black combined with a small quantity of red earth in a lime white matrix. Instrumental analysis of a sample from the black background of the wing fragment (sf 118) confirmed that both vermilion and red earth were combined with charcoal black, with the ratio of vermilion to red earth approximately 1:4. A similar combination of vermilion with charcoal black and red earth occurs in the wall-paintings of c1135 in Cormac's Chapel, Cashel (Ireland), where it was used for a purple colour on the south wall of the chancel (Howard 1991, 2).

In order to extend the palette further, extensive use was made of pigment mixtures and layering of colours. For example, an intense orange was achieved by mixing red and yellow earths, while charcoal black combined with vermilion in a lime white matrix was used for the greyish-purple colour in the torso fragment (sf 81). Lime white was combined with many of the pigments, serving both to modify their colour and to provide additional binding capacity.

The stratigraphy of the paint layers is remarkably varied, from thin single layers applied directly to the plaster to paint applied in considerable impasto, often over coloured grounds. In one sample from the lozenge-decorated rib (sf 120), a single layer of green earth combined with lime white, just 35μm thick, can be seen over the plaster. In a sample from the shield fragment (sf 135) (Plate 23), on the other hand, multiple paint layers including the lake glaze were applied to produce a brilliant red colour. The effect of porphyry on the shaft fragment (sf 125) (Plate 1) was achieved with loaded brush strokes of red, grey and white vigorously applied in impasto over a pink ground. In general, complex layering of brushstrokes is common, as on the 1916 fragment where green is applied in loose strokes over red, with the final details of the design added in black. In some instances the bare plaster substrate itself was employed as a creamy yellow background with details in black applied freely on the surface.

Original binding media

Analysis confirmed that the carbonation of lime was the principal binding mechanism, and that the paintings were executed partly in fresco. It also showed, however, that one or more organic media were employed for the application of particular pigments. Fluorescence stain tests suggested the presence of such a proteinaceous component in a sample of red lead, while FTIR analysis confirmed the presence of protein in a sample of green earth. The red lake glaze on the surface of the shield fragment (sf 135) was found to be particularly medium-rich, with preliminary GC-MS analysis (undertaken by Dr Perla Columbini of the University of Pisa) confirming the presence of protein, possibly casein or casein with animal glue.

Instrumental analysis of a number of other Romanesque wall-paintings has similarly shown them to be executed partly in fresco, but completed by the application of particular pigments in organic media. For instance, in the paintings of c1130 in St Gabriel's Chapel, Canterbury Cathedral, both protein and linseed oil have been identified as part of the original technique (Cather and Howard 1994, 144–146). In the late 12th-century paintings in Winchester Cathedral, a proteinaceous component has been identified in samples containing lead pigments, and also in a layer of calcium carbonate applied beneath an oil-based mordant for gold leaf (Howard 1995, 96). In polychrome sculpture, analysis of the late 12th-century figures from St Mary's Abbey, York, indicated that an egg tempera medium was employed, and glue as an adhesive for the gold leaf (Brodrick 1993, 26).

Conclusions

In their palette, and in the constituents of their plaster, the excavated fragments clearly form a coherent group, and the scientific examination has confirmed that the 1916 fragment belonged to the same scheme. While the masonry pattern fragment (sf 132) is exceptional in the simple nature of its painting and in the thinness of its plaster, analysis has shown that the constituents of this plaster are the same as those of the other fragments.

In general, the sophisticated technique of the paintings is typical of Romanesque wall-paintings of the highest quality. Executed partly in fresco, but completed with pigments applied in organic media, their rich and varied palette is fairly standard except in two respects: the absence of a mineral blue, and the exceptionally early use of red lake as a glaze. Many of the closest comparisons are provided by the scheme of c1175 in the Holy Sepulchre Chapel of Winchester Cathedral, which also includes red lake (though as part of an opaque paint layer) and conspicuous green modelling of the flesh tones.

The wide variation in the topography and stratigraphy of the plaster at Glasgow is again perhaps best paralleled by the Winchester scheme, where two plaster layers are apparent in some areas, and only one in others. A *sinopia* incorporating both vermilion and red earth occurs on the lower layer, and this may be the explanation of the traces of red paint on the two fragments at Glasgow exhibiting two separate plaster layers. Alternatively, they may provide evidence for a simple decorative scheme, itself of the late 12th century, executed shortly before the more complex figurative programme. The remains are simply too exiguous, however, for any firm conclusions on this point.

	context no./sample no.
Pinus sylvestris	
nave (N trench)	302/59; 304/39; 309/60; 382/40; 349/44; 390/62; 419/63; 423/41
nave (S trench)	501/42; 539/9; 551/15
crypt (W trench)	206/53; 209/54; 218/55; 223/57; 230/56
crypt (E trench)	102/45; 105/46; 115/47; 117/48; 117/49; 124/52
treasury	653/35; 655/36; 666/37
Quercus	
nave (S trench)	582/14

FIGURE 3.14

Wood samples from coffins

3.4 COFFINS AND COFFIN FURNITURE
by M J Richmond and S Bain

Wooden coffins

A total of 84 burials were recorded during the excavations of the crypt, nave, session room and W towers. Forty-two of these burials gave some indication that they were in wooden coffins. The majority of these date from the 18th and 19th centuries, but at least three are earlier than the mid 17th century. Wood was well preserved in some burials, particularly where lime had been used to treat the body. Some wooden coffins were little more than a stain and the remainder of coffin burials were represented by iron nails.

Wood identification
by S Bain and S Ramsay

Wood samples from 24 contexts from the nave, crypt and session room were examined (Figure 5.4 = 3.14). Fourteen of these samples were from identified coffins, the remainder were from loose fragments in other contexts, presumed to be from coffins. All the samples are from post-Reformation burials and the majority date from the 18th and 19th centuries. All the samples were of Scots pine (*pinus sylvestris*) with one exception, which was oak (*quercus*)

The use of pine and oak for coffin construction has been noted at other Scottish sites including Perth (J Stones 1989, 117) and presumably reflects local availability. The use of oak for a coffin may reflect higher economic status of the occupant. Cassel's *Household Guide*, published in 1874, lists the costs of various funerals; only the most expensive use oak (Morley 1971, 112). In England it appears to have been more common to use elm for coffins; elm was the most common species identified from Spitalfields, London (Reeve and Adams 1993, 80) and is also the common species for coffin construction in Cassel's guide.

Manufacture

The use of pine suggests that Scottish coffins were made from what was regionally available. The majority of coffin furniture, however, is likely to have been supplied directly by a large manufacturer, possibly one based around Birmingham which was a major metalworking centre at this time. None of the medieval graves survived well enough to determine the form of the coffins. The post-medieval coffins appear to fall into two designs: a simple trapezoid and the more familiar 'single-break' style with sides that flare out to accomodate the shoulders. Within the cathedral the preferred shape of coffin changes over time from the trapezoidal to the single-break. The trapezoidal coffins were identified in the nave (348, 534, 551). All must be earlier than the 18th century and some could date to the mid 17th century. The remaining coffins were all 'single break' and date from the 18th and 19th centuries.

Coffin furniture

'Coffin furniture' is the term for exterior metalwork of both decorative and functional nature. From the mid 18th century onwards it was common to cover the exterior of the wooden coffin in fabric, and further embellishment could be applied by using the metalwork available. The fabric was held in place with upholstery pins or strips of metal termed 'lace'. Sets of coffin handles or grips were frequently equipped with backing or grip plates which could be fastened to the sides of the coffin. Breast or depositum plates were fixed onto the lid and were often inscribed with biographical details. Other small pieces of decorative metalwork, escutcheons or 'drops', could be placed on the coffin to add to the overall design. The 'lace' and escutcheons were frequently of pressed tin and the grips of cast iron. Such items of coffin furniture would either have been bought by the undertaker ready-made or may have been produced by a local tin-plate worker from suppliers around Birmingham, copying designs from a trade catalogue (Reeve and Adams 1993, 83).

Phase	Area	Context	Sf	Description of coffin decorations
1	NN	403	533	Fe coffin fitting
2	NN	445	518	Fe coffin fitting
4	CW	244	723	Sn/Pb
4	CW	244	506	Fe coffin fitting
4–5	CE	111	295	Sn/Pb
5–6	CW	206	717	Sn/Pb
5–6	CW	209	718	Sn/Pb
5–6	CW	213		Tin-dipped stamped iron , fragment of winged cherub and cartouche
5–6	CW	218	719	Sn/Pb
5–6	CW	223	721	Sn/Pb
5–6	CW	234	722	Sn/Pb
5–6	CW	252	535	Fe coffin fitting
5–6	NN	322	604	Fe plaque with 5 holes, no decoration. 100 x 65 x 14mm
5–6	NN	322	728	Fe coffin decoration
6	NN	348	729	Sn/Pb. Plate frag of winged cherub and cartouche. Lace frag of raised circle type
6	NS	515	569	Fe coffin fitting
7	CE	143	496	2 frag of Fe coffin fittings
7	NN	304	726	Sn/Pb
7	NN	309	727	Sn/Pb. Lace frag of raised circle design
7	NN	309	491	4 frag of Fe coffin fittings
7	NN	312	524	2 frag of Fe coffin fittings
7	NN	417	730	Sn/Pb
7	NN	430	653	3 Sn/Pb frag of pressed coffin decoration
7	NN	431	731	Sn/Pb
7	NN	431	611	Fe
7	NS	548	732	Sn/Pb
7	SH	653	–	Sn/Pb. Lace frag of double diamond design
7	SH	656	–	Sn/Pb. 3 plate frag with winged cherub and rococo detail. 2 frag of lace, double wreathed oval design
7	SH	666	–	Sn/Pb. Frag lace, tri-fleur design
8	CE	105	195	Sn/Pb
8	CE	115	224	Fe
8	CE	117	249	Sn/Pb
8	CE	119	259	Sn/Pb
8	CE	119	733	Sn/Pb pressed plates with a decoration of winged cherubim, frag of coffin lace with a double diamond design
8	CE	122	418	Frag of Cu alloy coffin lining decoration
8	CE	122	265	Sn/Pb
8	CE	122	238	Sn/Pb
8	CE	124	734	Sn/Pb pressed plates with a decoration of winged cherubim, frag of coffin lace with a double diamond design
8	CE	124	277	Sn/Pb
8	CW	201	316	Sn/Pb
8	CW	220	720	Sn/Pb
8	NN	302	724	Sn/Pb
8	NN	302	520	7 frag of Fe coffin fittings
8	NN	302	725	Fe
8	NS	501	540	Fe coffin fitting
8	NS	501	556	2 Fe coffin studs and 1 decorative Fe fitting
8	NS	501	562	6 Fe decorative plates

FIGURE 3.15

Coffin fittings

Trade catalogues of the last century and other contemporary sources are very rare indeed, though the Victoria and Albert Museum in London, holds three catalogues of coffin furniture. One dates to the 1790s, the other to the 1820s and there is also a portfolio of loose prints from a second 18th-century pattern book. These were examined courtesy of Julian Litten of the Victoria and Albert Museum.

A total of 178 articles of coffin furniture were recovered from the cathedral excavations, including 94 iron coffin-grips, 84 fragments of tin and pewter coffin decoration and fittings, and a quantity of fabric, such as velvet and lace from coffin upholstery and silk ribbons from the shrouds. Only 60 of these items could be associated with a particular coffin or burial, the remainder were recovered from contexts where they had obviously been redeposited. The preservation of items of coffin furniture depends on a number of factors but, not surprisingly, it was clear that generally the bulkier iron grips and fittings

103

Phase	Area	Context	Sf	Description
4	CW	244	80	2 Fe coffin grips
4	NN	422	106	4 Fe coffin grips
4–5	CE	133	58	Fe coffin grip, length 180mm
5–6	CW	206	70	5 Fe coffin grips
5–6	CW	209	68	4 Fe coffin grips
5–6	CW	209	69	3 Fe coffin grips
5–6	CW	218	71	Fe coffin grip, length 240mm
5–6	CW	223	74	2 Fe coffin grip
5–6	CW	223	75, 76	2 Fe coffin grips. Out-turned terminals and central shield. 140mm length, 65mm drop
5–6	CW	234	72	2 Fe coffin grips. Out-turned terminals and central shield. 140mm length, 65mm drop
6	NN	348	323	2 Fe coffin grips and frag of 1 other. Out-turned terminals, round profile. Corroded. 110mm length, 7mm diameter
7	NN	304	324	7 Fe coffin grips
7	NN	386	320	2 Fe coffin grips
7	NN	417	321	Fe coffin grip
7	NN	420	103	5 Fe coffin grips
7	NN	431	104	5 Fe coffin grips
7	NS	548	109	5 Fe coffin grips
8	CE	111	282	Fe coffin grip. Conserved
8	CE	115	229	Fe coffin grip
8	CE	119	51	4 Fe coffin grips. 126mm length
8	CE	119	53	3 Fe coffin grips. 130mm length
8	CE	124	50	Fe coffin grip. 156mm length
8	CW	201	59	Fe coffin grip. 126mm length
8	CW	220	73	Fe coffin grip. 154mm length
8	NN	302	88, 91, 318, 319, 325	7 Fe coffin grips
8	NS	501	98, 107, 108	14 Fe coffin grips
8	WT	1002	1004	Possible coffin grip frag. Very heavily corroded. 106 x 16 x 9mm
8	WT	1005	1003	Coffin grip with a small projection at each end of its curved profile. Heavily corroded. 148 x 8 x 8mm
8	WT	1005	1002	Possible coffin grip frag, broken at both ends. The object tapers and curves smoothly approximately one third of the way along its length. Heavily corroded. 139 x 10 x 10mm
8	WT	1134	1007	Coffin grip of U-shaped form, with a slight widening at the terminals, to each of which a surviving frag of a looped fitting or eye bolt is attached. 84 x 38 x 8mm
unstrat	Nave	701	373	3 Fe coffin grips. 2 Fe coffin grips with plates
unstrat	SH	651	332	Fe coffin grip

FIGURE 3.16

List of iron coffin grips found during excavation

survived better than the thin pressed tin-pewter plates or the fabric.

Five coffins (348, 124, 223, 653, 656) warrant a detailed description of the coffin furniture because of their exceptional preservation and these are described in detail below. Other fittings are listed in Figure 3.15.

Coffin-grips

Of the 94 coffin-grips recovered from the excavations at Glasgow cathedral, the majority (52) were recovered from the trenches in the nave (Figure 3.16). All the coffins are post-Reformation and the majority appear to date from the 18th and 19th centuries. While 40 of the grips are associated with particular burials and represent the coffin in which the burial was made, the remaining grips were recovered from fills and layers loose, having been removed from their primary context during the continual re-digging of the ground for other burials.

Only two coffin-grips were cleaned and conserved, the remainder were lightly cleaned and wrapped in acid-free tissue paper. The grips all appear to be made from cast iron and the surface corrosion has made it impossible to identify any detailed decoration on all but two grips. The identification of the grips is therefore predicated on their basic shape. Five distinct shapes of grip were identified, although no typology or chronology can be deduced on stratigraphic grounds. All five shapes occurred in 18th- and 19th-century burials (Figure 3.17).

The use of grips on coffins appears to be as much a decorative as functional addition, and some coffins have no grips. The number and design of grips can give an indication of the social status of the deceased. Cassell's guide gives an indication of the cost and variety of funerals available in the 19th century. The

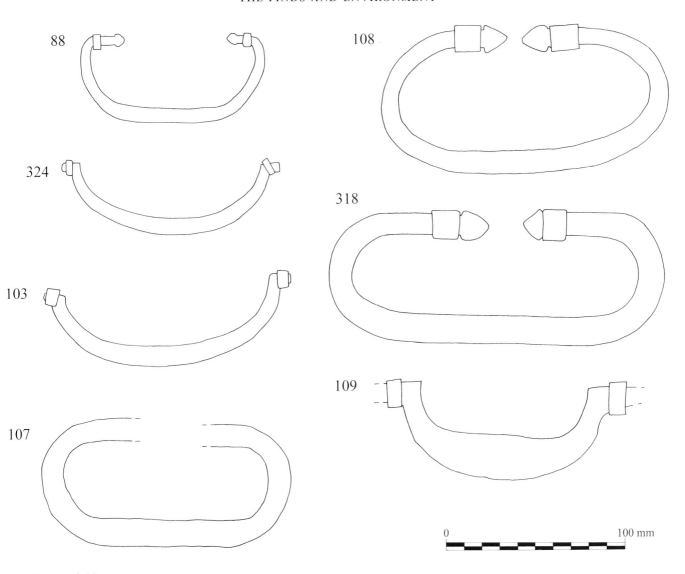

FIGURE 3.17

Sketch of coffin grips recovered from the excavations (sf 88, sf 107, sf 108, sf 109, sf 318, sf 324)

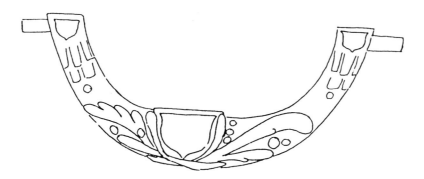

FIGURE 3.18

*Decorated coffin handle from Spitalfields of same design as sf 72 and 75
(after Reeve and Adams 1993, fiche 2, grip plate 14)*

FIGURE 3.19

Cherub grip plate of same design as on coffin 124 from trade catalogue. Courtesy of J Litten, Victoria and Albert Museum

cheapest option was in a plain elm coffin with no grips. For a little more expenditure one could get three pairs of grips and the upper range include four pairs of grips (Morley 1971, 112).

The excavation of Christ Church, Spitalfields, recovered 514 grips from burials dating between 1729 and 1852. Some of these grips could be accurately dated either from contemporary pattern books or because they were accompanied by dated depositum plates. This appeared to show that fashions in coffin furniture were slow to change, with some grip designs lasting for at least a century. Therefore the grip designs can give only a broad date range and at best a *terminus post quem*. Two grips from the crypt (sf 72 and sf 75) matched one recovered from Christ Church, Spitalfields, dated 1839–49 (Figure 3.18). The historical record indicates that burial in the crypt of Glasgow cathedral began around 1801 and finally stopped in the 1870s (see Section 2.2).

One coffin with grips was sealed under an internal partition wall (314) of the Outer High Kirk. The Kirk was established within the nave in 1647 but the partition may relate to the refurbishment in 1713. Two fragmentary grips were recovered (sf 323), both are a simple wide U-shape turning outwards at the terminals, with a small bulb or protrusion on the inside mid-point. The terminals are too corroded to determine the method of attachment to the coffin.

Grip-plates provide a decorative backing to the grips and are common on 18th- and 19th-century coffins (Reeve and Adams 1993, 83). They can be made from pressed iron, tin, tin-pewter or brass. Few identifiable fragments were recovered from the cathedral. The best preserved are part of the decorative assemblages discussed below.

A fragment of a grip-plate with part of an iron grip attached was recovered from coffin 124. The plate seems to be tin-plated iron and the reverse shows the outline of a pair of rococo-style flourishes. This piece forms the bottom part of a known motif consisting of a winged cherub's head beneath an oval convex cartouche, and parallels can be drawn with illustrations from both the 18th-century loose-leaf catalogue and the 1820s catalogue held by the Victoria and Albert Museum (Figure 3.19).

The occurrence of the same design of grips and grip-plates from cemeteries in London and Glasgow indicates that in the late 18th century designs fitted onto locally produced coffins were being chosen from national trade catalogues. The typology and dates of coffin furniture is an area which still needs further research, however it has the potential to aid in dating and to contribute to social history. The coffin furniture from Glasgow Cathedral supports the historical evidence; that the people buried within the cathedral were wealthy and influential.

'Lace'

Coffin 'lace' was used as a decorative method of fixing fabric coverings from as early as *c*1680 (Litten 1991, 109) and continued to be produced into the early 20th

PLATE 1

Late 12th-century part of a shaft with painting imitating porphyry (sf 125)

PLATE 2

Late 12th-century painted voussoir (sf 119)

PLATE 3

Late 12th-century voussoir painted with a shield above draperies (sf 135)

PLATE 4

Another view of the voussoir painted with linear decoration (sf 135)

PLATE 5

13th-century stone painted with masonry pattern (sf 132)

PLATE 6

Late 12th-century vaulting rib with painted lozenge decoration (sf 120)

PLATE 7

Another view of rib with painted lozenge decoration (sf 120)

PLATE 8

Late 12th-century fragment of a rib with painted decoration (sf 130)

PLATE 9

Late 12th-century stone painted with part of a torso with right arm raised (sf 81)

PLATE 10

Late 12th-century fragment of wall painting with imitation drapery (sf 129)

PLATE 11

Late 12th-century stone painted with a profile head and a cross (sf 86)

PLATE 12

Late 12th-century fragment of wall painting with imitation draperies (sf 114)

PLATE 13

Late 12th-century painted fragment (sf 115)

PLATE 14

Late 12th-century painted fragment (sf 116)

PLATE 15

Late 12th-century stone painted with a wing against a starry background (sf 118)

PLATE 16

Late 12th-century stone painted with diagonal sweeping lines (sf 122)

PLATE 17

Late 12th-century painted voussoir discovered in 1914–16

PLATE 18

Detail of a fragment painted with draperies (sf 129), showing a single layer of coarse lime plaster over the tooled sandstone support. Copyright Courtauld Institute

PLATE 19

Detail of the rib (sf 120) showing two layers of plaster, with remains of red paint on the lower layer. Copyright Courtauld Institute

PLATE 20

Detail of a fragment painted with draperies (sf 114), showing the rough surface texture of the plaster with large particles of aggregate penetrating the paint layer. Copyright Courtauld Institute

PLATE 21

Thin-section from sf 116, showing a lime deposit above a thin layer of vermilion (appearing as a dark line), above lime brought to the surface by polishing (appearing as a pale layer below the vermilion). Copyright Courtauld Institute

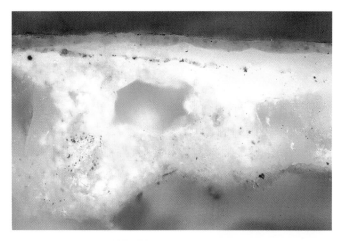

PLATE 22

Cross-section from the voussoir discovered in 1914–16, with green earth applied on a lime ground above a fine layer of red earth combined with charcoal black (the plaster layer appears below). Copyright Courtauld Institute

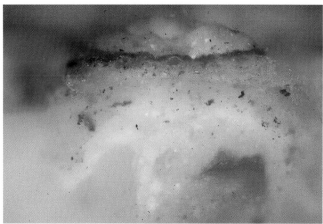

PLATE 23

Cross-section showing the red lake glaze on the fragment painted with a shield (sf 135). Beneath a lime crust on the surface, the glaze can be seen applied over a layer of vermilion combined with lime white. Copyright Courtauld Institute

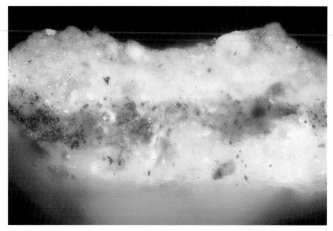

PLATE 24

Cross-section from the orange tip of the shield (sf 135), showing red lead applied over a lime white ground, over a layer of charcoal black combined with lime white. Copyright Courtauld Institute

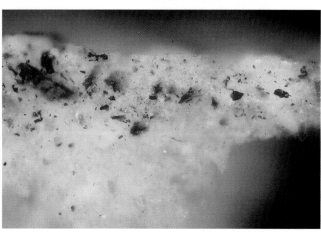

PLATE 25

Cross-section from the torso fragment (sf 81), showing charcoal black and lime white combined with a few particles of vermilion to produce a pale purple colour. Copyright Courtauld Institute

century. It could be a solid strip or an open design of filigree stamped from iron, brass or tin.

Fragments of coffin lace were recovered from the crypt, the nave and the treasury. The majority of fragments were recovered from grave fills or general layers and must have been redeposited during the frequent digging of new graves. Coffin lace was identified *in situ* on nine coffins. A number of fragments have been matched to contemporary trade catalogues of the 18th and 19th centuries. Two fragments of 'double diamond' pattern were recovered from coffin 213, a pattern also noted on coffins 124 and 653 and advertised in the 1820s catalogue.

Coffin 666 in the treasury yielded eight fragments of coffin lace. Despite its poor condition enough can be salvaged to establish that it does not have any similarities to designs illustrated in the trade catalogues. The die-cast stamped decoration is quite shallow and not as three-dimensional as the other lace recovered. The pattern is formed by a series of interlocking trefoil motifs. Two of the larger fragments show traces of shiny black enamelling or lacquering.

Two identifiable fragments of tin-pewter lace were recovered from coffin 309. One consists of a circular motif on a hatched background which bears traces of matte black colouring and can be matched with contemporary catalogue illustrations. The second fragment appears to be tin-plated stamped iron (*c*45 x 30mm) showing a flower garland border and the tip of a feathered wing (usually associated with the winged cherub head motif). Again this piece retains traces of what could be black paint. According to the coffin furniture catalogues both coffin lace and depositum/grip-plates could be selected in a variety of finishes, although the only examples of coloured coffin furniture recovered from Glasgow Cathedral have been black. According to the contemporary catalogues black was an expensive finish, more expensive than silver leaf.

Depositum plates and escutcheons

No examples of depositum plates bearing personal details such as name, date of birth or date of death were recovered. A feasible explanation for the absence of this type of furniture may be that the usual location for a depositum plate was the coffin lid, which usually collapses as the wood decays. It may also be, however, that since in some cases the biographical details were carried on the floor slabs (see Section 2.2) this obviated the need for a depositum plate. Two pieces of shield-shaped decoration which may have originally borne this information were isolated from the collection of fragmented coffin furniture.

An iron shield-shaped plate was recovered from the bedding sand for the nave floor (501). It is completely flat and badly corroded, it measures *c*70 x 60mm and may have been part of a larger decorative depositum plate similar to those illustrated in the 1820s catalogue. These examples come in both raised and flat shield form surrounded by designs such as the five-pointed crown, angels, winged cherubs, etc. The second of the shield-shaped plates forms part of the decorative assemblage from coffin 223, and is described in detail below.

Coffin 548 appeared to have been decorated with iron plate instead of the more common tin-pewter. One fragment (sf 677) is probably an escutcheon type of fitting (*c*30 x 30mm) roughly circular with a central hole and four lugs which square it off. The iron plates and studs found are listed on Figure 3.20.

Textiles

A quantity of fabric was recovered during the excavations, most of it velvet which would have been dyed black and used to cover the outer wood of the coffin (Figure 3.21). Some finer fabric may be from shrouds. Also recovered was silk ribbon used to decorate the shroud. The ribbon had been hand-sewn with silk thread either along one edge or along the centre of the ribbon which was then gathered up to form decorative ruffles. Some fragments of ribbon have small decorative copper-alloy hoops sewn on (sf 667). Copper-alloy shroud pins were used to pin the riffles to the shroud (see Section 3.5).

Phase	Area	Context	Sf	Description
6	NN	388	549	Decorative Fe coffin stud with mushroom shaped head. 38mm length, 30mm head diameter
8	NN	302	513	Fe coffin plate
8	NN	302	546	Decorative Fe coffin stud with mushroom shaped head. 52mm length, 24mm head diameter
8	NS	501	503	9 Fe decorated coffin plates
8	NS	501	564	4 decorative Fe coffin studs with mushroom shaped heads. Only heads are present
unstrat	NS	548	677	3 Fe coffin plate frag

FIGURE 3.20

List of iron plates and studs found during excavation

Phase	Area	Context	Sf	Description
5–6	CW	206	419, 421	2 frag of velvet coffin-covering
5–6	CW	207	659, 660	3 frag of velvet coffin-covering
5–6	CW	209	422	Frag of fine-weave textile
7	NN	304	649	5 frag of silk ribbon. The edges are frayed and the ribbon has been stitched with silk thread to form gathers. One frag is stitched along one edge, the others along the centre. Copper alloy pins are pinned through the ribbon crosswise at approx 45mm intervals
7	NN	305	650	Frag of velvet coffin-covering
7	NN	430	651	Frag of silk shroud-ribbon (15mm width). The edges are frayed and the ribbon is edge-stitched with silk thread and gathered. Three shroud pins (29–50mm) have been used to pin the ribbon
7	NN	430	652	5 frag of silk shroud ribbon with shroud pins. One frag is edge-stitched and drawn into gathers with a single frayed edge Two other frag (30mm wide) with no edge fray or gathers but are pinned with copper alloy pins. The remaining two frag have a double edge fray and are pinned with copper alloy pins
7	NN	430	654	Frag of velvet and silk thread on a coffin wood backing
7	NN	430	655	Multiple frag of layered silk and silk thread, possibly part of a shroud
7	SH	656	662	6 frag of velvet and the wooden backing for coffin decoration
8	CE	105	424	Frag of black velvet coffin covering
8	CE	115	656	Frag of velvet coffin covering
8	CE	124	429	Frag of velvet coffin-covering
8	CW	201	420	Frag of coarse woven textile
8	CW	215	64	Frag of textile, possibly from a shroud
8	CW	220	425	Frag of velvet coffin-covering
8	NS	501	99	Frag of black velvet coffin-covering and a frag of textile, possibly from a shroud or coffin-lining

FIGURE 3.21

List of textiles found during excavation

Other items

Along with the more decorative items of coffin furniture discussed above must go the more functional items of coffin construction. In the case of Glasgow cathedral these included iron nails, tacks and brackets. One hinge (sf 677) was recovered from a burial in the nave (548). This may represent a hinge for a lid, which would suggest a date in the 1870s or thereabouts (Litten 1991, 93).

Decorative assemblages from individual coffins

Coffin 348

Burial 348 is of an adult male in a trapezoidal pine coffin. The burial was sealed by an internal partition wall (314) of the Outer High Kirk, assumed to have been constructed after 1647, probably in 1713, after which burials ceased in this part of the nave. Litten (1991, 109) places the appearance of lace as a decorative motif *c*1680, which corresponds with the likely burial date.

The fragments recovered from coffin 348 included: a fragment of coffin lace with a circular motif on a hatched background identical to a fragment on coffin 309 and matched to a design in a late 18th-century loose-leaf catalogue; a fragment (*c*75 x 75mm) of a

winged cherub head/cartouche configuration in tin-pewter with a matte black finish all over. The cherub is below the cartouche as on coffin 213 and there is part of a rococo design to the left of the cherub's wing. Similar motifs are illustrated in Tuesby and Cooper's catalogue published in 1783 (Litten 1991) but no exact match has been found. This type of decoration has been popular since the end of the 17th century, as Litten (1991, 107) has remarked: 'Stamped iron *depositum* plates, tin-dipped and designed in the form of a concave oval cartouche encircled by a garland of flowers, first appeared at the end of the seventeenth century, so did grip-plates which were similarly oval with a repoussé design of winged cherubs' heads.'

The last identifiable fragment represents part of a design which was quite popular in England during the 18th and 19th centuries (Litten 1991). This motif is known as the 'flower pot' and often comes as part of a set including an angel. The fragment (*c*70 x 55mm) shows a fluted semi-circular bowl shape (the flower pot) sitting below a decorative swag of fabric. Several good matches for this can be found in both the 1820's catalogue and the 18th-century loose-leaf portfolio.

This burial appears to date to the early 18th century, but as has already been noted there was a remarkable longevity and popularity of designs within the funerary market. Unfortunately the typology and dating of coffin furniture is still in its infancy and a good chronology does not yet exist. The trapezoidal shape

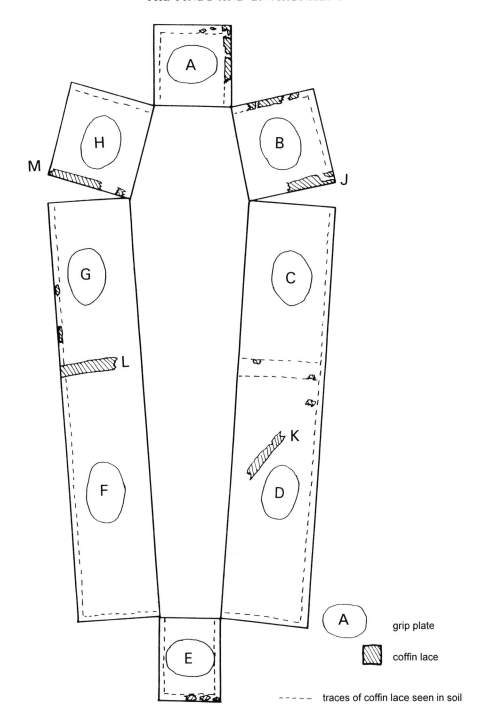

FIGURE 3.22

Sketch of coffin 124 showing locations of coffin furniture (not to scale)

of the coffin also suggests an early date but not conclusively.

Coffin 124

The skeleton of a mature adult female (sk 123) was discovered in a well-preserved coffin (124) in the crypt. The 'single-break' pine coffin was decorated with a number of items of coffin furniture. Eight grip-plates and coffin lace was observed on the coffin sides (Figure 3.22), although only three of the plates (D, G and F) and fragments of the lace were recovered. One plate still had the grip attached and a further six single grips were recovered. The remains of the silk cord used to lower the coffin into the grave-cut was still visible on some of the grips.

The grips are of cast iron and are quite heavily covered with corrosion concretion, rendering it impossible to ascertain whether they were decorated. They are 150mm in length with a drop of approximately 60mm. The terminals turn out and are attached

FIGURE 3.23

View of back of cherub grip plate in situ *on coffin 124*

to the grip-plate by two small iron nails, which can be seen from the reverse side with traces of coffin wood adhering to them.

The best preserved grip-plate, example D (Figure 3.23), measures 200mm x 140mm and is formed of an extremely thin metal, which analysis has shown to be a tin-pewter (70–80% tin and 20–30% lead). This is covered in embossed decoration consisting of a raised oval cartouche surrounded by rococo-style design which incorporates a pair of winged cherubs' heads. The surface has been damaged and the raised, embossed pattern is now quite flat. It is therefore difficult to be precise, but when viewed from the reverse side, it is possible to see the outline of the wings and the faces of a pair of cherubs above the convex oval. It is remarkably similar to the grip-plates on a coffin from Milton St John, Kent (Litten 1991, 115) which houses Eleanor Bell who died in 1827 and has 'a scarlet velvet upholstered elm case, with its cherub grip-plates, which might have been equally at home in the 1720s' (Litten 1991, 114).

The back of the grip-plate also has traces of fabric adhering to it, suggesting that when new, the coffin may have been upholstered with fabric which has now all but perished. This would not be unusual as most coffins after *c*1750 were fabric-covered, both for inhumation in the ground as well as deposition in a vault (Litten 1991, 103). The original colour of the fabric may have been red, black, blue or green. By the early 19th century a range of coloured velvets were utilised for coffin upholstery, whereas before this period the choice had been restricted to black or red (Litten 1991, 112). Since the grip-plate itself is of good quality (ie tin-pewter), it seems reasonable to assume that a high-quality covering such as velvet would have been used. Also, when closely inspected, there appear to be traces of pile to the fabric which suggests velvet.

Traces and fragments of the 'lace' which edged the coffin were noted and recovered. One piece, *c*110mm in length, has been conserved. Its pattern consists of two rows of diamonds separated by a double row of twisted cord. This matches a design from a catalogue of the 1820s where such lace was available in white (4/6d per dozen yards), white with black nails (5/6d), gilt lacquered (6/6d), gilt lacquered with black nails (7/6d).

Coffin 223

The burial of a mature adult male (sk 222) in a 'single-break' pine coffin was noted, not only because he possessed a fine set of false denture (see Section 4.2), but also because he was buried in an ornately decorated coffin (223).

The dominant item of coffin furniture was stamped tin-pewter decoration in the rococo style, backed with fabric, and featuring a non-figurative design not found in any of the catalogues. The largest piece measures *c*90 x 80mm and may be a rather wide and elaborate form of coffin lace, perhaps creating a panelled effect on the sides and lid of the coffin (Figure 3.24). Four fragments bearing the same pattern were recovered from the fill of grave (218) containing coffin 223 and were presumably once attached. The traces of fabric adhering to the lace are thought to be velvet.

The other furniture from this coffin included two pieces of stamped iron. One of these may be a rope type of border with a 'sun-ray' background, features which are illustrated as part of some depositum breast-plate patterns from the 18th-century loose-leaf catalogue in the Victoria and Albert Museum. The second iron fragment bears the impression of three raised roundels, possibly three berries in foliage as in an

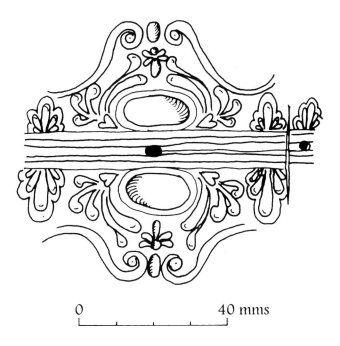

0   40 mms

FIGURE 3.24

Sketch of coffin lace from coffin 223

illustration of a depositum plate (the 1820s catalogue), or decorative beading found in part of a rococo style of decorative plate-border (18th-century loose-leaf catalogue). This motif was also noted at Christ Church, Spitalfields (Reeve and Adams 1993, fiche 2, grip-plate 25). One shield-shaped plate, 50 x 35mm, was also recovered. It is of raised form and has a bevelled border around the area where an inscription would have been. It appears to be made of tin-plated iron and the design was only visible from the reverse. It is similar to examples from Christ Church, Spital-fields (Reeve and Adams 1993, fiche 2, grip-plate 14).

Four grips were recovered from this coffin. They are all of cast iron and measure c140mm in length with a 65mm drop. The terminals turn out and are attached to the coffin by a cotter pin. The remains of the silk cord used to lower the coffin into the grave-cut was still visible on one of the grips. Although they are heavily concreted it is possible to determine that they were decorated, a central shield is visible at the centre of three of the grips. This is a motif noted on another grip from the crypt (sf 72) and from Christ Church, Spitalfield (Figure 3.18).

Coffin 653

One of two super-imposed mid 19th century burials excavated in the treasury. A number of fragments of coffin furniture were preserved on these 'single-break' pine coffins. The material recovered from coffin 653 includes five fragments of the 'double-diamond' type of coffin lace already identified from contemporary pattern books and identical to that recovered from coffin (124). The longest fragment is c75mm and has traces of matte black paint on the obverse. All the fragments have traces of fabric on the reverse. The remainder of the assemblage from coffin 653 consists of seven fragments of iron grips, three of which are still attached to pieces of iron grip-plates, and three fragments of iron plate decoration backed with fabric and wood. The only pattern visible is a common motif of rococo swags and flourishes.

Coffin 656

The other of the two super-imposed mid 19th-century burials from the treasury. The assemblage from coffin 656 consists of five lengths of coffin lace, four pieces of stamped tin-pewter decoration, and one piece of stamped iron plate decorated with rococo-style patterns. The coffin lace is tin-pewter which shows a double width of lace comprised of a series of small, raised ovals interleaved with a garland/wreath motif on a hatched background and edged with a raised 'rope' border. It can be matched with an example from the 1820s catalogue.

Only one of the fragments of tin-pewter stamped furniture has visible decoration, the others are too fragmentary. This shows a face and part of a wing (indicating either an angel or a cherub) fixed to the surviving wood with a copper-alloy (probably brass) tack. This could be part of a grip-plate. The stamped iron plate is likely to have been part of a lid decoration (perhaps a depositum plate). The decoration on this lid plate is the partial face of an angel or cherub with a fragment of wing and a 'necklace' of circular, raised shapes. These two fragments with a similar design motif suggest that coffin furniture was bought in matching sets.

Discussion

The recovery of coffins and coffin furniture from Glasgow Cathedral adds to a small but growing corpus of post-Reformation funereal items. The absence of dated depositum plates was unfortunate from an archaeological point of view, but even if they had survived they may have confirmed that, once a style or design in coffin furniture became popular, fashions were extremely slow to change. For example, elements of the designs for coffin furniture in Tuesby and Cooper's 1783 catalogue (Litten 1991), such as the border flower garland, the rococo-style designs, the oval cartouche and the winged cherub's head have many points of similarity with the grip-plate (sf 734) from Glasgow Cathedral which is believed on stratigraphic grounds to date from the mid 1800s.

It is assumed that those buried within the cathedral were part of the social élite and that their funerals reflected their social standing. The use of coffins was unusual for burials in the Middle Ages but increased in popularity throughout the 17th century. It would appear that the community buried within the cathedral adopted this practice and that the elaborate coffin furniture had become popular by the late 17th century. The coffins from the 18th and 19th century were decorated with mass-produced items typical of those sold throughout Britain as part of the 'industrialised' funeral business.

3.5 METALWORK

Small copper-alloy objects
by I Cullen

The majority of copper-alloy artefacts retrieved were shroud pins, but there were also a number of other pieces of metalwork (Figure 3.25). Three lace tags were recovered, all were formed by a small rectangle of copper-alloy folded into a tube. Laces can be used to fasten a variety of clothing, including shoes and shrouds. Other minor copper-alloy artefacts included: three buckle fragments, two buttons, two rings, a chain and a needle.

A large quantity of pins were recovered from grave contexts. Such 'shroud pins' were used to fasten clothing and other textiles to the coffin and body. All were of copper-alloy and the vast majority had round heads and were undecorated. Some of the larger pins had a spiral decoration on the heads (sf 441). The complete pins varied in length between 14 and 60mm, although larger pins were rare. In addition two small copper hoops (sf 667), measuring 11mm in diameter,

were recovered which appear to have been used as decoration on shroud ribbons. By far the most significant of the copper-alloy objects were the seal matrix and the mortars described below.

Seal matrix
by S T Driscoll

A shield-shaped copper-alloy seal (sf 96) was recovered from the backfill (346) of a grave-shaft (341) in the nave (N trench, phase 6). This object was used to seal letters and other documents with wax as a sign of authenticity. It is decorated with a central motif of a gatehouse with open door, surmounted by two birds separated by a fleur-de-lis, each with a fleur-de-lis in its beak. Around the edge is a continuous border inscribed with the following legend: S'| ADEM·LE | PORTIE |R (s[igillum] Adem le portier, seal of Adam the porter) (Figure 3.26).

Considerable skill has been employed cutting the seal matrix, which measures 26 x 24 x 2.2mm. The matrix is in fine condition and produces a crisp, clear impression, including idealised details of stonework on the gatehouse. The letters are a maximum of 2.5mm in height. No analysis of the metal composition has been carried out, but the weight of the seal suggests that it contains a significant proportion of lead. A high lead content would produce a softer medium to carve and aid in the production of a finer image. The suspension loop on the reverse appears to have been cast with the main body of the matrix. The rough edges were filed off leaving parallel scars. The loop was pierced after casting as indicated by the slight lip visible on one side. Traces of the suspension cord may be preserved in the corrosion within the loop. The excellent condition of the seal suggests that it was deposited shortly after manufacture.

The shield is triangular in shape and, although this is not a reliable guide to date, the lettering style appears to be late 13th or early 14th century (T A Heslop pers comm). The device alludes to the role of the porter as keeper of the gate or door of a castle or monastery, an important official within a religious house. In addition to keeping the keys, his duties included the distribution of alms ad portam monasterii (at the gate of the monastery; Black 1946, 669). The historical record is insufficient to establish whether there was indeed a gate-keeper, or holder of the office of porter at the cathedral or monastery, called Adam in this period. The suspension loop suggests that the matrix was worn as a badge of office and was in regular use. The proliferation of fleurs-de-lis might suggest that Adam was a Dominican monk, as this device forms the main charge on the heraldic arms of this Order. The Dominican Order arrived in Glasgow in 1256. Alternately the fleur-de-lis may have been intended to 'soften' any connotations of militarism

Phase	Area	Context	Sf	Description
4–5?	CE	110	46	Small copper-alloy circular bell constructed in two halves welded together forming a hollow sphere The bell has a small outer loop and is slightly bashed. 15 x 12mm
5–6?	CW	206	–	9 round-headed copper-alloy pins. 20–27mm length
5–6?	CW	209	57	Copper alloy ring, possibly a finger ring. 18mm diameter, 2mm thickness
5–6?	CW	209	439	1 oval headed shroud pin. 27mm length
5–6?	CW	209	448	9 round-headed copper-alloy pins. 20–27mm length
5–6?	CW	209	666	4 round-headed copper-alloy pins. 25–33mm length
5–6?	CW	209	667	2 copper-alloy rings; they were probably sown onto silk ribbon as a decoration for shrouds. 11mm diameter
6	NN	322	403	Frag of copper alloy
6	NN	322	405	Frag of copper alloy, and coal
6	NN	322	474	4 unidentifiable frag of copper alloy
6	NN	322	400	10 round-headed copper-alloy pins. 22–51mm length
6	NN	322	477	1 round-headed copper-alloy pin. 26mm length
6	NS	550	475	Unidentifiable frag of copper alloy
6	NS	552	479	Copper-alloy ferrule, possibly of brass, with no sign of wear. The ring is bashed and slightly discoloured at the edges. 25mm diameter, 8mm width
6	NS	575	476	Unidentifiable frag of copper alloy
7	NN	309	401	1 copper-alloy pin
7	NN	309	492	1 round-headed copper-alloy pin
7	NN	324	83	Copper alloy chain of split pins and links. 60mm length
7	NS	503	–	Copper alloy sewing needle
7	NS	503	487	Frag of copper alloy
7	NS	547	663	1 round-headed copper-alloy pin. 30mm length
8	CE	102	440	9 round-headed copper-alloy shroud pins (2 broken). 23–27mm length
8	CE	105	442	Copper-alloy sheet fragment. 12 x 9mm
8	CE	105	441/622	310 round-headed copper-alloy shroud pins (46 broken). Some of the larger of which have a spiral decoration on the heads. 20–60mm length (unbroken pins)
8	CE	110	203	55 round-headed copper-alloy shroud pins (8 broken). 14–35mm length
8	CE	110	45	Decorated T-shaped object, possibly a watch key
8	CE	110	201	Copper-alloy buckle hinge and Fe hinge pin. The copper alloy is bent round the iron pin and has a small hole punched through it. 20 x 10mm
8	CE	110	257	Frag of sheet copper alloy folded lengthways possibly around a wooden pin. The pin has an oval cross-section. 26 x 2mm
8	CE	110	289	A rolled tube of sheet copper alloy. The width of the tube tapers at one end
8	CE	111	209	7 round-headed copper-alloy shroud pins (3 broken). 25–32mm length
8	CE	114	216	28 round headed copper-alloy pins (1 broken). 18–35mm length
8	CE	114	215	2 possible belt pins formed from frag of sheet copper alloy bent around wooden pins. Also a small frag of sheet copper alloy. Pins: 20 and 22mm length with an oval cross-section of 2 mm; sheet fragment: 9 x 7mm
8	CE	115	225	33 round-headed copper-alloy pins (5 broken). 18–32mm length
8	CE	117	231	5 round-headed copper-alloy pins. length 23–35mm
8	CE	122	239	27 round-headed copper-alloy pins (11 broken). 15–50mm length
8	CE	133	56	Small flat circle of copper alloy with a loop attachment at back, possibly a modern button. 15mm diameter, 1mm thickness
8	CE	133	301	3 round-headed copper-alloy pins (1 broken). 25–34mm length
8	CW	105	671a	A decorated sheet with a punched circle and zig-zag decoration. 30 x 16 x 1mm
8	CW	105	671b	A rolled tube. 23 x 3 x 2mm
8	CW	201	443	Copper alloy wire. 60mm length. Frag of sheet copper alloy with two punched holes
8	CW	201		58 round-headed copper-alloy pins. 20–43mm length
8	CW	203	65	Circular button with small hoop, possibly a boot button. 11mm diameter, 4mm thickness
8	CW	203	66	Possible bootlace end formed from a small rectangle of copper alloy folded into a tube. 17mm length, 3mm diameter
8	CW	203	445	Copper-alloy wire. 40mm length
8	CW	203	444	3 round-headed copper-alloy pins. 24–30mm length
8	CW	204	446	3 round-headed copper-alloy pins. 35mm length
8	NN	302	668	28 round-headed copper-alloy pins. 20–27mm length
8	NS	501	478	1 round-headed copper-alloy pin. 26mm length
8	SH	651	340	Copper-alloy wire. 18mm length
8	SH	727	678	Unidentifiable copper-alloy object
unstrat	ED	800	360	Copper-alloy wire
unstrat	N	713	369	1 copper-alloy pin
unstrat	N	731	375	Unidentifiable copper-alloy object

FIGURE 3.25

List of small copper-alloy objects found during excavations

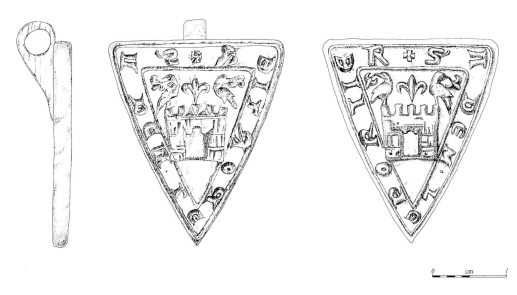

FIGURE 3.26

Seal of Adam le Porter (sf 96) and impression (on right)

expressed by the crenellated gate (T A Heslop pers comm).

Bronze mortars and iron pestle
by D Gallagher with K Forsyth

The two bronze mortars and an iron pestle recovered from a pit (150) in the NW corner of the Lady Chapel (crypt E trench, phase 7, context 143) (Figures 2.46 and 2.51) were buried together deliberately. One of the mortars (sf 61) is late 13th or early 14th century in date and had been much used before burial. The other is probably of slightly later date, but the pestle (sf 63) is likely to be several centuries later. It is unusual for a medieval pestle to be made of iron. Iron pestles do not appear to become common until the 16th and 17th centuries, so this may well be a replacement. It is rare to find a pestle so firmly associated with a medieval mortar.

Description

Mortar 1 (sf 61; Figures 3.27–3.28 and 3.31) is bucket-shaped with an everted lip and made of copper alloy. It has two 'rope' handles with attached iron rings. The body is encircled by two bands separated by raised mouldings. Cast in relief on the upper band is a legend in Lombardic capitals, ':WIL·EL·MUS: | :WUS·SCARD:'. The lower band has six simple, equal-armed crosses, also cast in relief. The base of the mortar has become convex through heavy use. 260mm height, 175mm diameter.

The variety of forms among the repeated letters and the six crosses indicates that each individual character was cut into the mould, rather than stamped. The reversals of the Ss may be a stylistic feature and need not suggest any incompetence on the part of the engraver. In the 13th and 14th century the use of trios of vertically arranged points is not unusual at the beginning and end of texts, or to indicate word division, but the use of single points within words to separate syllables is less common. The C, E, U and the Ws are enclosed by extended serifs. This feature was introduced in various media in the later 12th century but did not become universal until around the mid 13th century. Although Lombardic lettering ceases to be used on English seals around the mid 14th century, it can appear in other contexts considerably later, for example on two late 14th-century copper-alloy jugs (Alexander and Binski 1987, 524–525).

There are two possible candidates for the William Wischard (or Wishart) named in the inscription. The elder is the former archdeacon of St Andrews and royal chancellor of that name who became bishop-elect of Glasgow in 1270. This Wischard was an ambitious cleric whose tenure in Glasgow was short: he was elected bishop of St Andrews in 1273, never having been consecrated at Glasgow. He died in 1279 (for his career, see Watt 1977, 590–594; *Scotichronicon* 5, 381; Dowden 1908, 86). The mortar may represent a gift to the cathedral on his election in 1270. The practice of gift-giving became obligatory for all new members of the Chapter in the following century. The inscription does not identify William as *episcopus*, but, strictly, he would not have been entitled to style himself bishop until after consecration. William was a rich and powerful man but his association with Glasgow was short-lived and not without controversy. His younger namesake had a longer and more positive connection with Glasgow and for this reason he is perhaps more likely to be the donor of the mortar. The two Williams were close kinsmen, the junior being the

FIGURE 3.27

Bronze mortar 1 with WILELMUS WUSSCARD legend (sf 61)

FIGURE 3.28

Photo of WILELMUS WUSSCARD bronze mortar 1 (sf 61)

115

0   60 mms

FIGURE 3.29

Bronze mortar 2 (sf 62)

FIGURE 3.30

Photo of bronze mortar 2 (sf 62)

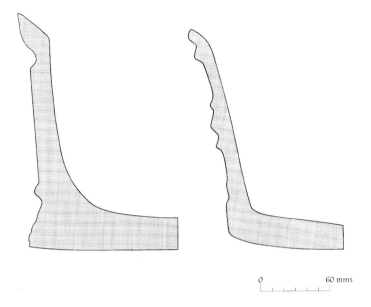

0   60 mms

FIGURE 3.31

Profiles of the two mortars (sf 62 on the left, sf 61 on the right)

nephew, or possibly even the son, of the senior. This would make the younger William the cousin, or possibly the brother, of the Robert Wischard who was consecrated bishop of Glasgow in 1273 (succeeding the senior William, his uncle or father, who had moved on to St Andrews; Watt 1977, 590). It is probably to bishop Robert that the younger William Wischard owed his very prominent position as archdeacon of Teviotdale, which he held for almost 50 years until his death *c*1320 (Watt 1977, 595).

Mortar 2 (sf 62; Figures 3.29–3.31) is a cylindrical mortar with splayed foot, made of copper alloy. It has two large and two smaller loop handles, all with diagonal slash decoration. Two copper-alloy rings are suspended from the smaller loops. The body of the mortar is decorated with eight equally spaced pilasters, each with moulded bases and capitals and two separate roll mouldings, one medial, the other just below the capital. There is a maker's mark cast in false relief in Lombardic letters: reversed IH, the H surmounted by a small equal-armed cross with expanded terminals. The angle where the body joins the rim is badly cast in places and there are signs of knife-finishing, a level of finishing typical of this type of medieval casting. The presence of copper-alloy, rather than iron, rings is a rare feature and otherwise unknown on mortars this large. The base is flat. 190mm height, 270mm diameter.

Maker's marks occur on a number of items of metalwork of Scottish provenance, although no exact parallel has been found for the *ih* mark on the mortar (sf 62). A bell from Monkton, Ayrshire is marked with the same letters, although not from the same stamp (Clouston 1949, 239–249). The lack of appropriate comparanda make this mortar difficult to date. In general cylindrical mortars appear to be somewhat later than those which taper (such as sf 61; St Mary's

York mortar, dated 1308). Mortar 2 (sf 62) may date, therefore, to the mid to late 14th century or 15th century.

The pestle (sf 63; Figures 3.32–3.33) is wrought-iron. The surface is badly corroded, but flat facets are visible on the surface of the shaft. The shaft splays out at either end, to diameters of 45mm and 50mm. 470mm max length, 50mm diameter.

Discussion

Medieval *mortaria* were used to grind various sub-stance for a variety of processes, both domestic and industrial. They were also used in the preparation of medicines. Metal mortars are depicted in illustrations of apothecaries and the inscription on the bronze mortar from St Mary's Abbey, York, indicates that it was a pharmacy mortar from the Abbey infirmary (Alexander and Binski 1987, 244). In Roger of Salerno's *Chiurgia,* a medical treatise written *c*1230–50, a mortar is shown in use while resting either on the ground or on a very low stand (Alexander and Binski 1987, 330). It appears, like mortar 1 (sf 61), to have loops suspended from two of its four handles. A mortar is depicted mounted on a table in another medical book, the *Herbarius zu Teutsch,* published in 1496 (Catalogue 1975, 67). Mortars were also used in the preparation of artist's materials such as the milling of gold for book illumination. Theophilus, writing in the 12th century, specifies that mortars for this purpose should be of a lead-free copper-tin alloy (Hawthorne and Smith 1979, 34). The massive size of the Glasgow mortars indicates that whatever the substance pounded therein, it was needed in some quantity. Their cathedral context suggests that they may have been used in the preparation of materials for the

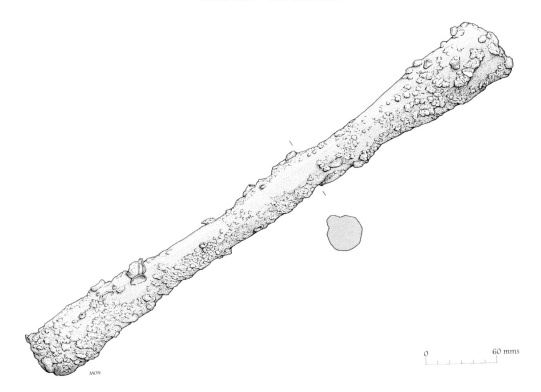

0   60 mms

FIGURE 3.32

Iron pestle (sf 63)

FIGURE 3.33

Photo of iron pestle (sf 63)

liturgy, ie incense. Large amounts of incense were burnt on important feast days: in 1486 James Lindsay, the Dean, made a gift for the annual provision of 4 pounds of wax and 2 pounds of incense for the High Altar on the feast of Kentigern (Eyre-Todd 1890, 480; Glasgow *Registrum ii,* 441).

No mortars are mentioned in the list of items belonging to the cathedral in 1432 (Dowden 1899), making it possible that they were purely secular objects buried simply to prevent theft at a time of disturbance.

Duffy (1992, 490–491) cites parallel instances of the concealment of church property in the floors of churches during the Reformation period in England. The considerable efforts taken to conceal the Glasgow hoard implies, however, that it had a significance far beyond its intrinsic value as scrap metal. Its burial position in the crypt near the Lady Chapel suggests sacred associations. The mortars were apparently several centuries old when buried, and one, at least, had been heavily used.

118

The concealment of ecclesiastical metalwork with ancient associations is attested elsewhere in Glasgow diocese. Two 'antique vessels' discovered at Galloflat, Rutherglen, in 1773 may or may not have been mortars. They were described as being of brass or copper, 'shaped like a porringer', each holding 'about a choppin' (ie a Scots half-pint, 0.85 litres), full of earth when found and 'white on the inside' (Ure 1793, 124). The ecclesiastical function of these objects is indicated by the fact that both had 'broad handles, about 9 inches [230mm] in length, having cut upon them the name *Congallus*, or *Convallus*' (Ure 1793, 124). St Conguall or Conval, patron of Rutherglen, was traditionally regarded as a disciple of Kentigern (Watson 1926, 169).

The ribbed mortar (sf 62) bears a striking resemblance to a, now lost, mortar discovered in 1877 on the site of the former Dominican Friary at Bell Street, a short distance from the cathedral (Anderson 1879, 48, fig 1). The two vessels are, in fact, virtually identical, both in form and size: the recorded dimensions of the Bell Street mortar are, height 7½" (c190mm), diameter 10¼" (c255mm) and the two share even small details of decoration such as the medial band on each pilaster. The two are surely the products of the same worship. The Bell Street mortar was found to contain a small cast brass figure in the shape of a lion (6" or c150mm tall) and another article, comprising brass-lined square plates decorated with twisted-wire filigree (Anderson 1879, 48–49), both now lost. The purpose of the latter is not know, although it may have been a reliquary; the lion, however, appears to be part of a candelabrum, probably ecclesiastical. The mortar, which showed signs of use, was discovered 'in forced earth', inverted over an iron 'lid' about 7½' (c2.3m) below street level; circumstances which also suggest deliberate burial.

The Bell Street mortar lacked rings when found, but a third apparently identical mortar is known, which did have rings intact. This third mortar, also now lost, was seen in the late 18th century by the traveller Thomas Pennant (1772, II, 74, pl vii, no 94). Pennant describes it as being of 'mixed metals' but gives no indication of its size. He saw it at the home of a Mr Dickinson of Locharwoods, Dumfries, and was told that it had been found in the neighbourhood. This area is, of course, within the diocese of Glasgow (archdeaconry of Teviotdale) and it is tempting to see this group of three or more mortars as somehow linked by liturgical practices associated with the cult of Kentigern, with the mortars perhaps even distributed through the diocese.

Pennant depicts another, decidedly bowed, mortar which is very similar, though not identical to the others: it has two not four handles and six not eight pilasters, each with double not single medial bands (1772 II, pl vii, no 74). No indication of size is given but it too may have been a Glasgow product.

Beyond the above examples, mortars are otherwise rare from medieval Scotland, in contrast to the high numbers of other metal vessels, especially cauldrons. The latter were collected by Scottish antiquaries from as early as the 18th century whereas mortars appear to have been regarded as utilitarian objects, their greater weight making them more susceptible to being melted as scrap.

Iron objects
by I Cullen

By far the majority of iron objects were nails and nail fragments, presumably from coffins and coffin fitments (Figure 3.34). Several heavily corroded nails were found, mainly represented by shaft fragments, but some exhibiting rectangular cross-sectioned shafts and rounded heads. All of the iron objects from the excavation are severely corroded, surface and constructional details only being visible on X-ray images.

3.6 COINS
by D Bateson

Twelve coins were recovered from Glasgow Cathedral. One English halfpenny dates to the late 12th–early 13th century and is associated with the construction of the current cathedral (phase 4). The remainder are all post-Reformation dating to the 17th and 18th century. All the coins seem to represent casual loss. In the following catalogue the context number appear in brackets before the sf number.

1 NS (4) (591) sf 322
England, cut halfpenny, from short cross penny-class, mint and moneyer uncertain; worn / 0.74 gm [11.4gr] / na. Short cross pennies were issued 1180–1247 and unlikely to have been lost in Scotland after 1250.

2 CE (7) (114) sf 41
ELIZABETH I, sixpence, 157– (im = eglantine 1574–78); worn / buckled / corroded / 2.40gm [37.1gr] / 0. Probably a 17th-century loss.

3 CE (8) (105) sf 37
CHARLES I, copper turner (twopence Scots), 1640s; slightly worn / struck off-centre both sides / 2.55gm [39.4gr] / 0.

4 CE (8) (105) sf 42
Similar, appears to be a forgery; worn / 1.85gm [28.6gr] / 180.

5 CE (7) (114) sf 40
CHARLES I-II, turner, 1640s or 1663; worn / 1.86gm [28.7gr] / na.

6 CE (8) (105) sf 39
WILLIAM II, turner or bodle, 1695, sceptres high, REX; very slightly worn / 2.41gm [37.2gr] / 180.

Phase	Area	Context	Sf	Iron nails	Other iron objects
1	NN	359	636	2	
1	NS	556	507	1	
3	NN	406	574	2	
3	NN	452	544	1	
4	CW	231	642	2	
4	CW	244	504	8	
4	NS	591	552	2	
4–5	CE	110	256, 633	32	1 plate
4–5	CE	111	210, 284	11	a bolt with a square shaft. 85mm length, 21mm width
4–5	CE	114	218	10	
4–5	CE	126	177	1	
4–5	CE	131	280, 531	15	
4–5	CE	133	304	6	1 sheet fragment
4–5	CE	139	630	1	
4–5	CE	148	631	2	
4–5	CE	149	619	11	
5–6	CW	206	607, 638	39	
5–6	CW	209	616, 632	108	
5–6	CW	218	617	6	
5–6	CW	223	612, 623, 628	76	
5–6	CW	230	624	20	
5–6	CW	234	615	10	
5–6	CW	240	614	4	
5–6	NN	388	548	6	
6	NN	322	510, 525, 603	103	
6	NN	345	577	4	
6	NN	346	509	16	
6	NN	349	497/572	38	
6	NN	350	543	13	
6	NN	357	634	1	
6	NN	360	541	1	
6	NN	364	493, 494	13	
6	NN	376	599	14	
6	NN	382	536	15	
6?	NN	386	291, 639	7	
6	NN	393	579	1	
6	NN	401	511	3	
6	NN	404	537	1	
6	NN	436	559	1	
6	NS	510	508, 519, 542	10	
6	NS	514	498, 553, 600	18	
6	NS	515	568	6	
6	NS	522	501	3	
6	NS	525	560	6	
6	NS	527	526, 567, 571	39	
6	NS	531	528	23	
6	NS	539	578	2	
6	NS	546	576	2	
6	NS	550	522	13	
6	NS	571	565	–	Unidentifiable iron object
6	NS	581	489	33	
6–7	NS	588	570	5	
7	CE	143	495	14	
7	NN	304	529	60	
7	NN	309	490, 547	45	
7	NN	312	523	10	
7	NN	324	530, 606	145	
7	NN	408	527	5	
7	NN	431	610	18	
7	NS	502	557	5	
7	NS	503	514, 515	30	
7	NS	503	516	–	Iron hook. 70mm length
7	NS	547	534	10	
8	CE	102	185	8	
8	CE	105	620	200	1 nut fragment
8	CE	115	228, 643	21	
8	CE	117	235, 245, 246	71	a bolt similar to sf 210. 53mm length
8	CE	119	261	53	

8	CE	122	270	–	2 pieces of wire twisted together at one end. 40mm length
8	CE	122	244, 268	63	
8	CE	124	613	56	
8	CW	201	315	43	
8	CW	203	640	2	
8	CW	204	645	8	
8	CW	214	644	3	
8	CW	220	625	3	
8	NN	302	512	12	a large iron bolt with square cross-section. 155mm length
8	NN	302	521, 545, 566	23	
8	NN	302	608	92	2 studs with mushroom-shaped heads; 2 bars
8	NN	302	635	6	2 plates
8	NS	501	499, 502, 539, 555, 561, 575	76	
unstrat	ED	800	361	4	2 coffin decorations
unstrat	ND	700	590, 593, 596	3	3 iron nails, 1 stud
unstrat	N	700	374	–	2 iron bolts; 2 unidentifiable iron objects
unstrat	N	–	637	2	
unstrat	WT	41	1001	–	Bar or file. Narrow, rectangular cross-sectioned bar, with one rounded and one squared terminal. A series of shallow serrations or teeth occurs along one of the long edges; the other is smooth. Where obscured by corrosion products, the serrations are visible on x-ray. Heavily corroded, with numerous accretions

FIGURE 3.34

List of iron objects recovered during excavation

7 CW (8) (201) sf 52
Similar, 1695/6, low sceptres, REX; worn / chipped / corroded / 2.48gm [38.3gr] / 180.

8 CW (8) (201) sf 55
17th century copper bawbee or sixpence, probably WILLIAM and MARY, 1692–24; worn / corroded / 6.81gm [105.1gr] / 180.

9 CW (8) (201) sf 47
17th century bawbee; worn smooth / 6.60 gm [101.8gr] / na.

10 CE (8) (105) sf 38
Ireland, WILLIAM and MARY, halfpenny, 1692; fairly worn / 7.48gm [115.5gr] / 0.

11 CE (7) (110) sf 43
Ireland, GEORGE II, halfpenny, 1742; worn / 7.71gm [119.0gr] / 180.

12 CW (8) (215) (no sf)
An unidentified fragment of copper-alloy coin.

3.7 POTTERY
by R S Will

A total of 201 medieval and post-medieval sherds were recovered along with 74 sherds from the 19th and 20th centuries. Most of the contexts contained a mixture of modern and medieval sherds (Figure 3.35).

Of the medieval sherds, 103 are in Scottish East Coast White Gritty Ware (SECWGW) type fabrics. This material is thought to have been made at several sites in the Borders, Lothian and Fife (Haggarty 1984), although the only excavated kiln site is at Coulston in East Lothian (Brooks 1980). Scottish white gritty wares date from the late 12th century (Kelso) through to the 15th century and are found in a wide area outwith their production centres. Several sherds of this material were identified from excavations as far away as Trondheim and Bergen in Norway (Reed 1990).

The material from Glasgow Cathedral appears to cover a range of fabrics and dates. A jug rim (sf 527) with part of a tubular spout may date to the 13th century. The largest group of material recovered, 66 sherds (sf 312), appears to date from the 15th century. One of the white gritty sherds (sf 358) has been rounded off and re-used, presumably as a counter or gaming piece.

Also recovered were 47 sherds of Scottish medieval redwares, which most likely represent local fabrics from the Glasgow area. To date no kiln sources have been identified for this type of material, although Hagg's Castle has been suggested (Sloan 1972). One sherd (sf 502) with a white slip over the red/orange fabric may be from Perth (MacAskill 1987, 91).

Many of the sherds in both the white and red fabrics seem to be from globular jars and jugs, although a bowl is also present (sf 503). The dating of these sherds is complicated by the small size of the sherds but most would date to the 14th and 15th centuries, although some sherds, particularly from globular jars, could be earlier.

The post-medieval period is represented by Scottish post-medieval reduced wares and the partially oxidised version (sf 220) which is very similar to that found at Throsk (Caldwell and Dean 1992). These sherds are all from jugs and date from the 15th–18th centuries (Haggarty 1984).

One sherd of a 17th-century Westerwald stoneware vessel (sf 322) was recovered. These vessels with their

Phase	Context	Sherds	spmrw	we	smr	swgw	ting	other
1	556	2				2		
3	406	4				4		
4	327	1			1 gj			
4	591	13				13		
5	322	24	2		13 gj	8		1 17thC German stoneware
5	373	14				14		
6	204	1				1		
6	346	1				1 gj		
6	350	2				2 14–15thC		
6	358	1				1 gaming piece		
6	388	1				1		
6	411	1		1				
6	436	2		2				
6	514	1			1 handle			
6	527	2			1	1 12–13thC		
6	543	1	1					
6	716	2			2			
6	723	5			3	2		
7	110	3				3		
7	117	4	3	1				
7	122	2	1	1				
7	206	6		1	3		2	
7	209	6		2	1	1		1 Wedgwood
7	223	1		1				
7	302	7	3	1	1	1		
7	304	1					1	
7	312	75	23		19	32		1 daub
7	321	1	1					
7	324	2			1			
7	380	1				1		
7	408	3	1			2		
7	502	2			1	1		
7	503	2			2			
7	510	1				1		
7	711	1			1			
8	102	7	1	3	1			1 brick
8	105	27	4	8	7	1	3	4 wasters
8	111	8		3		4		
8	126	1			1			
8	133	1			1			
8	201	6		2	1		2	
8	203	3		2	1			
8	214	3		1	1		1	
8	220	3		1	1			1 spmow
8	234	2	2					
8	501	7	2	1	2	2		
8	651	7		4	3			
8	700	5		3		1		
8	800	2		2				

spmrw = Scottish post-medieval reduced wares
we = white earthenware
smr = Scottish medieval redwares
swgw = Scottish white gritty ware

ting = tin glaze
spmow = Scottish post-medieval oxidised ware
gj = globular jar

FIGURE 3.35

Distribution of pottery types across the sites

distinctive grey body and cobalt blue decoration were first imported into Britain in the early 17th century and production continues to the present day. The commonest forms are jugs and drinking mugs or tankards (Jennings 1982). Unfortunately the cathedral sherd is too small to identify the type of vessel.

Several sherds of late 18th- to early 19th-century tin glaze were recovered and could be from Glasgow potteries, although the sherds are too small and lack distinctive marks or decoration, making identification impossible. There is a group of kiln wasters (sf 105), including partly-fired sherds and kiln furniture which

Phase	Area	Context	Sf	Description
6	NN	346	455	1 frag of clay-pipe stem
6	NN	350	456	1 frag of clay-pipe stem
7	CE	115	669	Frag of clay-pipe stem
7	CE	117	49	Spurred bowl with crudely executed floral decoration and a running leaf design disguising the seams; 5/64"; c1750–1850
7	CE	122	433	1 frag of clay-pipe stem
7	CE	124	434	1 frag of clay-pipe stem
7	CW	209	430	1 frag of clay-pipe stem
7	NN	408	458	Bowl, bottered, with 3/4 milling; 7/64"; Scottish; c1660–80
7	NN	422	398	1 frag of clay-pipe stem
7	NS	515	461	1 frag of clay-pipe stem
8	CE	105	436	4 frag of clay-pipe stem, 3 are undecorated and 1 has a yellow glaze
8	CE	111	435	Small basal frag of a bowl; no measurable stem bore; Dutch; probably 18th century
8	CW	201	432	1 frag of clay-pipe stem
8	CW	214	685	2 frag of clay-pipe stem
8	N	702	370	Thick-walled bowl of cutty style pipe; 6/64"; Scottish; post-1850
8	NN	302	397	Stem frag decorated with a band of plain broad spiral grooves, alternate grooves having pellets, burnished length 10mm; 6/64"; Glasgow; c1680–1730
8	NN	302	397	Stem frag with part of a band of spiral decoration, similar to 5 and possibly from the same pipe, burnished; Glasgow; c1680–1730. 3 undecorated stem frag
8	NS	501	459	Stem frag with part of a roller stamp, having COLHOUN within a pellet border; 7/64"; James Colquhoun of Glasgow; c1680–1730. 2 undecorated stem frag
8	NS	502	460	1 frag of clay-pipe stem
8	SH	651	342	Bowl, bottered, full milling with diagonal tooth pattern, incuse G on base, mould-imparted tree and bird/ bell and fish in relief on sides of base; 7/64"; Glasgow; c1660–80. 3 undecorated stem frag
unstrat	ED	800	357	Stem frag with W.WHI[TE]/[GLA]SGOW; 6/64"; William White of Glasgow; post-1806. 1 undecorated stem frag
unstrat	N	700	353	Stem frag with McDOUGALL/GLASGOW; 4/64"; Duncan McDougall of Glasgow; post-1846. 5 undecorated stem frag
unstrat	N	700	353	Stem frag with OBAN on one side, preceded by a maker's name which is obscured by slag; 5/64". No Oban maker has been previously recorded.

FIGURE 3.36

List of clay tobacco pipes. The descriptions are arranged in the following order: brief description; stem bore measurement; possible place of manufacture; suggested date range

stylistically pre-date 1820 (G Haggarty pers comm). This material was presumably brought in as hard-core from a local pottery.

The other 19th- and 20th-century sherds are a mixture of red and white earthenware with a variety of hand-painted and transfer-printed designs from a number of different factories that cannot be identified due to the small size of the sherds.

3.8 CLAY TOBACCO PIPES
by D Gallagher

A total of 41 clay tobacco pipe fragments from 20 contexts were recovered (Figure 3.36). These consisted of 5 bowl fragments, 4 mouthpieces and 32 stem fragments.

This assemblage, although very small, contains a number of unusual items (Figure 3.37). There is an elegant bowl (sf 342) marked with an initial G and the elements of the Glasgow burgh arms: a tree, bird, bell and fish. The placing of a symbol on the base of the pipe, which identified the burgh where the pipe was manufactured, follows the practice established in

Edinburgh. The single letter G on the base is uncommon but not unknown in a Scottish context; there are pipes from Stirling marked with an S (Gallagher and Harrison 1995). More common are triple letter marks which combine the maker's initials with the place of manufacture (Gallagher 1984). The marking of this pipe, however, departs from the custom followed by most Scottish pipemakers in the 17th century in that it does not have the initials of the maker on the side of the base. Instead there are the elements of the Glasgow burgh arms, the first recorded example of a 17th-century Scottish pipe with the symbols of the burgh in this position. It may be influenced by Dutch pipes with symbols on the side of the bowl (Düco 1981, 377) or those produced later in the century which are decorated with complex armorial designs (Düco 1981, 252). Dutch pipes were common imports to Scotland from the early decades of the 17th century (Davey 1992, 280). The stem marked Colhoun (sf 459) is a product of James Colquhoun; two persons of that name dominated pipemaking in Glasgow during the period 1670–1730 (Gallagher 1987, 38–39). Colquhoun pipes marked with roller stamps were found in the wreck of the HMS Dartmouth, which sunk in 1690 (Martin

123

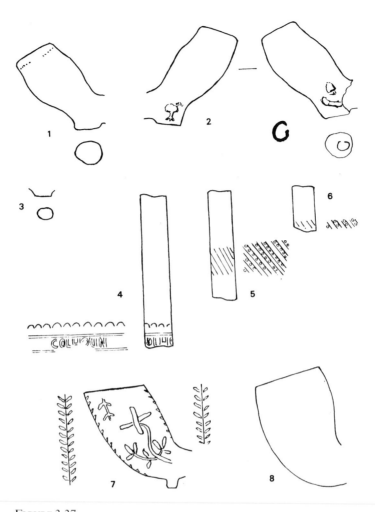

FIGURE 3.37

Clay pipe fragments from the excavations. 1: sf 458, 2: sf 342, 3: sf 435, 4: sf 459, 5: sf 397, 6: sf 397, 7: sf 49, 8: sf 370, 1:1.

1987a, 227). The date range for their usage is unknown. The other roller stamp design (sf 397), is also likely to be a Glasgow product, although no exact parallels with the design have been found.

The 19th-century stems contain examples from the major pipe factories of Glasgow, being those of William White and Duncan McDougall (sf 357 and 353). There is one stem marked Oban (sf 353). It was usual for names on stems to indicate the maker and place of manufacture. As there are no pipemakers listed in the local directories (Martin 1987b), this may be the first evidence for pipe manufacture in that town, although there is the other possibility that it may be advertising a local retailer. The probable maker's name, which preceded OBAN, is unfortunately obscured by slag.

3.9 OTHER FINDS AND MATERIALS
by I Cullen

Other finds and materials were recovered from the excavation in lesser quantities. Those derived from the excavation of the western towers (WT), completed in 1983, are prefixed by 100 in this catalogue to avoid duplication. Fragments of tile and daub derive mostly from post-medieval contexts (Figure 3.38), together with finds of worked stone (Figure 3.39) and roofing slates (Figure 3.40). Fragments of iron slag were also found (Figure 3.41).

A large number of glass fragments from both windows and bottles was recovered (Figure 3.42). All appeared to be modern in origin. Glass objects were less abundant (Figure 3.42). One glass button, possibly from a boot, was recovered and probably represents a casual loss. The spectacle lens came from the bedding sand for the floor slabs and it too represents a casual loss.

The organic material found includes items of personal adornment, such as shoes and buttons. One fragment of leather with copper-alloy rings is presumably part of a shroud or burial clothing. The other items were not found in grave contexts but may have been disturbed and redeposited (Figure 3.43).

The identifiable lead artefacts are of two distinct groups: window cames and coffin furniture. A number

Phase	Area	Context	Sf	Description
7	CW	209	683	1 frag of red tile or chimney pot with a curved profile
7	CW	209	-	1 frag of tile
7	NN	312	693	2 frag of burnt daub
8	CE	110	254	2 frag of red tile with black paint on one face of each fragment. The tile surfaces are smooth and even. 28mm thick
8	CE	111	212	1 coarse white tile with a green glaze
8	CE	111	284	1 frag of red tile or chimney pot with a curved profile
8	CE	111	-	1 frag of tile
8	CE	131	387	1 frag of unglazed red tile; 28mm thick
8	CE	133	299	4 frag of unglazed red tile with irregular surfaces, the other pieces are fragmentary. 43mm thick
8	CH	002	3	1 frag of modern tile
8	CH	002	5	1 frag of modern tile
8	NN	302	389	1 frag of unglazed red tile

FIGURE 3.38

Tile and daub

Phase	Area	Context	Sf	Description
4	NN	413	735	Small flake of dark brown flint
6	NN	346	699	Small frag of worked shale with a squared edge
6	NN	383	105	Flint core possibly for use with a flintlock firearm
7	NS	502	457	Semi-circular fragment of worked shale, possibly a broken gaming piece. 86mm diameter, 11mm thickness
8	NN	302	411	Small frag of burnt stone
8	NN	302	427	Small frag of stone, possibly iron stone
8	NS	501	459	3 disks of flat, oval, worked shale, possibly intended as gaming pieces. 2 of these are smooth, regular and finished in appearance (30 x 24 x 4mm, 28 x 25 x 2mm). The third is thicker and more irregular and appears to be a rough-out (30 x 24 x 12mm)

FIGURE 3.39

Worked and miscellaneous stone

Phase	Area	Context	Sf	Description
8	CH	2	16	Frag of slate covered with mortar. 89 x 84mm
8	CW	201	309	Frag of roofing slate with a nail hole 7mm in diameter. 70 x 53mm
8	NN	302	458	Irregular square shaped roof slate with a nail hole 14mm in diameter. 90 x 90mm
unstrat	SH	651	345	Roofing slate

FIGURE 3.40

Distribution of roofing slate

of lengths of modern lead came were recovered. Two strips of lead that would have decorated a coffin were also found. An unusual find were the four lead shot balls recovered from a burial (see below). The remaining artefacts appear to represent scrap and waste, indicating some processing of lead on site; perhaps associated with constuction and repair activities on the fabric of the building (Figure 3.44).

Four lead shot balls (sf 97) were recovered from the body of a young adult male (353) buried in the nave (N trench, phase 6). Three were recovered from within the cranium, the fourth from below his chin. At least one entrance wound was identified on the left where a shot had smashed the frontal bone (see Section 4.2; Figures 4.19 and 4.20). Three of the balls are slightly oval in shape, 14mm in diameter and have a pitted surface. The fourth is flattened to form an oval discus 7mm thick. Once musket balls appear in Europe around the end of the 15th century they do not change significantly over time, although earlier musket balls tend to be less spherical and use less pure lead. They are normally used in firearms that fire one shot at a time, but by the end of the 17th century are being used in pieces of artillery to produce a shotgun effect (S Woods pers comm). The 14mm diameter balls are appropriate for either a musket or pistol, but are perhaps most likely to be late 17th-century pistol balls. The presence of several balls perhaps suggests execution rather than an injury

Phase	Area	Context	Sf	Description
1	NS	556	488	Bloomworking debris, 1 frag
3	NN	459	408	Bloomworking debris, 1 frag
4	CW	244	505	Bloomworking debris, 1 frag
4	NS	591	175	Fe lump associated with stone cross. 130mm length
6	NN	322	407, 602	Slag, 5 frag
6	NN	322	481	Cinder, 6 frag
6	NN	322	482	Bloomworking debris, 1 frag
6	NN	346	483	Bloomworking debris, 1 frag
6	NN	404	538	Slag, 1 frag
6	NN	410	412	Highly magnetic bloomworking debris, 1 frag
6	NN	410	629	Slag, 1 frag
6	NS	514	554	Bloomworking debris, 1 frag
6	NS	527	404	Vitreous slag, 6 frag
6	NS	581	409	Bloomworking debris, 1 frag
7	NN	312	480	Bloomworking debris, 1 frag
7	NS	502	558	Bloomworking debris, 2 frag
7	NS	503	486	Cinder, 1 frag
8	CE	105	200	Slag, 4 frag
8	CE	122	243	Vitreous slag, 1 frag
8	NN	302	402	Cinder, 1 frag
8	NN	302	609	Slag, 1 frag
unstrat	ED	800	359	Slag, 1 frag

FIGURE 3.41

Iron slag

in open battle. The use of a pistol for close-range execution would be more likely than a musket.

Two small gold hoop, hinged ear-rings (sf 60), 12mm in diameter, were found *in situ* in a grave (207) in the crypt W trench (phase 5/6). Although very similar they do not match exactly.

Post-medieval gravestones
by S T Driscoll

One fragment of a gravestone or memorial plaque (sf 136) was recovered from the crypt E trench. It is dated 1693 (Figure 3.45) but was found in a context probably disturbed in the 19th century. A further 59 fragments were recovered from the treasury, all of them dated to the 19th century. Several fragments bore inscribed lettering, but apart from those noted in Figure 3.46, these were too fragmented to be reconstructed.

Plasterwork
by S Bain

The plasterwork recovered from the nave and the choir appears to be from modern repairs to the stonework, including the fleur-de-lis fragment (Figure 3.47). A full catalogue is listed in the Appendix. The material recovered from the crypt is probably medieval wall plaster: some fragments bore traces of paint. The descriptions of colour given in the catalogue are as they appear and may not be the original colour.

Pigments obtained from organic sources discolour in an alkaline pH. Other pigments discolour for a variety of reasons (Cronyn 1989).

Mortar
by S Bain

A total of 17 samples of mortar from 14 different contexts were collected from trenches in the nave and crypt. These included samples from all major building phases of the cathedral. The analysis attempted to identify similarities and differences in the mortar in order to aid the phasing sequence. The mortar samples were subject to a visual examination using a hand lens. The visual analysis, although not always conclusive, was helpful for resolving some questions regarding masonry phasing. Mortar analysis would have proved more valuable if a wider sampling programme had been undertaken since, in retrospect, the samples proved not always to be from the most revealing places. Chemical analysis would have enhanced the value of the mortar evidence. A full description of each sample appears in the Appendix.

3.10   ENVIRONMENTAL EVIDENCE

Introduction
by S T Driscoll

Conditions within the cathedral are not favourable for the preservation of palaeo-environmental materials,

WINDOW GLASS

Phase	Area	Context	Sf	Frag
4	NN	327	698	2
4–5	CE	110	202	2
4–5	CE	111	293a	6
4–5	CE	114	220	13
5–6	CW	249	468	1
5–6	NN	388	550	1
6	NN	322	462	17
6	NN	346	469	1
7	NN	304	379	1
7	NN	309	384a	1
7	NN	311	381	2
7	NN	312	472	1
7	NN	321	467	1
7	NN	324	385	4
7	NN	408	470	4
7	NN	422	380, 473	7
7	NS	547	471	1
8	CE	102	181a	1
8	CE	105	199a	30
8	CE	115	230	1
8	CE	117	251, 673	1
8	CE	117	673a	2
8	CE	122	264a	3
8	CW	201	314b	50
8	CW	203	450	42
8	CW	214	452	1
8	CW	220	453	1
8	NN	302	382, 386, 454, 464	83
8	NS	501	465, 466, 670	32
unstrat	N	700	592a	1
unstrat	ND	716	589	1

GLASS VESSELS

Phase	Area	Context	Sf	Description
4–5	CE	111	293b	Bottle, 1 frag. Indeterminate, 1 frag
4–5	CE	133	303	Bottle, 5 frag
5–6	CW	206	451	Bottle, 1 frag
6	NN	322	383	Bottle, 1 frag
7	NN	309	384b	Bottle, 1 frag
8	CE	102	181b	Bottle, 4 frag
8	CE	105	621	Bottle, 2 frag. Fine ware, 7 frag
8	CE	117	673b	Indeterminate, 2 frag
8	CE	122	264b	Bottle, 1 frag
8	CE	124	274	Bottle, 1 frag
8	CH	002	4	Modern glass, 3 frag
8	CW	201	314b	Bottle, 4 frag
8	NN	302	378	Bottle, 3 frag
8	NS	501	672	Blown, 1 frag
unstrat	ED	800	356	Glass, 6 frag
unstrat	N	700	592b	Bottle, 1 frag
unstrat	N	700	366	Glass, 9 frag
unstrat	N	711	364	Glass, 1 frag
unstrat	SH	651	344, 346	Glass, 2 frag
unstrat	SH K	651	328	Glass
unstrat	SH K	651	329	Glass

GLASS OBJECTS

Phase	Area	Context	Sf	Description
4–5	CE	1110	44	A black glass ovoid button possibly from a boot. There is an iron fitting on one side and the upper surface is scratched and worn. 14mm length x 13mm width x 8mm thickness
8	NN	302	–	Spectacle lens, 1 frag

FIGURE 3.42

Distribution of glass across the sites

Phase	Area	Context	Sf	Description
6	NN	346	92	Fragment of shoe sole
6	NN	346	95	Unidentifiable fragment of leather
7	CW	222	664	Natural sponge. 110 x 80 x 40mm
7	NN	310	647	Fragment of leather with two copper alloy rings attached, associated with the cranium of sk 310
7	NN	324	82	Shaped shoe sole with stitch holes and a pointed toe. The stitch holes are close to the edges and appear irregular and hand sewn. Possibly from a ladies shoe. 128 x 75 x 3mm
7	NS	547	454	Short length of twine of natural fibre
8	CE	115	657	Short length of twine of natural fibre
8	CE	120	48	Mother of pearl button, with 4 holes, possibly from a shroud garment.12mm diameter, 2mm thickness
8	CW	201	658	Fragment of leather with a single punched hole
unstrat	N	700	372	Unidentifiable fragment of leather

FIGURE 3.43

Organic material

Phase	Area	Context	Sf	Description
3	NN	373	484	2 frag of waste run lead
3	NN	406	485	2 frag of waste run lead
5	NN	434	675	Fragment of sheet scrap lead
6	NN	322	406	Lead came. 68mm length
6	NN	322	605	Iron nail with a lead head decoration in the shape of a diamond folded to form a triangle
8	CE	105	665	Lead came. 42mm length
8	CE	115	647	Frag of sheet scrap lead
8	CE	115	676	2 frag of sheet scrap lead
8	CE	117	250	2 frag of waste lead
8	CE	122	267, 455	4 frag of waste lead
8	CW	201	307	Decorative lead band with punched hole decoration. 29 x 13 x 3mm
8	NN	302	399	Decorative lead strip, folded lengthways. 72 x 10 x 2mm
8	NN	302	410	3 frag of waste run lead with irregular surfaces
unstrat	SH K	651	327	Milled lead came with an H-profile. 270mm length
unstrat	WT	123	1005	2 conjoining frag of a piece of waste sheet with irregular edges. One has a short slit near to its centre, probably cut by a knife. 105 x 50 x 1mm
unstrat	WT	123	1006	Small frag of waste sheet with irregular edges. 46 x 32 x 1mm

FIGURE 3.44

Lead objects

apart from human remains. Most of the areas below the paving are dry and well-drained. Where damp does prevail, as in the NW corner, the moisture levels fluctuate. It was never anticipated that excavations would be rich in materials for environmental study, nevertheless provision was made to seize such opportunities as presented themselves. Within the cathedral the subfloor conditions are quite heterogeneous. Localised conditions have established some pockets where there has been good organic survival. The small quantities of materials which were recovered have rather limited the following studies, but, despite these limitations, it is gratifying that the studies illuminate both the earliest and most modern phases.

Within the nave all substantial concentrations of charcoal were sampled. The most substantial was in a hearth, and has produced a radiocarbon date of 772–980 (see Appendix). Coffins survived in several locations, permitting the timber to be analysed across

a broad chronological range. Very little in the way of faunal remains was encountered in these excavations. Given that human bone survives well in the ground, this would suggest that there was never much to be found. This scant evidence of food debris is complimented by a small pottery assemblage (see Section 3.7) which goes to suggest that over its varied history, little in the way of domestic rubbish has accumulated in the cathedral.

Carbonised plant remains
by S Ramsay

Flots (>1mm and >250μm), sorted residues and unsorted fine residues (200ml subsample) from processed soil samples were examined for carbonised plant remains. Many of the samples contained modern plant rootlets and other recent material all of which

FIGURE 3.45

Inscribed gravestone recovered from below floor of crypt (sf 136)

was uncarbonised and very fresh in appearance. These modern botanical remains were not included in the following analysis because they were obviously not contemporary with the carbonised remains. The modern material was all identifiable as coming from *Betula* (birch) and was in the form of seeds, female catkin scales and an entire male catkin and had probably contaminated the samples during the excavation. In general the charcoal recovered was very fragmented and small fragments (approx 2–5mm) were not identified. No measurable roundwood fragments were identified from the contexts, probably as a result of the fragmentary nature of the charcoal rather than an absence of these remains. The results of the analyses are shown in Figure 3.48 (carbonised seeds and fruits) and Figure 3.49 (charcoal). Figure 3.50 gives the common English names of all the taxa found as well as the families to which they belong. Nomenclature follows Stace (1991).

Results

Context 359: ground hearth, Ph 1, NN

This context contained the richest plant assemblage of all those examined. Barley (*Hordeum* sp), including six-row barley (*Hordeum vulgare*), and oats (*Avena* sp) were both present. These cereals in association with numerous fragments of hazelnut (*Corylus avellana*) shells suggest some form of domestic activity. The other seeds from this context include *Chenopodium album*, *Rumex acetosa*, *Rumex acetosella* and *Urtica dioica*. These are all species associated with cultivated land and grassland. This context also had the greatest variety of tree taxa represented by charcoal. *Quercus* (oak) was the dominant taxon, with *Alnus* (alder) and

Phase	Area	Context	Sf	Description
unstrat	SH	–	581	Frag of white marble memorial stone
unstrat	SH	–	582	Frag of white marble memorial stone with decorated border
unstrat	SH	651	580	Frag of white marble memorial stone. 60 x 54 x 35mm
unstrat	SH	651	586	Frag of white marble memorial stone with decorated border
unstrat	SH	651	588	Frag of white marble memorial slab, decorated and with traces of lettering
unstrat	SH	651	349	Frag of decorated memorial stone
unstrat	SHK	651	334	25 frag from a limestone memorial plaque inscribed: '. . .one. . . | G[l]asgow. . . | [o]f ill health. . . | . . .of th[is] Tru. . . | . . .Magistra[te]. . . | . . .[f]or his s[on]. . .'. Erected in the Rennie family vault (see Section 2.4)
unstrat	SHK	651	335	Frag of memorial stone
unstrat	SHK	651	336	Frag of lettered memorial stone
unstrat	SHK	651	337	Frag of lettered memorial stone
unstrat	SHK	651	338	Frag of decorated memorial stone
unstrat	SHK	651	339	Frag of sculpted memorial stone
unstrat	SHK	651	348	3 frag of sculpted memorial stone
unstrat	SHK	651	350	7 frag of sculpted memorial stone
unstrat	SHK	651	351	14 frag of lettered memorial stone
4	CE/W	–	136	Gravestone frag inscribed: '. . . | Glas. . . | thei. . . | 1693 A. . . | . . . also. . .' 560 x 490 x 160mm (Figure 3.45)

FIGURE 3.46

Post-medieval gravestones

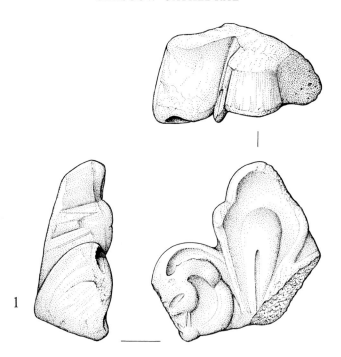

FIGURE 3.47

Plaster fleurs-de-lis recovered from the choir (sf 1), 1:2

	Contexts					
Taxon	359 ground hearth	363 ditch fill	393 grave fill	403 ditch fill	413 silt layer	441 small hearth
Avena sp	5	–	–	–	4	–
cf *Bromus* sp	2	–	–	–	–	–
Carex disticha	1	–	–	–	–	–
Carex pilulifera	–	–	–	–	1	–
Chenopodium album	1	–	–	–	–	–
Corylus avellana nut shell*	28 F	6 F	–	8 F	5 F	10 F
Eleocharis cf *palustris*	–	–	–	–	3	–
cf *Galeopsis* sp	–	–	–	–	1	–
Hordeum vulgare	5	–	1	–	2	–
Hordeum sp	3	–	–	–	–	–
cf *Hordeum* sp	1	–	–	–	–	–
Indet cereal	2	–	–	1	–	-
Montia fontana	1	–	–	–	–	–
Poaceae (small)	2	–	–	–	–	–
Prunus padus	–	–	–	–	1	–
Ranunculus flammula	–	–	–	1	–	-
Rumex acetosa	3	–	–	–	–	–
Rumex acetosella	3	–	–	–	1	–
Rumex cf *conglomeratus*	–	–	–	–	1	–
Urtica dioica	2	–	–	–	–	–
Urtica urens	–	–	–	–	1	–

* *Corylus avellana* (hazel) nut shells were only found as fragments

FIGURE 3.48

Carbonised seeds and fruits, showing number of seeds and fruits in each sample

Corylus (hazel) present in moderate amounts and *Betula* (birch), *Prunus* type (cherry) and *Taxus* (yew) in trace amounts. This suggests wood collected from mixed woodland with oak perhaps being favoured.

Yew is often associated with religious sites and rarely occurs as a component of mixed woodland. It may have been collected from a tree growing very close to the site.

Taxon	Contexts					
	359 ground hearth	363 ditch fill	403 ditch fill	413 silt layer	441 small hearth	465 grave fill
Alnus	2.0 g [39]	0.5 g [9]	1.2 g [18]	2.1 g [35]	<0.1 g [1]	0.6 g [4]
Betula	0.1 g [4]	0.9 g [10]	0.5 g [7]	1.5 g [40]	<0.1 g [1]	–
Corylus avellana	1.6 g [28]	0.1 g [5]	0.2 g [10]	1.6 g [52]	–	–
cf *Prunus*	<0.1 g [1]	–	–	–	–	–
Quercus	9.9 g [93]	1.6 g [18]	2.0 g [45]	3.1 g [67]	0.4 g [36]	5.6 g [33]
Taxus	0.2 g [3]	–	–	–	–	–
Indeterminate bark	– –	–	–	–	<0.1 g [2]	–
Indeterminate	2.0 g [36]	2.2 g [29]	1.3 g [16]	1.2 g [46]	0.4 g [5]	–
Unidentified	6.6 g	4.4 g	2.8 g	3.1 g	0.4 g	0.5 g

FIGURE 3.49

Charcoal. Numbers of charcoal fragments are shown in brackets under the weights

Taxon	Common name	Family
Alnus	Alder	Betulaceae
Avena sp	Oats	Poaceae
Betula	Birch	Betulaceae
cf *Bromus* sp	Brome	Poaceae
Carex disticha	Brown Sedge	Cyperaceae
Carex pilulifera	Pill Sedge	Cyperaceae
Chenopodium album	Fat-hen	Chenopodiaceae
Corylus avellana	Hazel	Betulaceae
Eleocharis cf *palustris*	Common Spike-rush	Cyperaceae
cf *Galeopsis* sp	Hemp-nettle	Lamiaceae
Hordeum vulgare	Six-row Barley	Poaceae
Hordeum sp	Barley	Poaceae
cf *Hordeum* sp	Barley	Poaceae
Indet. cereal	-----	Poaceae
Montia fontana	Blinks	Portulacaceae
Poaceae (small)	Grass	Poaceae
Prunus padus	Bird Cherry	Rosaceae
cf *Prunus*	Cherry	Rosaceae
Quercus	Oak	Fagaceae
Ranunculus flammula	Lesser Spearwort	Ranunculaceae
Rumex acetosa	Common Sorrel	Polygonaceae
Rumex acetosella	Sheep's Sorrel	Polygonaceae
Rumex cf *conglomeratus*	Clustered Dock	Polygonaceae
Taxus	Yew	Taxaceae
Urtica dioica	Common Nettle	Urticaceae
Urtica urens	Small Nettle	Urticaceae

FIGURE 3.50

List of all taxa found

Context 363: ditch fill, Ph 1, NN

This context had a mixed assemblage of charcoal with alder, birch, hazel and oak all present, again suggesting a mixed woodland origin. The only non-wood finds from this context were six fragments of hazelnut shell.

Context 393: grave fill, Ph 6, NN

Only one grain of *Hordeum vulgare* (six-row barley) was found in this context and it is impossible to draw any conclusions from this isolated find.

Context 403: ditch fill, Ph 1, NN

Hazelnut fragments were again present in this sample along with one indeterminate cereal grain suggesting minor domestic activity. One seed of *Ranunculus flammula* (lesser spearwort) was also identified in this sample. This species grows in wetter places and may have colonised the ditch during a period of waterlogging. The mixed woodland assemblage of charcoal was again present (ie alder, birch, hazel and oak).

Context 413: silt layer, Ph 4, NN

The silt layer was the second richest sample in terms of carbonised seeds. Oats, six-row barley, hazelnut shells and one fruit stone of *Prunus padus* (bird cherry) were present indicating a degree of domestic activity on the site. *Carex pilulifera*, cf *Galeopsis* sp, *Rumex acetosella* and *Rumex* cf *conglomeratus* are all indicative of grassland with *Urtica urens* a coloniser of cultivated or nitrogen enriched land. *Eleocharis* cf *palustris* indicates areas of wetter ground. The same assemblage of charcoal was found in this context as in most of the others: alder, birch, hazel and oak.

Context 441: small hearth, Ph 3, NN

Very little charcoal was recovered from this context but that which was identified (alder, birch and oak) was indicative of mixed woodland. Fragments of hazelnut shell were also found.

Context 465: grave fill, Ph 1, NN

This grave fill contained no seeds and a charcoal assemblage which differed from all the other contexts. A small amount of alder was present but the vast majority of the charcoal identified was oak. This suggests oak had been specifically selected for use in connection with this context.

Discussion

These contexts span four of the major phases of activity on the site, from the earliest recorded feature (465), an early medieval burial dated to 677–860, the double ditches (363, 403) which pre-date the early 12th-century cathedral, the hearth (441) associated with the later 12th-century construction phase, to the grave (393) and deposit (413) asssociated with the later 13th-century construction. Some general conclusions can therefore be drawn regarding the vegetation present in the area prior to the construction of the present cathedral.

Woodland

The tree taxa represented by the charcoal remains are all native to Scotland (although *Taxus* is an unproven native). They are all taxa which would have grown in the area in stands of mixed deciduous woodland. *Corylus* and *Prunus* type generally grow as understorey

vegetation in *Quercus* (oak) woods. *Alnus* usually grows in wetter parts of mixed woodland, for example in damp hollows or along the sides of streams. *Betula* is a component of many woodland types, capable of rapidly colonising a wide variety of habitats.

Taxus (yew) is an unproven native in Scotland although the oldest living tree in Scotland is the Fortingall Yew with an estimated age of between 1500–3000 years (Dickson 1993). This tree is in the churchyard at Fortingall, Perthshire, emphasising the long association between yew trees and sacred or religious sites.

Cereals, seeds and fruits

The cereals identified from the site were barley (*Hordeum* sp), including six-row barley (*Hordeum vulgare*), and oats (*Avena* sp). Six-row barley has always been the main cereal crop to be cultivated and used in Scotland (Boyd 1988). The number of cereal grains found was not large but probably sufficient to indicate domestic activity on or close to the site especially when considered in conjunction with the significant number of hazelnut shell fragments also present. The only other possible food plant remains to be identified were one fruit stone of *Prunus padus* (bird cherry), the fruit of which is very sour, and one seed of *Chenopodium album* (fat-hen). Although sometimes collected for food, fat-hen is equally or more likely to be present as a result of being a common opportunist weed of disturbed and fertile soils associated with human habitation. The other carbonised seeds identified are mostly from weeds of arable or pastoral cultivation although there are several species, such as *Carex disticha*, *Eleocharis* cf *palustris*, *Montia fontana* and *Ranunculus flammula*, which are plants of wet or marshy ground.

Conclusions

The carbonised botanical remains from Glasgow Cathedral indicate limited domestic activity on the site prior to the building of the present cathedral. The charcoal remains would appear to be the remnants of fuel collected from mixed deciduous woodland in the area. Only the grave fill (465), which is dominated by oak charcoal, suggests the use of wood for some purpose other than everyday fuel.

The animal bones
by H Loney

The mammal species present included sheep, cattle, pig and dog. There were also a few birds, mostly domestic. The bones were in a fairly fragmentary condition, with few whole elements. In the following, species only are recorded.

The mammal bones

The majority of the finds were sheep bones, followed by cattle. The sample included leg and toe, skull, rib, vertebra, and pelvis. The bones were in a highly fragmented state, which can be attributed in some cases to processing for food, but which in most cases was due to post-depositional processes, including the use of the deposits for construction. There were a few butchery marks, mostly visible on ribs, but almost no sawn ends of long bones or other marks. Only a small number of pig bones were identified, along with a few trace dog bones and an unidentifiable medium mammal. Most of the sample consisted of mature animals, with a small proportion of immature animals represented by a few unfused sheep long bones, and in one case an unfused sheep metapodial. In one context (362), the entire sample consisted of extremely small, burned fragments. The pieces were very well reduced.

The bird and fish bones

There were very few bird bones, almost entirely chicken. In addition, there was a single fish vertebrae, which was not speciated. Given the small quantity of bird found in samples, there is little more that can be said about their presence, except to speculate that chicken was far less a popular food item than either cow or sheep.

HUMAN SKELETAL REMAINS

4.1 INTRODUCTION
by S T Driscoll

Large numbers of burials were expected before the excavations began. In order to maximise this unique opportunity the team included a specialist in the study of archaeological human remains, Sarah King. This ensured that skilled observations could be made on fragile materials or materials that could not be lifted and certainly contributed to the comprehensiveness of the skeletal records.

The sample is significant for a number of reasons. It is one of the longest continuously used burial place to have been investigated and has produced one of the larger assemblages from detailed archaeological excavation in Scotland. It is also a group which is relatively well-dated by virtue of the architectural history complemented by the post-medieval coffin typology. Possibly most important is the historical quality of the sample which spans the medieval to modern world and allows one to make comparisons between the population of a modest sized burgh with that of a great imperial city. For these reason it was determined to conduct a detailed analysis of all the disarticulated as well as the articulated materials, including a full programme of metrical and non-metrical studies, and analysis of insect larvae. Burials have also been excavated outside the cathedral in recent years. The opportunity has been taken to bring shorter reports on those discoveries together here.

During the excavation a number of soil samples were taken from the gut region of six burials, which seemed to have been relatively undisturbed post-interment. It was one of the few opportunities to secure palaeobotantical samples and was particularly attractive as it would allow them to be linked with individuals. The results of this experiment were inconclusive but suggest that given the right conditions this could be a valuable technique in the future.

4.2 THE SKELETAL REMAINS FROM THE NAVE, CRYPT, CHOIR AND TREASURY
by S E King

Introduction

During the 1992–93 excavations of Glasgow Cathedral a total of 84 burials were recorded, five of which were left *in situ* due to poor preservation or excavation limitations. The remaining 79 skeletons were recovered for analysis. Of these, 22 date from the 17th to 19th centuries, and 55 were from the 14th to 17th centuries, with only fragments surviving from the early medieval period. Analysis of the sample was limited to a comparison of two broad phases (6: 14th to 17th centuries, n = 56; 7: 17th to 19th centuries, n = 21). Large quantities of disarticulated remains were also collected from the soil surrounding the burials. These bones were briefly observed to identify pathological conditions and establish the minimum number of individuals represented.

Before analysis began, the skeletons were washed and long bones, crania and remains with pathological lesions reconstructed. Detailed observations were also made of those skeletons left *in situ*. An inventory of all teeth and bones from the burials was made using diagrams and record sheets (deposited in the NMRS) which form a permanent record of the human remains destined for reburial. This chapter presents information regarding the preservation, age, sex, stature, health and disease of the skeletal remains.

Methodology

The preservation of a skeleton was determined by the quality of surviving bone and the completeness of remains. Descriptions of preservation were made during excavation and under laboratory conditions.

Age estimations were determined for each individual using several methods. For subadults (less than 18 years of age), age estimates were based on dental formation and eruption (Ubelaker 1989), bone growth (diaphyseal length) (Sundick 1978) and fusion of epiphyses (Brothwell 1981; Ubelaker 1989). For adult skeletons, age estimations were determined by observing cranial suture closure (Meindl and Lovejoy 1985), dental attrition (Brothwell 1981), pubic symphysis metamorphosis (Todd 1920; McKern and Stewart 1957; Gilbert and McKern 1973; Katz and Suchey 1986; Suchey *et al* 1988), morphological changes to the ilium auricular surface (Lovejoy *et al* 1985) and degenerative changes to the sternal ends of ribs (Isçan *et al* 1984; 1985).

Despite recognised limitations with the methodologies (Ubelaker 1989; Sundick 1978; Saunders 1992), age categories are narrow for subadults. This is due to the fact that the skeleton and teeth undergo several changes during the growing years (Johnston and Zimmer 1989). Due to poor preservation and lack of completeness of the subadult remains, only one of the above methods could be applied in all but four cases. In two of these cases (sk 533 and sk 580) dental age and diaphyseal length determinations were compared. In one case (sk 378), dental age and epiphyseal fusion were compared and in another case (sk 396) all three methods could be applied (sk 396). Age estimations based on dental formation/eruption and diaphyseal length were found to correspond most closely.

Adults

Age estimations based on dental attrition were appropriate for most of the Glasgow Cathedral adult skeletal sample as the method used was developed on British populations from the Neolithic to medieval times (Brothwell 1981). This method was used in association with other techniques in order to determine broad age categories. Almost half of the skeletal sample (sk 34) had dentition to analyse and there were only three cases (sk 356, sk 387, sk 396) where the results from this method did not correlate with other aging techniques. In these cases there was little or no molar wear, where the individuals were estimated to be either 'middle' or 'mature' adults by other methods. These discrepancies may be due to differing diets, jaw sizes or chewing stresses (Brothwell 1981).

Three methods for determining age at death (for each sex) based on metamorphoses of the pubic symphysis were applied to the Glasgow Cathedral sample. There has been an abundance of literature discussing the problems of each.

There are problems with all ageing techniques, although some are thought be more accurate than others. When possible, age was determined by comparing and combining all applicable methods. All techniques could only be applied to five of the 65 adults analysed. The majority of skeletons aged beyond the 'adult' category required the application of at least three methods. When precise methods could not be applied, the skeletons were aged at a very gross level, such as subadult or adult (based on size, suture closure, dental attrition, and whether the epiphyses were fused). The predicted age ranges for adults were usually broad, but the mean age of each individual was placed into a standardized (University of Bradford) age category.

Sex analysis

When possible, 24 different criteria were observed on the skeleton to determine sex (subadults were not sexed due to methodological problems, see Saunders 1992). These observations included: (1) assessments of morphological features of the cranium, pelvis, sacrum and sternum (outlined by Phenice 1967; Bass 1987; Brothwell 1981; Ubelaker 1989; Steele and Bramblett 1988; Sutherland and Suchey 1991; White 1991) and (2) measurements of the femora (head diameter and bicondylar width), humeri (head diameter), radii, (head diameter), glenoid fossae (cavity width) and clavicles (maximum length) (Bass 1987). The cranium and particularly the pelvis are considered the best indicators for determining sex (St Hoyme and Isçan 1989). However, as with ageing techniques, as many indicators as possible were assessed. Robusticity (muscular markings and relative weight of bone) was also noted.

Just under half of the adult skeletons could be sexed by observing all criteria (various morphological features of the cranium, pelvis and metric traits). Where two methods could be applied, the age was felt to be reliable, especially if the pelvis was present. In those cases where only a few measurements could be assessed, the sex was often assigned with a question mark. Generally, it was found that most observations provided comparable results and that there was obvious sexual dimorphism. Some females (sk 007, sk 017, sk 227 and sk 523), however, had very male cranial features (eg supraorbital ridges, and/or pronounced external occipital protuberances), and some males (sk 387, sk 545, sk 551, sk 215 and sk 222) had wide sciatic notches, although all other features of the pelvis were masculine.

Confident sex determinations were not possible for all skeletons due to the lack of completeness in the material. In total there were 42 (66%) cases where sex could be determined with confidence, 19 (29%) cases where sex could not be as confidently assessed and three (5%) cases where sex could not be determined. It is rarely possible for analysts to determine sex in more than 80–90% of the skeletons in a sample (St Hoyme and Işcan 1989).

Stature analysis

Stature was estimated using regression equations for white adult males and females (Trotter 1970). Where possible, the length of the femur (femora) and the length of the tibia (tibiae) were added and the appropriate equation applied. The number of cases where this was possible is illustrated in Figure 4.1. Since the age ranges were broad, exact correction values for individuals over the age of 30 (middle and mature adults) could not be made. It is noted, however, that an individual of 75 years would have a correction value of only –2.7cm.

It is well known that differences in body proportions exist between various populations through time and space. The application of Trotter's (1970) equations (derived from modern North American populations) on the Glasgow Cathedral skeletal sample will have resulted in greater standard errors. Furthermore, errors increase depending on which bone(s) were present for measurement (see Figure 4.1). Despite these problems, the equations were useful for estimating stature (within several cm) and for observing patterns of height within the sample.

	Females (n)	Males (n)	Standard Error (± cm) Females	Males
Femur + Tibia	10	13	3.55	2.99
Femur	5	4	3.72	3.27
Tibia	5	4	3.66	3.37
Humerus	0	2	4.45	4.05
Ulna	0	1	4.30	4.32

FIGURE 4.1

Bones used to estimate stature (in order of increasing standard error as devised by Trotter 1970)

Disease analysis

Five types of dental diseases were systematically recorded: calculus, caries, dental enamel hypoplasia, periodontal disease and abscesses. Calculus was graded according to Brothwell (1981), caries were described following Lukacs (1989), periodontal disease was scored according to Brothwell (1981), dental enamel hypoplasia was described as pits, lines or grooves (also drawn and measured from cement/enamel junction to defects) and abscesses were recorded according to tooth position and type of drainage (internal or external).

Due to differential outcome of studies based on variable methodologies and analyses (see Bridges 1993), a simple overview of joint changes present in the sample was provided. Any changes on articular surfaces which involved osteophyte formation, pitting (subchondral porosity), eburnation and changes to the joint shape were described and recorded. For the cranial and appendicular skeleton, the severity of joint changes was graded using criteria modified from Jurmain (1990): eburnation, or pitting, or osteophyte formation, or any combination of these changes, where < 10% of the articular surface is affected (slight), >10% and <90% of the articular surface affected (moderate), and >90% of joint surface or entire surface affected (severe).

Changes in the spine were graded according to Sager (1969), although Grade I was described as 'slight', Grade II 'moderate' and Grade III 'severe' (for both vertebral bodies and apophyseal joints). Furthermore, the side most affected (if significant) and the general shape of the vertebrae (if altered) was noted (for example, triangular shaped). Schmorl's nodes were also recorded and described if unusual in shape. For analysis, the severity was based on the portion of the vertebral bodies or apophyseal joints which were the most greatly affected. Comparisons between phases and sexes were not attempted due to the small numbers of individuals.

There are many different indicators and criteria used for grading and defining the presence of osteoarthritis. For example, osteophytes alone have not been considered to be indicative of osteoarthritis unless associated with pitting and/or eburnation, whereas the presence of eburnation alone has been considered to be a 'Grade II' severity (Waldron 1992). In other studies (eg Jurmain 1990) the presence of any one of the above changes denotes arthritic changes.

All pathological lesions with evidence of infection were recorded and a selected number of the most severe were photographed and radiographed. Diagnoses were made with the aid of Manchester (1983) and Ortner and Putschar (1981).

Observations of trauma were recorded and drawn. Unusual cases were also photographed and radiographed.

Results

Preservation

Bone quality varied from poor or fair to good (based on the degree of erosion, cracking, flaking, crystallization, and/or fragmentation). In some cases, the preservation was exceptional, and there was preservation of hair and fabric on several of the crania from phase 7. Some of the burials (sk 398 and sk 422) were represented only by sandy outlines and no skeletal remains

Skeleton Completeness	Poor	Fair	Poor/ Good	Fair/ Good	Good	Total
80%>			1	7	9	17
50–80%			3	9	7	19
<50%	15	5	2	6	15	41
Total	**15**	**5**	**6**	**22**	**31**	**79**

FIGURE 4.2

Preservation: quality of bone condition v completeness

could be recovered for analysis. The various states of preservation will be discussed in detail below.

Preservation of bone varied dramatically within and between skeletons. Figure 4.2 gives an idea of the relationship between skeleton completeness and quality of preservation. Most of the well preserved bones from incomplete skeletons represent burials which were disturbed or could not be completely excavated.

There did not appear to be any differences in preservation by sex, but subadult remains were poorly represented. The incompleteness of this age category would seem to be due to taphonomic factors. Of the 12 infant and juvenile burials, six (sk 248, sk 317, sk 318, sk 326, sk 339 and sk 580) were in good condition but incomplete due to post-mortem disturbance. Two other burials were relatively complete (sk 343 and sk 378) and an additional two were truncated by an excavation baulk (sk 247 and sk 020). Only two cases (sk 367 and sk 533) occur where the incompleteness was due to poor bone quality.

The skeletal remains from both phases were often stained purple, black or green. Purple staining was also noted in the Spitalfields sample and identified as a fungus-yeast (Molleson and Cox 1993). A brief analysis revealed, however, that no yeast-like structures were present on the purple and black samples of bone from the cathedral sample (D Clarke pers comm). The green colouring may be due to the corrosion of copper alloy although no artefacts were found associated with these stains.

The remains of spores (sk 390) and insect pupae (sk 207) were also found on the crania of two skeletons from phase 7. The spores were identified as belonging to the genus *Myxomycete* (D Clarke pers comm) and must have developed after excavation. The insect remains are discussed below (see Section 4.6).

Several of the phase 7 skeletons from the nave (sk 305, sk 310, sk 416, sk 419, sk 430 and sk 547), had a white powdery substance covering the bones. The bones were also permeated with white crystal deposits, destroying the integrity of the bone. These crystallized areas have been identified by X-ray diffraction as brushite, formed by the degradation of bone mineral and hydroxy-apatite (D Turner and G Curry pers comm). In these cases, the entire skeleton was usually affected, leaving less than 30% intact. Conversely, the coffin wood of these burials was extremely well preserved. A sample of powder from the coffin wood was also analysed by X-ray diffraction and identified as gypsum (D Turner and G Curry pers comm). Two samples of coffin wood without white powder (one from an individual with brushite changes and one from a skeleton with no bone degradation) were also analysed for comparison, and found to be free of gypsum.

Mineral samples of gypsum and brushite were also recovered from the skeletal remains in the crypt of Christ Church, Spitalfields (dated 1729–1857; Molleson and Cox 1993). Interestingly, it appeared that these individuals were buried five to nine days after death. The findings from Spitalfields suggest that this treatment may have been restricted to corpses that, for whatever reason, could not be buried immediately.

Three individuals had crystallization of bone (not associated with the gypsum substance) in the region of the cranium (sk 118, sk 211 and sk 390). Two of the individuals were from phase 7 and were buried within the crypt. One (sk 390, phase 6), was buried in the nave. The crystals were both rounded and spicular in appearance, relatively localised, destructive to the bone and, in one case (sk 390), associated with purple/black discolouration. Both skeletons from phase 7 had well preserved hair on the crania. Without further research, it is not possible to determine the taphonomic/diagenetic processes involved in these changes.

Discussion

Overall, the majority of the skeletons were in good condition but incomplete. Post-mortem disturbance by construction and grave digging and limitations on the extent of the excavation were responsible for the lack of completeness. Particularly, it appears that infant burials were often disturbed at some time after burial. This may be due to multiple internments of children within the same location (such as sk 317 and sk 318) or due to small bones being overlooked when later adult graves were dug.

All states of preservation occurred in all chronological phases and in all areas of the cathedral. The soil conditions in the nave varied from dry sandy conditions (eastern portion of nave) to wet sandy conditions (western portion of nave). There did not seem to be, however, a difference in bone preservation among the soil types. Many individuals from the later phase also had hair preserved on the crania, probably more a factor of time than of taphonomic processes.

Age estimations

Fifteen subadults (19%) and 64 adults (81%) were represented in the sample (Figure 4.3). The individuals excavated in the cathedral comprised mostly of adults, 75% of which were living until middle or mature adulthood. This percentage includes a large number of 'adult' individuals (23) who were likely to be either middle or mature adults. It is believed that most of the 'mature' individuals, with a few exceptions, were probably close to 50 years of age. It is not possible to determine if the individuals were living to a greater age in one of the phases.

An overview of the unstratified human bone suggests that at least 93 individuals were represented in the soil surrounding the burials (from all areas of the cathedral). The majority of individuals (87%) were adults, and 13% were subadults, supporting the finding that most of the individuals buried within the cathedral were living until adulthood.

Subadults may have been equally represented through time (19% of burials in each phase were subadults) although a larger sample size would provide more convincing support for this finding. The majority, 10 (67%), of the subadults seemed to have died before or near the age of five years. It has been suggested that respiratory infections and gastroenteritis were the main causes of infant death in the past (Manchester 1983). Unfortunately, the incompleteness of the subadult remains omits the possibility of growth investigations.

Age Category*	Total	Phase 6	Phase 7
Subadult (< 18yrs.)	1	1	0
0–1 yr	4	4	0
2–5 yrs	5	3	2
6–9 yrs	2	1	1
10–12 yrs	0	0	0
13–17 yrs	3	2	1
Subtotal	**15**	**11**	**4**
Adult	23	16	7
Young Adult (18–25 yrs)	5	1	3
Middle Adult (26–45 yrs)	15	14	1
Mature Adult (46+ yrs)	21	14	6
Subtotal	**64**	**45**	**17**
Total	**79**	**56**	**21**

* ages do not represent actual chronological age

FIGURE 4.3

Age distribution of skeletal remains recovered

Sex determinations

The Glasgow Cathedral sample consisted of 26 female adults, 35 male adults and three unsexed adults (Figure 4.4). When the total sample is considered the ratio of females to males is 1:1.3. In phase 6 the ratio is 1:1.7, and in phase 7 the exact opposite ratio of 1.7:1.

	Female (?F)	Male (?M)	Unsexed
Adult			
Phase 6	1 (4)	3 (6)	2
Phase 7	2 (2)	0 (2)	1
Young Adult			
Phase 6	0 (0)	1 (0)	0
Phase 7	2 (0)	0 (1)	0
MiddleAdult			
Phase 6	6 (1)	7 (0)	0
Phase 7	1 (0)	0 (0)	0
MatureAdult			
Phase 6	4 (0)	10 (0)	0
Phase 7	2 (1)	2 (1)	0
Total	**18 (8) = 26**	**23 (10) = 33**	**3**

FIGURE 4.4

The distribution of females and males by age category and phase

Stature estimations

Stature was estimated for 20 females (77% of the females) and 25 males (73% of the males), representing 68% of the total adult sample. Phase 6 females (n = 14) ranged in stature from 147.50 ± 3.72cm to 160.00 ± 3.55cm with an average of 156.50cm. Phase 7 females (n = 6) ranged in stature from 147.20 ± 3.55cm to 163.20 ± 3.55cm, an average of 157.10cm. Phase 6 males (n = 22) ranged in height from 160.50 ± 2.99cm to 187.70 ± 2.99cm, averaging at 174.10cm. Phase 7 males (n = 2) had statures of 181.30 and 182.00cm.

Out of the total sample, the stature of the females ranged from 147.20 ± 3.55cm to 163.20 ± 3.55cm with an average of 156.70cm. The males ranged in height from 160.50 ± 2.99cm to 186.40 ± 2.99cm with an average of 172.20cm.

The stature estimate indicate that females were shorter than males but exhibited little overlap and the range of heights was wide for both sexes. Phase by phase, it appeared that the average heights were slightly shorter during the medieval period. Interestingly, the mean heights of the female individuals from the sample lie towards the high end of the range exhibited by other medieval Scottish populations, whereas the males may have been slightly taller (Figure 4.5). It is also possible that the individuals from the 17th to 19th centuries may have been taller than their Scottish contemporaries.

Site	Time period	Females (n)	mean stature (cm)	Males (n)	mean stature (cm)
Glasgow, phase 6	**14th–17th cent**	**(14)**	**156.5**	**(22)**	**174.1**
Whithorn	late medieval	(117)	156	(103)	170
Aberdeen	medieval		160		168
Linlithgow	medieval		156		170
Perth	medieval			(1)	170
Glasgow, phase 7	**17th-19th**	**(6)**	**157.1**	**(2)**	**181.7**
St Ronan's, Iona	post-medieval	(26)	152.6		

FIGURE 4.5

Stature estimates from Glasgow Cathedral and various Scottish medieval cemeteries: Whithorn (Cardy 1997) Aberdeen, Linlithgow and Perth (Cross and Bruce 1989) St Ronan's Church, Iona (Lorimer 1994)

Pathology

In this section an attempt is made to describe and interpret pathological lesions observed on the skeletal remains. The presence and frequency of certain diseases can help elucidate the health and disease of a population group. It cannot, however, reveal the whole picture. One problem for palaeopathologists is that many diseases do not affect bone, or an individual may die before a disease has progressed sufficiently enough to affect the bone. There are also problems of diagnosis, exemplified by fragmentary and incomplete material. Furthermore, theoretical issues regarding the relationship between disease, culture and environment must be tackled when interpreting pathological lesions (Ortner 1991). Despite these cautionary notes, pathological states can provide clues as to what an individual (or group of individuals) may have suffered from during life or at death. With additional evidence (for example, archaeological, historical, environmental) it is possible to make hypotheses regarding health and disease.

Dental disease

A total of 660 permanent teeth from 34 adults (17 female and 17 male) and 56 permanent teeth from two subadults (sk 378 and sk 396) were observed for dental disease. All individuals had at least one type of oral pathology.

CALCULUS

During life, plaque is formed on the surfaces of teeth by a build up of bacteria embedded within a matrix (manufactured by bacteria and by proteins in the saliva which can mineralise into calculus). Nutrients from the diet diffuse into the dental plaque affecting its rate of growth (for example, sucrose in the diet causes plaque to grow faster). The presence of calculus may provide information on diet type and oral hygiene.

Calculus is ubiquitous in this sample. In total 94% of all individuals with teeth and 78% of all teeth had calculus deposits. It appeared that male teeth were more affected then females in both phases (phase 6

females = 73%, males = 86%; phase 7 females = 57%, males = 68%) and in the total sample (females = 68%, males = 84%). It also appeared that more teeth were covered with calculus from the earlier phase.

CARIES

Caries were present in 50% of all individuals with dentition and in 6% of all teeth with an average of 2.3 lesions per individual. In phase 6, subadults had the highest frequency of carious teeth (9%). Overall, the highest percentage of carious lesions were present in mature adults. In phase 6 there did not appear to be a large difference between females and males when caries were quantified by tooth counts (females = 6%, males = 5%). In phase 7 the males seemed to be more affected (females = 8%, males = 15%).

DENTAL ENAMEL HYPOPLASIA

Horizontal lines, grooves or pits on the enamel surface are indicative of dental enamel hypoplasia (Hillson 1986). They are deficiencies in enamel thickness resulting from temporary halts in enamel matrix production (Goodman 1991). Defects which occur during years of growth usually remain on the teeth in adulthood. Based on studies by Goodman (1991), the presence of dental enamel hypoplasia may suggest increased stress (eg disease and/or under nutrition). Other causes include congenital defects, inborn errors of metabolism, neonatal disturbances, local trauma and local infection (see Hillson 1986). The number of observable dental enamel hypoplasia lesions may have been limited by the high frequency of dental calculus and attrition in the Glasgow Cathedral sample.

Dental enamel hypoplasia was present in 17% of the individuals with dentition and in 6% of all teeth. There were no females in phase 6 and no males in phase 7 with dental enamel hypoplasia. Due to the small number of individuals with dental enamel hypoplasia (six), it was difficult to determine the significance of this pattern. When the total sample was observed, the males appeared to have been more affected in both 'individual counts' (females = 6%, males = 18%) and 'tooth counts' (females = 3%, males = 6%). The two subadults with dentition had the highest frequency of dental enamel hypoplasia (tooth counts = 18%). More individuals appeared to have dental enamel hypoplasia in phase 6 (19%, phase 7 = 11%), although a greater percentage of teeth were affected in phase 7 (7%, phase 6 = 5%). These numbers are too low to draw any firm conclusions.

Estimates were made of the ages of hypoplasia episodes using charts from Schour and Massler (1941). There are problems with these estimates, primarily due to the fact that they are for modern populations. It generally appeared, however, that the individuals with dental enamel hypoplasia acquired the defects between birth and five years of age.

ABSCESS (PERIAPICAL INFLAMMATION)

All abscesses observed were periapical. In total 19% of all individuals with dentitions had at least one abscess and 2% of the total number of sockets observed had an abscess associated with it. No male individuals had an abscess in phase 7, and female and male individuals were equally affected in phase 6 (both at 20%). It also appeared that more individuals had abscesses in phase 6 (phase 6 = 22%, phase 7 = 11%).

PERIODONTAL DISEASE

Periodontal disease was the second most frequently observed dental disease in the sample, affecting 64% of individuals with dentition. A higher percentage of individuals had periodontal disease in phase 7 (78%) than in phase 6 (59%). The frequency and severity of this disease by age and sex was determined for the total sample. It appeared that males were more severely affected by it than females in each age category, and it was generally found to increase in severity with age.

ANTEMORTEM TOOTH LOSS

Periodontal disease and caries may result in antemortem tooth loss (Brothwell 1981). From all the dentitions examined 155 of the teeth were lost antemortem. In phase 6 more female teeth (12%) were lost antemortem than male (6%). However, there was no differences in female and male tooth loss in phase 7 (both 31%). Both female and male individuals in phase 7 lost more teeth than individuals in phase 6.

FALSE TEETH
by H Noble

A partial denture (sf 222) was discovered *in situ* in a grave (217) in the W trench of the crypt (phase 7). It belonged to a mature adult male (sk 222) and it was composed of tooth crowns of human teeth embedded by gold rods into a hard base of hippopotamus ivory (Figures 4.6 and 4.7). The denture is approximately 16mm wide and 15mm high. The false teeth replaced both mandibular first incisors and the right second incisor. The tooth crowns are attached to the ivory base by gold posts which, after being firmly screwed into the tooth crowns, have been fitted into the holes drilled into the ivory base with the exposed ends flattened to rivet them in place. The partial denture has been held in place by silk or linen ligatures which anchored it to the necks of the neighbouring teeth. Holes have been drilled for this purpose through to the lingual surface of the denture. The colour of the crowns, the size and the degree of wear suggest that they may be from the teeth lost from the individual. It is possible that the teeth may have been knocked out, then made into a false set. The tooth sockets were well-healed (although there was some postmortem damage) suggesting that the individual lost the teeth at least three months before death. In order for the crowns of the 'false' teeth to have been equal with the other teeth, the base must have rested on the gum.

If the teeth were not from this individual, there are many possible ways in which they could be obtained. During the 18th century, teeth were often acquired from corpses '. . .in hospitals, from the executioner, from cemeteries, and, chiefly, from battlefields' (Hoffmann-Axthelm 1981). The teeth could also have come from a poor individual who willingly sold their teeth (D Lunt pers comm). This specimen exhibits dentistry of a high quality from a technical, functional and aesthetic point of view. It could possibly be the work of a Glasgow dentist, but is perhaps more likely to have been obtained in Edinburgh or London. It is not likely to have been produced earlier than 1750 nor later than 1850. Certainly, an individual with a finely crafted set of false teeth must have been socially advantaged. His burial place, near St Kentigern's tomb in the western portion of the crypt, corroborates the wealth or importance of this individual.

DISCUSSION

The most common dental diseases are caries, calculus and periodontal disease, all of which are related to the presence of plaque deposits (Hillson 1986). One individual (sk 007) with severe dental enamel hypoplasia, calculus, periodontal disease and abscesses will have to stand for the many (Figure 4.8). Certainly, these diseases are frequently observed in the Glasgow Cathedral sample. Calculus is by far the most common condition, present in all individuals with permanent teeth regardless of age, sex or phase. Some interesting patterns in calculus frequency were apparent however. More individuals (and teeth) were affected by calculus in phase 6 than in phase 7, and males were generally more affected than females in both phases. It is possible that changes in diet and/or ideas regarding oral hygiene may be responsible for these differences.

Bread, one possible source of fermentable carbohydrates, has consistently been an important part of the British diet (Wilson 1973; Hammond 1993). In the Scottish medieval period there were several different types of bread which varied in quality. Even the white,

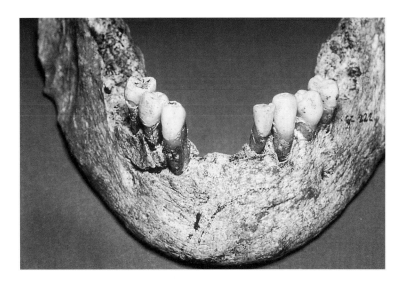

FIGURE 4.6

Mandible without denture (sk 222)

FIGURE 4.7

Partial denture, labial aspect (sk 222)

well-bolted breads (usually eaten by the gentry) were grey, coarse and 'distinctly solid' compared to modern standards (Mayhew 1993). Is it possible that the consumption of coarse starchy foods, requiring heavy mastication, producing the fermentable products and the neutral oral environment necessary for calculus deposits to form. Although this is one possible suggestion, it is likely that several other factors (for example, sugars in the diet, attrition, oral hygiene) were responsible for the differences in calculus deposition between time periods and sexes.

Calculus and fermentable carbohydrates must also be present for carious lesions to develop (Hillson 1986). Although calculus was more frequent in the early phase, a higher percentage of teeth had caries in the later phase (phase 6: 5.6% of the teeth; in phase 7:

9.9%). These findings roughly correspond to the prevalence figures of other Scottish population groups (medieval period = 6.2%; 16th–19th century = 16.0%) (complied by D Lunt, pers comm). It must be noted , however, that the differences in the sample are not significant at the 0.05 level. Generally there appears to be a trend of increasing caries in Britain through time, culminating in the last *c*150 years (Manchester 1983). Furthermore, there was more antemortem tooth loss in phase 7 which may be due to higher frequencies of caries. Sugar-rich diets have been demonstrated to be the most cariogenic (Hillson 1986). It is probable that the individuals buried within the cathedral had access to sugar and refined foodstuffs which were increasing prevalent in Britain from the 12th century onwards (Hardwick 1960).

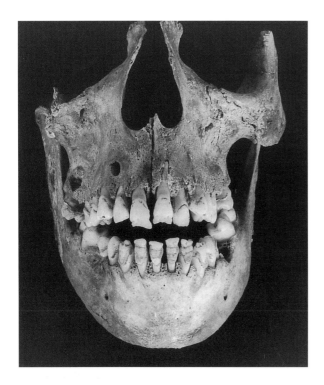

FIGURE 4.8

Skeleton 007 with severe DEH, calculus, periodontal disease and abscesses

There did not appear to be differences in rates of caries between the sexes in phase 6, although in phase 7 a higher percentage of males had caries than females. This difference, however, is not statistically significant (p>0.05). By age, caries were most frequent in mature adults, which supports the hypothesis that caries prevalence has been related to age (Lunt 1986). The caries experience of this individual may be anomalous, perhaps due to diet or hereditary factors (Hillson 1986).

The presence of calculus may also be partially responsible for the high frequency of periodontal disease and antemortem tooth loss in both phases. Another factor may be the high percentage of middle and mature adults in the sample. Adult periodontis is more prevalent and more severe in older age groups (Hillson 1986). In the cathedral sample the severity of periodontis was found to increase with age. Particularly, it appeared that males may have been more severely affected than females in each age category. This may be partially due to higher frequencies of calculus in males.

It is interesting to note that the six individuals with dental enamel hypoplasia included two subadults (sk 378 and sk 396), two young adults (sk 353 and sk 007), and two middle adults (sk 405 and sk 410). This may suggest that these individuals had histories of poor health and died at relatively younger ages.

Joint changes

OSTEOARTHRITIS

Osteoarthritis (OA) is a common disease in antiquity and in modern times. Thirty-two (50%) of the adult individuals had at least one diarthrodial joint slightly to severely affected; 38 (61%) (including the spine) had one or more of the above features (Figure 4.9). There was no evidence of joint disease in the subadults.

Age	Phase 6		Phase 7		Total sample	
	Female	Male	Female	Male	Female	Male
Young adult	0	0	0	0	0	0
Middle adult	3 (43%)	6 (86%)	0	0	3 (38%)	6 (86%)
Mature adult	4 (100%)	10 (100%)	1 (33%)	1 (33%)	5 (71%)	11 (85%)
Adult	2 (40%)	1 (11%)	2 (50%)	1 (50%)	4 (44%)	2 (18%)

FIGURE 4.9

Number (%) of individuals with joint changes (including joints with only marginal osteophytes) by age, sex and phase (n=31) (not including the spine)

Age	Phase 6		Phase 7		Total sample	
	Female	Male	Female	Male	Female	Male
Young adult	0	0	0	0	0	0
Middle adult	2 (29%)	2 (29%)	0	0	2 (25%)	2 (29%)
Mature adult	3 (75%)	7 (70%)	1 (33%)	0	4 (57%)	7 (54%)
Adult	0	0	2 (50%)	0	2 (22%)	0

FIGURE 4.10

Number (%) of individuals with joint changes (excluding joints with only marginal osteophytes) by age, sex and phase (n=17) (not including the spine)

When all diarthrodial joint surfaces with the presence of only marginal osteophytes were ignored, only 18 (27%) individuals (25 or 39% including the spine) were considered to be affected by osteoarthritis (Figure 4.10).

The percentage of individuals with joint disease differs depending on whether the analyst includes cases of osteophytes without other changes as an indicator of osteoarthritis. The sample sizes, however, were too small to make any convincing conclusions.

Several skeletons (sk 123, sk 149, sk 341, sk 387, sk 410, sk 535 and sk 582) expressed single lytic lesions (often not more than 2mm in diameter) on a joint surface. Commonly, these lesions were observed in the hands and feet, particularly on the proximal end of the proximal phalanx of the big toe.

Due to the incompleteness of many of the skeletons, and the lack of standardized methodological conventions, frequencies of joint involvement were not attempted. An overview of joint changes observed does, however, illustrate possible trends. The spine was most commonly affected, followed by the acromioclavicular joint, hip and foot. The joint surfaces of the ACJ were usually covered with medium sized porous lesions. The hip was often affected either bilaterally or on the right side. The first metatarsophalangeal articulation was the joint most affected by osteoarthritis in the foot. If marginal osteophytes are indicative of osteoarthritis, it would appear that the shoulder, elbow and knee were also commonly affected joints. Only five individuals had joint changes which involved eburnation. If the diagnosis of osteoarthritis is made primarily on the presence of eburnation (for example, Waldron 1992), then it would appear that there was very little evidence of joint disease in the sample. Only two of these cases (knee in sk 227 and elbow in sk 341; Figure 4.11) were considered to be severe, involving deep grooving, marginal osteophytes and porosity.

Spinal joint disease is frequently observed in individuals past middle age (Ortner and Putschar 1981). Osteophytosis of the vertebral bodies and osteoarthritis of the apophyseal joints are often most frequent in areas of curvature in the spine where stress is the greatest (C5/6, T7/8 and L3/4) (Manchester 1983). Studies of spinal arthritis have attributed mechanical (activity related) stress as a significant factor in its pattern of expression (for example, Bridges 1994; Lovell 1994).

The 22 individuals with spinal joint disease also had osteoarthritis in other parts of the skeleton; seven individuals had only spinal joint disease, and nine had joint disease affecting only the appendicular skeleton. Figure 4.12 shows that spinal joint disease is most frequent in the older age categories.

Cervical vertebrae 4–7, T5–T8 and L1–L4 were the most severely affected vertebrae. It is interesting to note that (generally) when one grade of severity peaks, the other troughs, except in particular vertebrae (C6,

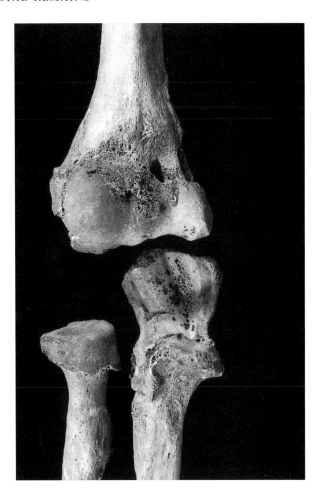

FIGURE 4.11

Osteoarthritis in the right elbow of skeleton 34

Age group	number of vertebrae observed	number (%) of affected vertebrae
Young adult	70	12*(17%)
Middle adult	209	62 (30%)
Mature adult	249	168 (67%)
Adult	20	17 (85%)
Total	548	259 (47%)

*Schmorl's nodes were the only changes observed in the young adult category

FIGURE 4.12

Age analysis of individuals with spinal joint disease

?T7 and L4) where there were high percentages of both degrees of severity. Overall, the cervical and thoracic vertebrae were most frequently slightly affected, whereas the lumbar vertebrae were more often moderately affected. The cervical vertebrae, however, were more severely affected than any other part of the spine (Figure 4.13).

A brief analysis of the apophyseal joints suggested that the cervical and thoracic surfaces were most often moderately affected whereas the lumbar surfaces were most frequently slightly affected (Figure 4.14).

	n	% Slight	% Moderate	% Severe
Cervical	43	47	30	23
Thoracic	129	60	26	14
Lumbar	47	47	51	2

FIGURE 4.13

Severity of vertebral body joint disease (n = total number of affected vertebrae)

	n	% Slight	% Moderate	% Severe
Cervical	7	14	57	28
Thoracic	12	17	50	33
Lumbar	9	67	22	11

FIGURE 4.14

Severity of apophyseal OA (n = total number of vertebrae affected in at least one apophyseal surface)

Ankylosis (fusion of osteophytes) occurred in three individuals (sk 017, sk 310 and sk 364). Sk 017 was an adult female with fusion of the articular processes of C6 and C7, sk 310 was a mature adult ?female with a candle-wax like fusion of T10, T11 and T12, and sk 364 was a mature adult male with fused T6 and T7.

SCHMORL'S NODES

Schmorl's nodes are observed as round or oval depressions in the superior and inferior surfaces of vertebral bodies. Degenerative and traumatic changes to an intervertebral disc can result in herniation which may then protrude into a vertebral end-plate (Ortner and Putschar 1981).

Of 29 individuals with spinal joint changes, 12 had lytic lesions which have been diagnosed as Schmorl's nodes, and four of these (sk 338, sk 356, sk 353 and sk 007) had only Schmorl's nodes with no other changes to the spine. These latter individuals include two middle adult females, a young adult male and a young adult female. The thoracic vertebrae were most often affected, followed by the lumbar vertebrae. There were no cases of Schmorl's nodes on the cervical vertebrae.

One middle adult female (sk 338) and two mature adult males (sk 381 and sk 387) from phase 6 had semi-circular lytic lesions on the anterior portions on some of the thoracic and lumbar vertebral bodies. These lesions have also been identified in some of the individuals from the late medieval cemetery at Whithorn (Cardy 1997) and described as intervertebral osteochondrosis. In sk 381 the right side of the T12 has collapsed slightly due to the severity of the lesion. This individual probably had a slight scoliosis (medial-lateral curvature) of the spine.

Joint changes in the axial and appendicular skeleton are the second most common disease observed in the sample. The high frequency of arthritic changes may be partially due to the age distribution of the sample:

osteoarthritis is a disease which is most frequently observed in older age groups (Ortner and Putschar 1981).

In spinal joint disease, the general patterns observed are consistent with what might be expected given an upright posture: that is, arthritic involvement which peaks in the areas of greatest spine curvature and which is minimal in areas lying along the centre of gravity. Also, the lower spine is most often affected due to greater weight-bearing demands in that region (Bridges 1994). There does, however, appear to be a high frequency of thoracic vertebrae which were 'slightly' affected. Whether this involvement is due to factors other than age or weight-bearing is difficult to suggest without further studies and comparisons with other samples. The high number of Schmorl's nodes in this region may suggest, however, the existence of additional biomechanical stresses.

Infection

PRIMARY PERIOSTITIS

Primary periostitis is often a result of trauma or infection, although it is sometimes impossible to determine which of these conditions resulted in a particular lesion (Ortner and Putschar 1981). Secondary periostitis occurs as a response to a specific disease process (for example, leprosy) and will be discussed in more detail below.

Sk 242 (phase 6) was an adult ?male only represented by the lower extremities. The left tibia and fibula were slightly thickened with irregular but smooth (well-healed) new bone formation on the mid to distal (anterior, lateral and posterior) portions of the shafts. The lesions appeared to be unilateral and the only other changes to the bones were DJD on the calcaneal articular surfaces of the talus (possibly secondary arthritis). Non-specific periostitis is common in the tibia and may be due to the fact that this bone is near the skin and more prone to direct trauma (Ortner and Putschar 1981).

Sk 387 (phase 6) was a mature adult male with extensive periosteal lesions (raised plaques of greyish striated and/or porous new bone formation with irregular thickening of the shaft, having a smooth or spiculed appearance). The lesions were observed on the right femur, tibial shafts, fibulae, left talus and fifth metatarsals (Figure 4.15). Fusion occurred between the distal right tibia and fibula and between the right tibia and talus. The periosteal lesions were probably secondary to a fracture of the right fibula (see below). The sharp ends of the displaced compound fracture probably protruded through the skin, resulting in infection. Although the fracture was well healed at the time of death, the presence of both healed and active periosteal lesions suggest that there may have been haematogenous spread of the infection to other areas of the skeleton. This individual probably suffered from

144

FIGURE 4.15

Fracture, infection and fusion of the right tibia, fibula and talus (sk 387)

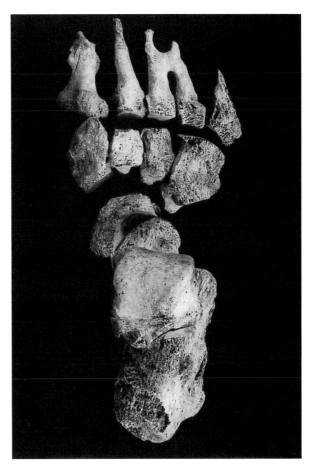

FIGURE 4.16

Leprous changes to the foot (sk 551)

chronic pain in the limbs and reduced mobility, at least in the right ankle.

LEPROSY

Leprosy is a chronic infectious disease caused by *Mycobacterium leprae*. The infection primarily affects the nervous system and secondarily involves the skin, mucous membranes, soft tissues and arterial blood vessels (Manchester 1983; Ortner and Putschar 1981). The signs and symptoms of the disease can develop from two to seven years after the disease was contracted and progression of the disease extends over decades. Skeletal changes can involve osteomyelitis, periostitis, resorption of the nasal spine, rounding and widening of the nasal aperture, partial resorption of the premaxillary alveolar process with or without loss of the upper incisors and concentric remodelling of the finger and toe bones (Manchester 1983).

Sk 551 (phase 6) was a middle adult male excavated from the nave. A complete skeleton revealed tibiae and fibulae with areas of irregular smooth thickening (well-healed lesions), raised plaques of porous new bone formation (active lesions), striated grey bone and spiculed bone formation. The left tibia and fibula were more severely affected than the right side. There were also changes to the bones of the feet involving fusion

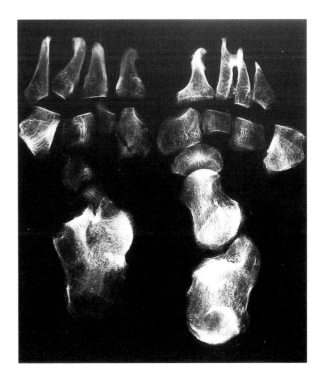

FIGURE 4.17

X-ray of leprous changes to the feet (sk 551)

145

of the left calcaneus and talus, new bone formation on several of the tarsals, resorption of the left medial cuneiform and the metatarsals (having a knife edge appearance) and cortical thinning of the phalanges (Figures 4.16 and 4.17). No changes were observed in the hands or the face. These findings were diagnosed as lepromatous leprosy (low resistance type). This individual also suffered several fractures to the ribs (see below).

DISCUSSION

There was a relatively low frequency of infection/ infectious diseases present in the Glasgow Cathedral sample (7%). The presence of chronic conditions, such as leprosy, may suggest that an individual was healthy long enough for lesions to develop on the bones. By contrast, many acute infectious diseases result in rapid death leaving no traces of their existence on the bones. It is probable that several individuals from the sample, particularly the infants and children, may have suffered from acute infectious diseases (for example, typhus and dysentery), although it is impossible to determine by the skeletal remains alone. Certainly these diseases, along with war and famine, were prevalent in Scotland until the 18th century (Hamilton 1981).

Leprosy seemed to be at its highest peak in Europe during the 13th century (Manchester 1991; 1992), although it is known to have continued in Scotland until the 1700s where the last case was recorded in Orkney (Hamilton 1981). In Glasgow, a leprosy hospital was present south of the Clyde (Hamilton 1981).

Skeletal malformation

The only malformation observed in the sample was a case of spina bifida occulta in a middle adult female (sk 356). This is an asymptomatic condition involving incomplete fusion of the spinous processes of the sacrum. Spina bifida occulta is commonly mentioned in archaeological reports, and it has been suggested that there may be a genetic component to its expression (Ortner and Putschar 1981).

Tumours

A middle adult female (sk 523) from phase 6 had a single small circular bony growth (5mm diameter and 3mm thick) on the left zygomatic bone. It is probable that this lesion was a button osteoma, a type of benign tumour which is relatively common and usually found only on the skull.

An oval lytic lesion (approx 10mm diameter) was present on the medial portion of the scapular spine (right side) of sk 545, a middle adult male (Figure 4.18). The edges were sharp but it appeared as if there was a fine fibrous ring around the opening of the lesion. The internal surface was rough with a small amount of porous, raised new bone formation. This

lesion may be a benign cyst although a differential diagnosis of trauma could also be possible.

Stress indicators

CRIBRA ORBITALIA

Cribra orbitalia is a term used to describe porotic lesions which occur in the orbital roof. This type of lesion may be due to a number of different pathological processes. One of these processes is anaemia. Only one skeleton (sk 551) from the sample had cribra orbitalia. A small focal area (approx 4mm diameter) of small coalescing porosities were symmetrically present on the mid to lateral, superior, portions of the orbits. This individual was a middle adult male who also suffered from lepromatous leprosy. It is not surprising to observe these lesions in an individual with a chronic infectious disease. It is possible that the immune system was working against the disease, resulting in decreased levels of iron absorption and anaemia.

HARRIS' LINES

Harris' lines are metaphyseal transverse lines of lamellar bone (usually observed on long bones by radiographic examination). They result from temporary disturbances of cartilage and bone cells during the growth period. Harris' lines were observed macroscopically on one juvenile (sk 400). A horizontal line of bone approximately 6mm from the distal articular surface was exposed on a fragmented tibial shaft. This is the only case of Harris' lines observed, however radiographs were not routinely taken. It is possible that this individual may have suffered from one of the aetiological factors discussed above.

Other

PAGET'S DISEASE

Paget's disease (osteitis deformans) is usually found in older individuals. The cause of this disease is not known. It can be widespread in a skeleton or localized to one bone. It is characterized by thickening of the bone due to a 'pathological speedup and distortion of the normal remodeling mechanism' (Ortner and Putschar 1981, 122). The bone may be bent as well as thickened (Apley and Solomon 1988). The skeleton of individual 552 (adult ?female) was very poorly preserved, with only 40% of the remains recovered. The left tibia, talus and calcaneus (the left fibula was missing) had a thickened cortex and trabeculae, the cortex having a thick lattice pattern in some areas and rough, disorganised new bone formation in other areas. Areas on the tibia also showed 'pumice' type bone subperiosteally. The tibia was thickened and bowed anteriorly but narrow laterally and medially. The bones were extremely fragile, being powdery and brittle to touch. No other bones present for observation appeared to have been affected. The pathological tibia is considerably smaller than the normal tibia. This would have resulted in a limp during walking.

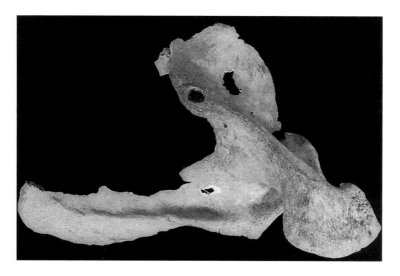

FIGURE 4.18

A possible cyst on the scapular spine (sk 545)

This lesion may be due to Paget's disease although a differential diagnosis of *fibrous dysplasia* (developmental abnormality of bone) may be possible.

BOWING

Several individuals had long bones which were bowed (medio-laterally). In three cases the femora were slightly bowed (sk 310, sk 149 and sk 523), two had bowed fibulae (sk 123 and sk 349), one had bowed humeri (sk 534) and one skeleton had a bowed left ulna. These changes were observed in adult females and males from both phases. At present, it is not possible to determine what factors may be involved in bowing, although occupational related changes or rickets in childhood are possibilities.

CHANGES IN AREAS OF MUSCLE ATTACHMENT

Spicules of bone in areas of tendinous attachment, depressions and ridges (new bone formation) were often observed in areas of muscle attachment. These types of changes have been attributed as occupational stress markers in conjunction with other evidence (for example, Lai and Lovell 1992). In two cases (sk 353 and sk 387) the tibial tuberosity was reduced in size whereas the area of attachment for the patellar ligament was greatly enlarged.

Trauma

There was relatively little evidence of trauma in the sample, affecting only 11 (17%) of the adults. Of these cases, ten traumatic lesions were observed on males. It is probable that at least four of the individuals (sk 353, sk 411, sk 381 and sk 531) may have suffered intentional violent trauma. In at least one case (sk 353), and possibly sk 411, death occurred as a result.

WEAPON WOUNDS

The most dramatic fractures observed were gun shot wounds to the head of a young adult male (sk 353) from phase 6. Three lead balls were found in the cranium during excavation and one more in the region of the hyoid bone, that is under the chin. An entry wound (bevelled endocranially) was present on the left side of the frontal bone in the area of the temporal line (Figure 4.19). The lesion was completely circular (approx 15mm diameter) with at least three curving radiating fractures extending from it. A second wound (beveled mostly ectocranially) occurred on the posterior portion of the right parietal (Figure 4.20). It was roughly circular in shape (approx 24mm diameter) with three radiating fractures extending away from it. It was probably an exit wound. Not surprisingly, no healing was evident on the lesions. It was not possible to determine whether there were any other entry (or exit) wounds. There were too few cranial fragments surviving from the right side of the face to make reconstruction in this area possible. It is possible that the weapon from which the lead balls came was a blunderbuss or short gun with a large bore firing many balls at once (see Section 3.9). Since there was only one clear entry wound, however, it is difficult to determine whether the lead balls derived from one or several gunshots.

It was noted that there were well-marked muscle attachments on this skeleton, especially for the deltoid on the right humerus. Bilateral thickening on the posterior proximal portion of the tibial shafts just above the nutrient foramina was also evident.

A possible case of antemortem trauma was present on the sternum of a mature adult male (sk 411) from phase 6. A cut (approx 9mm on the anterior side and

147

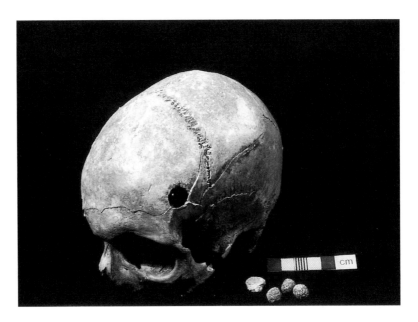

FIGURE 4.19

Gun shot entry-wound to cranium (sk 353)

FIGURE 4.20

Gun shot exit-wound to cranium (sk 353)

12mm on the dorsal side), probably from a pointed knife, penetrated the sternum (Figure 4.21). The edges were sharp and slightly raised on the antero-superior portion and slightly depressed on the antero-inferior portion of the cut. A dry bone would not demonstrate this flexibility. The cut was at a slight angle with a small terminal radiating fracture at the superior end. Terminal fractures are usually associated with larger weapons; the presence of a terminal fracture with a small wound is suggestive of considerable applied force. Although it is unlikely that this wound alone was fatal, concurrent wounds to the soft tissues may

have been the cause of death. In any case, the individual died prior to healing of the bone.

FRACTURES

Evidence of cranial trauma was also observed on the frontal bone of a mature adult male (sk 381). A roughly oval depression (approx 9mm x 13mm with a small 2mm lytic lesion in the centre of the depression) was present on the mid to left side of the frontal bone. It was not possible to determine whether there were changes on the endocranial surface. This lesion appeared to be a well healed depressed fracture which

FIGURE 4.21

Knife cut on sternum (sk 411)

may have been intentionally inflicted or accidentally substained.

Healed fractured nasal bones were observed in a mature adult male (sk 531) from phase 6. Both nasal bones were fractured on the infero-anterior portion and were slightly displaced (depressed) with some fusion. It is possible that this wound was intentionally inflicted by a blow to the face.

Sk 387, a mature adult male, suffered from an compound oblique fracture to the distal end of the right fibula. The fracture was displaced by approximately 10mm and slightly rotated medially. The sharp edges of the fracture probably protruded through the skin surface resulting in secondary infection (see above) although the fracture itself was well healed.

A non-united transverse fracture of the styloid process of the left fifth metatarsal was observed in a mature adult female (sk 535) from phase 6. The fractured ends had some evidence of healing with irregular but smooth surfaces associated with several medium sized porous lesions.

A middle adult male (sk 551) with leprosy had several (minimum of 11) healed fractures to the ribs. The exact ribs could not be determined, but it appeared that the middle and lower right and left ribs were affected. Many of the ribs had at least two fractures.

The ribs were well healed with slight callus formation and very little displacement (except in two cases).

The last case of fracture is the least dramatic. An adult male (sk 588) had a well-healed, slightly displaced, oblique fracture of a proximal phalanx (side unknown) from a foot.

ENTHESOPATHIES

Enthesopathies are bony outgrowths in areas of tendinous or ligamentous attachment which occur as a result of elevated levels of habitual strain, or it could be part of a disease process. There was only one enthesopathy observed in the sample from a middle adult male (sk 405) from phase 6. A small amount of new bone formation was present in the area of attachment for the tibial collateral ligament (distal medial portion of femur, superior to the articular condyle) on the right femur. It is possible that this type of trauma may be related to occupation.

Pathological conditions on unstratified bone

The unstratified bone recovered during the excavation was collected and briefly examined for pathological conditions. Although there were several cases of typical dental disease, and arthritic changes, a few interesting pathological cases merit a brief discussion.

TRAUMA

An adult male mandible (CE 115) had a focal area (approx 20mm in diameter) of reactive porous new bone formation on the left ramus, just superior to the gonial angle. It appeared that this individual may have had a blow to the jaw which was in the process of healing at the time of his death.

An adult individual (CW 234) had a fractured neck of the right femur. The length of the neck was reduced and slightly displaced inferiorly. Smooth, but irregular (well-healed) new bone formation surrounded the margins of the femoral head (and surrounding the fovea capitis). There were only slight changes to the shape of the femoral head.

An adult individual (NS 556) suffered a compound fracture of the right femoral shaft. The fracture occurred in the proximal/midshaft region, and was slightly displaced anteriorly and laterally from the distal portion of the shaft. The fracture was well-healed with extensive smooth new bone formation.

There were three cases of postmortem trauma in the form of autopsy (NS 501, CE 115, NS 514). The sectioned skulls belonged to two adult individuals (Figure 4.22) and a subadult of approximately 12 years (based on dental formation and eruption). There was no evidence of any other pathological lesions on the crania.

INTERNAL FRONTAL HYPEROSTOSIS

This condition is usually restricted to the endocranial surface of the frontal bone, which becomes thickened

FIGURE 4.22

Skull sawn in half for an autopsy

and irregular. It almost always affects females, particularly after menopause (Ortner and Putschar 1981). These types of lesions occurred in three frontal bones of adult individuals to varying degrees (NS 501, NN 322). At least two of the crania appeared to be female, both from the same context.

INFECTION

A calvarium from an adult ?female (NS 501) had a large circular lesion in the region of the glabella (on the frontal bone). The lesion was lytic, approximately 22mm by 17mm in diameter, with sharp remodeled edges and fine porosity surrounding portions of the lesion. The lesion exposed the frontal sinuses; the left sinus had slight thickening of the bone surface with increased porosity. There was also slight porous bone formation in small diffuse patches on the left side of the frontal bone in the area of the supraorbital ridge. Some postmortem damage occurred in the area of the nasal bones, but it appeared that there was some remodelling of the nasal bones. Plaques of new bone formation were present on the sutures between the frontal and the nasal bones. Without the post-cranial skeleton, diagnosis is difficult. These lesions, however, may be due to treponemal disease (for example, syphilis) or perhaps trauma.

Two adult tibiae and a right proximal femur (from one individual NN 302) had extensive periosteal new bone formation on the shafts. The bones were greatly thickened and heavy. The changes on the tibia were symmetrical, suggesting a haematogenous spread of infection (possibly secondary periostitis).

The left tibia of an adult individual (NS 503) had striated plaques of new bone formation (healed) covering ¾ of the shaft. The bone surface was irregular and thickened.

ANKYLOSING SPONDYLITIS

This disorder of unknown aetiology is common in males with onset in early adulthood. It is an inflammatory condition which affects the apophyseal joints of the spine, costovertebral joints and sacroiliac joints (Ortner and Putschar 1981). Six lower thoracic vertebrae, L2 to L5, sacrum and innominates (from one adult male NN 322) had pathological changes characteristic of ankylosing spondylitis. The sacrum and innominates were bilaterally fused, slight to moderate osteophytes occurred on the lumbar vertebrae, and two thoracic vertebrae were fused with a 'bamboo' appearance. There was also ossification of ligamentous attachments on the ischial tuberosities and iliac crest. These areas of ossification are also common in diffuse idiopathic skeletal hyperostosis (a condition characterized by this phenomenon).

RICKETS

Both tibiae from an adult individual (NN 302) demonstrated marked medio-lateral bowing. It is possible that this individual suffered from a childhood episode of rickets.

Summary conclusions

Before any conclusions can be made, the limitations of the cathedral sample must be addressed. Firstly, the sample size is small. Secondly, comparisons with other archaeological samples present problems of compatibility due to different analytical methods. Furthermore, there are few Scottish skeletal samples (and published reports) from similar time periods to facilitate a comprehensive comparative analysis. Thirdly, the phases of the sample span over six hundred years, during which time small variations in mortality and disease patterns may be overlooked. Despite these problems, it is believed that the findings from skeletal analysis of the 79 burials are likely to be consistent with what might be expected of the select group of individuals for whom the privilege of burial within Glasgow Cathedral was an option.

Age at death

The sample (phase 6 and phase 7) consisted mainly of adult females and males, the majority of whom lived to be middle or mature adults (26–45 and 46+ years). Generally, it has been believed that life expectancy was relatively low in the past. For example, in 17th century Scotland, the general population could not expect to live to over 30 years of age (Hamilton 1981). At least two possibilities could explain the high life expectancy of the cathedral sample. First, it is possible that the ageing techniques used on the sample overestimate the true age of the individuals. This is unlikely, however, as studies of ageing techniques have shown that there is actually a tendency to underage older adults (Molleson and Cox 1993). Second, another possibility concerns the socio-economic class of the individuals. A comparison of the age distributions of other Scottish archaeological samples suggests that the individuals from the medieval phase of the cathedral sample outlived their contemporaries. In the late medieval cemetery of Whithorn (n = 1553), it has been estimated that only 10% of the individuals survived to late-middle or old age (Cardy 1997). In archaeological samples from Aberdeen (n = 93, late 14th to early 17th centuries) and Linlithgow (n = 227, early 14th to 17th centuries), both considered to represent a section of the local population buried within friary buildings and graveyards, the life expectancy was found to be relatively low. In the Aberdeen sample, females did not live past young adulthood and males did not live past middle adulthood. At Linlithgow, deaths of females and males peaked in young adulthood (Cross and Bruce 1989). It seems possible that privileged individuals who were not exposed to the hardships of life experienced by the general population were buried within the cathedral.

In the Whithorn and Aberdeen sites, females were found to die slightly younger than males (Cardy 1997; Cross and Bruce 1989). High female mortality in young adulthood has been attributed to increased malnutrition, infection and birth complications during the reproductive years (Cross and Bruce 1989; Grauer 1991). Other explanations, however, such as migration, may also be involved (Grauer 1991). The cathedral sample lacks this exaggerated mortality of young females. Better nutrition and living conditions may be partly responsible for this difference.

Low subadult mortality

When compared to other Scottish sites, the percentage of subadults represented in the cathedral sample was relatively low (19%). In the Whithorn sample, approximately a third of the individuals were immature (Cardy 1997). In the Aberdeen sample 36% of the burials were immature, and 59% of the Linlithgow sample were immature, less than 18 years of age (Cross and Bruce 1989). The small number of subadults in phase 6 of the cathedral may suggest a low mortality rate in this age group, at least when compared to other broadly contemporary medieval sites. It is also possible, however, that infants and subadults are under-represented due to differential burial practices.

Population health

A number of factors suggest that the individuals buried within the cathedral were relatively healthy. One is the percentage of individuals living to middle or old age. While stature is primarily determined by genetics, it may also be influenced by environmental factors, for example, nutrition and climate (Brothwell 1981). The male individuals from the cathedral sample may have been slightly taller than their Scottish contemporaries, at least during the medieval period (females were within the ranges, although on the high end, of other samples). Males averaged 174.10cm, 4.10cm taller than the males from Whithorn, Aberdeen and Linlithgow (Cardy 1997; Cross and Bruce 1989). This could partially represent better nutritional status.

The presence or absence of diseases within a sample may provide information regarding living environment, nutritional status and hygiene. One interesting observation in the cathedral sample was the lack of cribra orbitalia, a condition which can be indicative of environmental stresses, for example infection, parasitism, or iron-deficient diet (Stuart-Macadam 1989). This condition is usually common in archaeological samples. In Whithorn, for example, 30% of the sample had cribra orbitalia. The virtual absence of this condition may suggest that the individuals lived with fewer stresses than the general Scottish population. No other nutritional deficiency diseases (for example, vitamin C, vitamin D) were observed except for a possible case of rickets among the unstratified skeletal remains.

There was a relatively low percentage (7%) of individuals with infection/infectious diseases in the cathedral sample. The presence and severity of infectious disease is dependent on both innate and acquired immunity of the host to the pathogen. Innate immunity is influenced by the nutritional status, socio-economic status, and living conditions of the individual (Manchester 1992). These factors could be responsible for the low frequency of infectious disease, although it is also possible that individuals may have died before infectious diseases could have affected the bone. The high percentage of middle and mature adults in the sample suggests that most of the individuals survived exposure to infectious diseases during their younger years.

There was one interesting case of leprosy in the cathedral from phase 6, and a possible case of treponemal disease (possibly syphilis) among the unstratified bone. Certainly, both types of disease were common in Scotland during the Middle Ages, syphilis first appearing as an epidemic in 1497 (Hamilton 1981). The presence of these diseases may be largely, but not exclusively, an urban phenomenon (Manchester 1992).

Arthritic changes were most frequently observed in the spine. Analysis of the affected vertebrae suggested that upright posture and old age were probably the main aetiological factors involved in its expression. Generally, the presence of joint disease in this sample simply reflects what might be expected in an ageing group of individuals (with the possible exceptions of sk 227, sk 341 and sk 531).

Relatively few individuals had serious fractures which would have required medical attention. All fractures observed were well healed without observable infection, with the exception of one compound fracture of the fibula (sk 387). An individual buried near St Kentigern's tomb in the crypt (phase 7) may have lost his lower incisors by a traumatic accident. In any case, they were replaced by a finely crafted set of false teeth, suggesting access to a skilled dentist.

Analysis of the skeletal remains suggests, as might be expected, that the individuals buried within Glasgow Cathedral were of high socio-economic status. They probably had better living conditions and better nutrition than the general population compared to the medieval burials from the cemetery at Whithorn, for example. Despite better nutrition, the individuals from the cathedral suffered from caries, possibly due to the consumption of refined foodstuffs and sugar. Sugar, or sucrose, was introduced to England in the 12th century and there was vast trade in the product (mainly for the wealthy) by the early 15th century. During the late 16th century sugar was mainly used in the manufacture of marzipan and sweetmeats, and luxury commodities for the rich. By the 17th and 18th centuries, sugar consumption had increased and finer flours became available (Hardwick 1960).

Overall, very few differences were observed between the skeletons of the two phases. Partially, this is due to the small number of skeletons from the later phase. Both may have enjoyed a privileged life. The presence of females, males and children in both phases suggests that the sample represents a normal familial community.

One difference may be an increase in stature over time. Another change may have occurred in the shape of the head, with a change from broad to average or medium sized heads. This trend has also been observed in other Scottish samples (Cross and Bruce 1989). One pathological condition, the presence of calculus, was significantly different between the phases. Calculus was more frequent on the teeth of individuals from phase 6, and males were more affected than females.

This finding may suggest a change in diet and ideas regarding oral hygiene over time.

4.3 TWO SKELETONS FROM THE NW TOWER
by J A Roberts

Preservation

The skeletons were contained in two shallow depressions and were already badly damaged, the skull, pelvis and various other bones having been removed sometime in antiquity. The burials followed the typical Christian practice of extended E–W orientation. The remains were in a very poor, fragmentary condition, a situation that worsened upon attempted cleaning of the bone.

Sk 1152 was less than 30% complete, and the bones were fragmentary. There was a moderate amount of surface erosion and the vertebrae and pelvis, in particular, were soft, partially disintegrating upon careful washing. Skeletal elements represented were: the right and left femur, the right and left ulna and radius, right and left metacarpals and carpals, right metatarsals, fragments of pelvis including the right auricular surface, left iliac crest and right and left acetabulum, fragments of right and left rib, and a minimum number of four lumbar and four thoracic vertebrae.

Sk 1153 was less than 25% complete. All the bones were very fragmentary except for the right femur and right ulna. The skeletal elements represented were predominantly from the right side of the body: the right ulna, right proximal radius, right femur, right and left metacarpals, and fragments of vertebra, pelvis and sacrum.

Results

Sex

Sk 1153 was male and sk 1152 was probably male. These determinations of sex were based on the morphology of the sciatic notch, the auricular surface and the pre-auricular sulcus of the pelvis in both skeletons, and also the acetabulum in sk 1153. With the exception of the bicondylar breadth of the humerus from sk 1152 (which was ambiguous) all the post cranial data indicated a male sex for both skeletons (Figure 4.23).

Age at death

The age at death of sk 1152 was estimated as being between 17 and 20 years, based primarily on epiphyseal fusion. The epiphyses of the distal radius and proximal femur were recently fused, and the iliac crest

	sk 1153	sk 1152	male	female
Femur: vertical head diameter	52.9 (R)	50.8 (R)	>48	<43
		48.6 (L)		
Femur: bicondylar breadth	81 (R)	NA	>78	<72
Radius: maximum head diameter	25.3 (R)	25 (L)	>24	<21
Humerus: epicondylar width*	NA	60.1 (L)	63.9	56.8

*Male and female values given are mean values: male = 63.89 ± 3.59; female = 56.76 ± 3.32

FIGURE 4.23

Post-cranial metric data (measured in mm) (sk 1153 and sk 1152)

was partially fused. The one sternal end of rib present indicated an age of 17 to 23 years and the auricular surface of the ilium suggested an age at death of between 19 and 24 years.

Estimation of the age of sk 1153 was less accurate as epiphyseal fusion was complete. A broad age category of 40 to 50 years at death (or 'mature adult') was assigned, on the basis of the appearance of the auricular surface of the ilium (42 to 50 years), and generalised degenerative change, which included osteophytes around the fovea of the femoral head (M F Bruce pers comm).

Stature and build

It was not possible to determine the stature of sk 1152 as no complete long bones were present. The individual was of average build and displayed a degree of asymmetry, the articular surfaces of the right radius and femur being larger than the left. Both the right and the left femur were platymeric, the meric indices being 84.3 and 80.8 respectively. The smaller femoral head and the greater antero-posterior flattening of the proximal left femur may have been related, in part, to a pathological process (discussed below).

The estimated stature of sk 1153 was 169cm based on the length of the femur, and 158cm based on the length of the ulna. As the standard error is greater when stature is based on upper rather than lower limbs, the height of 169cm was considered to be the more accurate estimation. This is considerably shorter than the mean statures of both the 13th–17th century and the 17th–19th-century burials from within the cathedral (Figure 4.5). The right (and only surviving) femur of sk 1153, was visibly flattened antero-posteriorly and had a meric index of only 66. This shorter stature and extreme platymeria, may have been due to nutritional deficiencies, although there was no pathological evidence of osteomalacia (caused by lack of vitamin D) or scurvy (caused by lack of vitamin C). Evidence of iron deficiency anaemia might have been present in the skull, as *cribra orbitalia* or *porotic hyperostosis* (Ortner and Putschar 1981; Grauer 1993), but as both crania were missing, this could not be assessed. The lateral aspect of the proximal femur was

enlarged at the insertion point of *vastus lateralis,* and the insertion groove for *obturator internus* was particularly well defined. *Vastus lateralis* is one of the quadricep muscles responsible for extension of the knee joint, and *obturator internus* is a lateral rotator of the thigh, assisting also in flexion and extension of the trunk when walking. The enlargement of the insertion points of these muscles may be indicative that this individual consistently walked for long distances.

Non metric traits

Post-cranial non-metric traits were recorded as being either present or absent, standards being taken from Finnegan (1978). The only non-metric traits identified were plaque on both femoral heads/necks of sk 1152, and a third trochanter on the left proximal femur of the same skeleton. No valid conclusions can be drawn from this information, as the poor preservation of the skeletal remains meant that these data were almost certainly not an accurate representation of the traits present.

Pathology

As with non-metric traits the recognition of specific diseases is dependent on the survival of specific skeletal elements. Even if the appropriate bones are present, a sample with little or no evidence of pathology does not necessarily indicate a healthy population. The individuals concerned may have died quickly from an infectious disease before bony involvement developed, or from a condition which would not have affected the skeleton, such as cardio-vascular disease, or fatal soft tissue traumatic injury. Each skeletal element in the assemblage was examined for evidence of pathology, which was then classified according to cause (Manchester 1983). The following types of pathological condition were found to be present.

Degenerative joint disease

The most common type of joint disease found in any archaeological population is osteoarthritis, which is often termed degenerative joint disease. Studies have shown that certain joints do appear to be more frequently affected than others, most notably the lumbar spine, the elbow, the shoulder, the knee and the hip (Larsen 1984; Lovell 1994).

153

Degenerative joint disease of moderate severity was observed in the right hip and lumbar spine of sk 1153. In the hip, this was characterised by porosity and osteophytes on and around the femoral head, and osteophytes around the rim of the acetabulum. The lumbar vertebrae were fragmentary, but five fragments of body had porosity on the inferior and superior surfaces, and osteophytes around the margins of these joints. Fragments of the sacrum showed similar changes, and osteophytes were also present on the superior articular facets. Slight osteoarthritis was present in the right knee of the same skeleton, characterised by porosity of the femoral condyles, and slight porosity and osteophytes on the lateral condyle of the tibia. These manifestations may have caused some pain and stiffness, particularly in the hip and lower back.

Sk 1152 was younger than the above individual, and therefore a lack of degenerative changes in the joints was expected. There was, however, slight osteoarthritis of the left elbow, characterised by slight porosity of the medial aspect of the trochlea, and quite marked porosity of the radial head and olecranon fossa. In addition Schmorl's nodes were identified on the twelfth thoracic, and first, second, third and fourth lumbar vertebrae. These lesions represent herniation of the contents of the intervertebral discs onto the superior and inferior surfaces of the vertebral body, a condition associated with repeated flexion and lateral bending, and heavy lifting in general in younger individuals (Kennedy 1989). Congenital predisposition is also thought to be a contributory factor (C Roberts pers comm).

Circulatory disorders/trauma

Osteochondritis dissecans is a condition whereby part of the articular cartilage and underlying bone becomes detached at the joint. The cause is believed by some to be a direct result of trauma and the impaction of one joint surface against another (Forrester and Brown 1987), and by others to represent aseptic vascular necrosis (Ortner and Putschar 1981). It is most frequently seen in adolescent or young males, most commonly affecting the distal femur and proximal tibia.

The condition was identified in both skeletons. In the younger sk 1152, a small lesion, measuring 3.6mm maximum diameter, was present on the distal articular surface of the right radius. In sk 1153, a raised 'plug' of bone, on the medial condyle of the right femur, measuring 8.8mm maximum diameter, represented an almost healed lesion. If Forrester and Brown's interpretation of the aetiology of the disease is accepted, then its presence in the latter individual may have been associated with the previously discussed features attributed to prolonged walking.

Congenital disorders

In sk 1153 the spinous processes and posterior arches of two thoracic vertebrae were fused together, while the bodies remained separate. There appeared to be no underlying trauma, degenerative or infectious disease, and therefore a congenital cause is thought to be the most likely explanation. The condition was probably asymptomatic.

The left proximal femur of sk 1152 appeared to be deformed. The head was flattened and uneven on the superior surface, and the angle between the head and the neck was less acute than normal, although the head did not appear to be dislocated. These abnormalities were thought to constitute some form of congenital hip dysplasia but unfortunately the acetabulum was too fragmentary to allow a more precise diagnosis. Slight porosity of the femoral head may have represented the early stages of degenerative change, precipitated by alteration of the normal stress forces through the joint. The condition may have caused this young man to walk with a slight limp, although the incomplete acetabulum and femur, and the absence of the lower leg, meant that the full extent of his problems could not be determined.

Infectious disease

Only one example of superficial infectious change was identified, on the mid shaft of a left rib belonging to sk 1153. An area of lamellar bone (32.20mm x 6.10mm) was located on the inner surface of the fragment below the sub-costal groove. This type of new bone growth is indicative of partially healed or long-standing infection that was probably not active at the time of death. It may have been an isolated area of infection or one of several patches, which together may have represented a chest infection. Unfortunately the fragmentation and loss of the majority of the ribs, made it impossible to tell which diagnosis was correct.

The lack of evidence of infectious disease on both skeletons may have been due to the poor preservation of the remains. In particular, the absence of the tibiae, the most common site for periostitis in archaeological specimens, may have biased the results.

Conclusions

The two skeletons analysed were those of a male aged 40 to 50 years at death 1153, and a probable male aged 17 to 20 years at death (sk 1152). The former was approximately 169cm tall. It was not possible to determine the stature of the latter.

Sk 1153 suffered from moderate arthritis of the right hip, lumbar spine and sacrum, and slight arthritis of the right knee. Sk 1152 had moderate and large Schmorl's nodes on five of the seven vertebral bodies preserved, and signs of early degenerative change in the left elbow. Although these pathological conditions have complex aetiologies, they are often associated with an arduous lifestyle which involves heavy physical labour and indicates that those buried inside the cathedral were not unused to the rigours of life. This would be consistent with the well-developed muscul-ature observed in sk 1153.

Both showed virtually no evidence of infectious disease or trauma and the cause of their deaths must remain unknown. The relatively short stature and platymeria seen in sk 1153 may be indicative that this older male had suffered from malnutrition in his youth, but the remains were too incomplete for a definite diagnosis to be made.

4.4 HUMAN REMAINS FROM THE SURROUNDINGS OF THE CATHEDRAL
by J A Roberts

The skeleton (sk 2003) was located below the sloped ground to the east of the graveyard wall of the cathedral at a depth of 0.7m below the topsoil (see Section 2.6). It was orientated E–W, approximately 0.5m away from the cemetery wall and was lying supine with the right arm extended by the right side and the left arm loosely flexed across the pelvis. The preservation of the bones was good. The skeleton was fully articulated, but had been truncated just below the pelvis during the digging of the cable trench.

The skeleton was that of a 35–45 year old female of slender build, measuring approximately 156–158cm in height. Asymmetry of the upper limb bones suggest that she was right-handed.

There was little pathology present on the bones. The spine showed signs of mild degenerative change in the lower cervical and thoracic vertebrae and more severe arthritis affecting the fifth lumbar and first sacral vertebrae. There were also some associated arthritic

changes in the heads of ten of the ribs. The individual had suffered from mild sinusitis and had also incurred a traumatic injury to the right little finger. The teeth were in good condition suggesting a non-gritty, pos-sibly meat-based diet.

4.5 BOTANICAL ANALYSIS OF SOIL FROM THE PELVIC REGION OF SIX SKELETONS
by J J Miller

Dietary remains have occasionally been found in entire corpses (for example, Helbaek 1950; 1958; Holden and Núñez 1993) but the retrieval and verification of a faecal mass from a skeleton is much more problematic (Reinhard et al 1992). During recent renovations at Glasgow Cathedral, the discovery of several 14th–17th century-skeletons faced the excavators with just such a task. Samples were taken for analysis for dietary remains, but given the density of the medieval burial in the nave, there is a distinct possibility that the soil in the graves may derive from pre-existing burials.

Method

Following the methods described by Reinhard et al (1992) the excavators took three samples from each of the six skeletons found, namely the top and bottom of the pelvis and a control from the top of the bones; 200 ml volume was analysed where possible, and sieved in the usual manner through 500μm and 10μm sieves. Soil texture was described and the fragments observed by low power microscopy. The pelvic bottom sample, judged to be most likely to produce results (Reinhard et al 1992), was analysed first to see if comparative controls were required. All samples producing seeds

	sk 523 pb	sk 531 pb	con	sk 535 pt	pb	sk 551 bp	sk 545 pb	sk 571 pb	pt	con
Betula charcoal	–	1	–	–	–	–	–	–	–	-
Quercus charcoal	–	–	1	–	–	–	–	–	–	–
unident charcoal	ab	co	ra	ra	fq	co	ab	ra	ra	ra
Chenopodium album	–	–	–	–	1	–	–	–	–	–
Cyperaceae sp	–	1	–	–	–	–	–	–	–	-
Sambucus nigra/ racemosa	–	–	–	2	3	–	–	4	–	-
Juncus effusus/ conglomeratus	–	–	6	–	–	–	–	–	–	–
roots	ab	co	–	–	–	co	ra	–	–	–
Cenococcum geophilum	21	–	co	ra	fq	–	–	10	–	-
bone frag	sp	sp	sp	sp	sp	–	sp	sp	sp	–
fish bones	–	–	–	–	–	–	–	1	1	1
small snail shell	–	–	–	–	–	–	–	1	–	-
insect frag	–	–	ra	–	ra	–	–	3	–	-
tested for gut nematode oocysts	n/a	n/a	n/a	neg	neg	–	–	neg	neg	neg

FIGURE 4.24

Organic remains from the pelvis of six skeletons (quantification after Hubbard and Clapham 1992). Abbreviations: pb — pelvic bottom, pt — pelvic top, con — control, unid — unidentified, ab — abundant, co — common, fq — frequent, sp — sparse, ra — rare

sk	Soil texture
523 pb	Heavy, clay soil, gravel <20mm diameter, sand and sandstone prevalent. Much silt. Coal occasional, <2mm
531 pb	Gravel and sandy dry crumb. Gravel <10mm, coal occasional, <5mm
535 con	Very sandy, brown and silty soil. Gravel <10mm coal and slate occasional, <10mm
551 pb	Dry, sandy crumb texture. Small gravel, occasional coal and slate, <10mm
545 pb	Medium clay, with aggregate, sandstone, sand and silt
571 pb	Gravelly dry crumb. Gravel <15mm, rare coal
571 con	As for 571 pb, coal <5mm

FIGURE 4.25

Description of soils from colon samples. Abbreviations: pb — pelvic bottom, con — control

were tested for gut nematode parasite oocysts after Dainton (1987).

Results

Samples varied greatly, both in soil morphology and organic content. In all cases, charcoal and tiny cancellous bone fragments accounted for the major part of the organic material, with contamination roots prevalent in several. The results obtained are shown in Figures 4.24 and 4.25.

Discussion

Clearly the soil variation may have had a differential effect on the preservation of organic remains. Sandy soils tend to be poor preserving environments due to their open texture, while the anaerobic environment in heavy clay would be expected to retain more. Variation in the water content of the soil may explain the scarcity of organic remains, and the abundant roots in several samples implied contamination.

The only two skeletons found to have any remains of plants likely to have been consumed are sk 535 and sk 571. The species of seed found are as follows:

Chenopodium album (fat hen). One seed found in sk 535. This is often recovered from archaeological deposits (for example, Dimbleby 1975; Greig 1976). It has a nutritious leaf, rich in iron, calcium and vitamins B1 and C, as well as having seeds which are a good substitute or supplement to cereals in times of famine (Stuart 1989; Hedrick 1972). It has been discovered in the last meal of Tollund and Grauballe men (Helbaek 1950; 1958) and Lightfoot (1777, 149) states that 'in Isla I observed the people boiled and eat it as greens'. The species, however, is also an opportunist weed, frequently occurring on disturbed and enriched soils associated with human occupation (Stace 1991; Godwin 1975). Therefore accidental deposition cannot be ruled out, and as one seed certainly does not constitute a meal, such an arrival must be considered likely.

Sambucus nigra (elder) or *Sambucus racemosa* (red berried elder) were found in sk 535 (6 seeds) and sk 571 (4 seeds). The discrimination between *S nigra* and

sk	Length	Width	Description
535 pt	3.40mm	1.80mm	entire
	n/a	n/a	frag only
535 pb	3.60mm	1.80mm	entire
	3.00mm	1.90mm	entire
	3.10mm	1.50mm	entire
	n/a	n/a	frag
571 pb	3.80mm	2.00mm	entire
	3.60mm	1.90mm	entire
	4.00mm	2.00mm	split (measurements estimated)
	3.90mm	1.90mm	split (measurements estimated)

FIGURE 4.26

Sambuscus nigra/racemosa *seed sizes*

S racemosa is a difficult process, depending on size and widths of seeds (Fredskild 1978; Lempiäinen 1992). Sizes of seeds found on this site are outlined in Figure 4.26. Following Fredskild (1978) and Lempiäinen (1992) it appears that all seeds are larger than the mean size for *S racemosa*, and indeed some could only be *S nigra*. As *S racemosa* is introduced (Stace 1991) the seeds found are most probably *S nigra*.

S nigra is a vigorous species which is often found on disturbed and enriched soils around human occupation (Stace 1991). The berries and flowers are edible (Hedrick 1972) so that the fact that some seeds were broken could suggest mastication, but this is inconclusive. Similarly, the carbonised *Rumex* sp (dock) seed could have been ingested with cooked grains, as it is an arable and wasteland weed (Stace 1991). However it could just as easily have been mixed in with the tinder which produced the charcoal also recovered from this context.

The *Juncus effusus* (soft rush)/*conglomeratus* (compact rush) and Cyperaceae sp (sedge) seeds found are likely to have derived from the natural seed bank.

The two fish bones found in sk 571 are indicative of intestinal contents and are unlikely to have derived from the surrounding soil naturally. The discovery of another fish bone fragment in control (sk 571) would imply, however, contamination from a pre-existing burial, and introduction via the tunnelling behaviour of small mammals cannot be discounted. Further expert identification of the species of fish may help reduce speculation. The small snail shell found is likely to be a natural contamination.

No nematode gut parasite eggs were found in any of the samples tested.

Conclusion

The samples from the skeletons excavated from Glasgow Cathedral did not yield unequivocal evidence of dietary remains. Many had extensive root and charcoal contamination, and those which did contain seeds were inconclusive. The fish bones and broken seeds do suggest ingestion, but again, not definitely. The lack of nematode gut parasite eggs in seed-producing samples is only a further indication of an accidental deposition, and it is likely that the lack of roots in seed producing samples is coincidental. There was no definite evidence of internal remains in any of the samples tested.

4.6 INSECT FAUNA FROM WITHIN THE CRANIUM OF SKELETON 570
by P Buckland

Only one species was recovered from the cranium, 54 individuals of the so-called coffin beetle, *Rhizophagus parallelocollis* Gyll. This has been widely recorded from cemeteries in Europe (Horion 1960), and Megnin (1894), in a study of exhumed corpses, noted the beetle in large numbers on bodies two to three years old. There has been some doubt, however, over what the beetles feed upon. Palm (1959) assumed that they consumed the fatty substances of the corpse, while Horion (1960) and Koch (1989) considered the species a feeder upon fungi on the body or in the mouldy wood of the coffin. In a review of the available habitat data consequent upon fossil finds from an old forest fauna at Thorne, South Yorkshire, Buckland (1979) pointed out that the occurrence of the beetle in large numbers in the stone, lead-lined coffin of Archbishop Greenfield (d 1317) inside the Minster at York, seemed to preclude mouldy wood as the food source and suggested, as both Blair (1922) and Johnson (1962) had previously done, that the species was a predator on the numerous phorid, such as coffin flies, likely to be on the corpse. In York Minster it was associated with another predatory species tolerant of particularly foul conditions, the staphylinid *Quedius mesomelinus*. Peacock (1977), while quoting Buckland's then unpublished review (Buckland 1979), says that it remains unknown whether it fed upon the body, moulds or dipterous larvae. While also recorded under bark (Peacock 1977), *R parallelocollis* is essentially subterranean (Thompson 1995), and must once have been more widespread in foul compost and damp litter-rich soils. In urban deposits in York, Kenward notes it from deposits ranging from the Roman (Hall and Kenward 1990) to the Anglo-Scandinavian period (Kenward and Hall 1995), and it also appears in a 15th-century cess pit at Pluscarden Priory in Moray (Buckland 1995). As well as the unpublished record from York Minster, Girling (1981) records the beetle from the body of Abbot Dygon from St Augustine's Abbey in Canterbury, and notes that the examples discussed by Stafford (1971) came from the body of Ann Mowbray, who had died in 1481. The sealed nature of the burials of both Dygon and Greenfield caused both Girling (1981) and Buckland (1979) to suggest that the beetles had oviposited onto the bodies before interment and that they had maintained breeding populations inside the closed stone sarcophagi. The Glasgow fauna includes many teneral individuals, suggesting a breeding population on the corpse, but it contains no evidence for phorids or other Diptera, and the food source of the beetle remains uncertain. Medieval towns would have had abundant habitats to sustain *R parallelocollis*, and graveyards were probably one of the last urban refuges for the species, before it largely succumbed to more hygienic burial practices.

5

CONCLUDING DISCUSSION

S T Driscoll

The investigations described in the preceding chapters were the first large-scale excavations ever to have been undertaken in a Scottish cathedral. Their most important contribution has been to reveal the distinct architectural forms assumed by the cathedral over the course of the 12th century. We know now that three successive constructions occupied the same sacred space above the tomb of St Kentigern, but each was executed in a different architectural idiom. More importantly, dramatic increases in scale were documented. At the end of the 12th century the newly designed cathedral was more than double the size of its precursor, an increase which reflects the dramatic growth in the popularity of the cult of Kentigern and in the wealth of the diocese. Also important is the contribution to our understanding of the evolving use of the cathedral through new and detailed evidence of changing worship and burial practices through the late medieval and into the modern periods made by the excavations.

The solidity and purity of the existing 13th-century cathedral at Glasgow tends to obscure the complex development of the site and to make the subtle traces of the earlier building works seem relatively insignificant. The search for traces of the early cathedrals was one of the main objectives of the excavations. Reconsidering these early structures allows us to rethink how the cathedral fitted into the pre-existing ecclesiastical landscape of the middle Clyde. Recent work at Govan has reinforced the view that prior to the 12th century, the ecclesiastical centre of the district lay south of the river. The decline of Govan dovetails nicely with the rise of the cathedral (Driscoll 1998).

Probably the most surprising result of the excavations was the recovery of a wealth of architectural evidence relating to the pre 13th-century work. Substantial portions of the two cathedrals built succesively in the 12th century, including *in situ* remains of both the naves, were discovered. These and other remains allow the structural development of the cathedral to be traced over some 850 years.

Burial and worship

Eighty-seven burials and large quantities of disarticulated bones were excavated, largely from the nave. Although relatively few graves were present elsewhere, disarticulated human remains were encountered in all trenches. The analysis of these remains has made an important contribution to our understanding of the relationship between the cathedral and those who worshipped there. The two principal contributions of burial studies were, firstly, in charting the changes in burial practices from the 13th to the 19th century and, secondly, in providing baseline data for assessing population structure and health in medieval Glasgow and beyond.

The earliest religious activity on the site is a cemetery of simple dug graves, several of which are stratigraphically earlier than the earliest 12th-century cathedral building. Although the early burials were fragmentary they have provided two vital radiocarbon dates, which substantiate the existence of an early medieval Christian presence at Glasgow. The earliest dated burial was made between AD 677–860, which at the lower limit takes us to within a few generations of the historical Kentigern, and at the upper limit into the Viking Age. The burial establishes that there was indeed a Christian cemetery here during the early medieval period, which in turn adds some historical

FIGURE 5.1

Interior of Antwerp Cathedral *by Pieter van Neefs the Younger (1620–75) showing how the altars in the nave may have looked. Note the position of the grave markers in the floor pavement. Copyright Hunterian Art Gallery, University of Glasgow*

weight to the traditional veneration of Glasgow as the burial place of Kentigern.

From the 7th century, a cemetery around a holy tomb is likely to have been accompanied by a church (although no trace of one was discovered). The early burial ground at Glasgow appears to have been situated within a wider sacred lansdcape which included a holy well (now incorporated into the cathedral itself in the SW corner of the crypt). The Molendinar burn, as the bathing place of the saint, may also have formed part of this sacred landscape.

The other radiocarbon-dated burial was located near the north wall of Jocelin's nave where it was cut by the construction trench. It has been dated to AD 1169–1263, which seems to indicate that the individual was buried within the nave of John's cathedral. This is the earliest evidence of a tradition which was to become widespread following the completion of the new nave in the 13th century. Initially these nave burials appear somewhat disorganised, but as coffins become more common the disposition of the burials

becomes more formal. This formality was visible mostly in the three vaults or lairs recognised in the middle of the nave, where mortar spreads left from the 13th-century construction work allowed the grave cuts to be seen. In these deep, straight-sided shafts burials were repeatedly made in the same grave plot. The precision with which subsequent burials were located presumably indicates that the lairs were marked with inscribed slabs.

The creation of these lairs may be linked to the foundation of altars at the nave piers. John Durkan has gathered together a collection of data which gives a flavour of the considerable enthusiasm for these altars from the mid 15th century onwards (Durkan 1970). At the third pier on the north side of the nave an altar dedicated to St Manchan was founded and endowed in 1459 by the cathedral Chancellor, Patrick Leitch, who established a chaplaincy, preferentially granted to his kin, and supported by an income from property and rents. The altar itself was made of cut and polished stones. The creation of an associated family lair at such an altar would be the expected consequence of such a dedication. Corporate bodies also made endowments, for instance the Weaver's altar to St Severus/Serf at either the first or second pier on the north side. It is difficult to establish exactly who was being buried at these trades-corporation altars, but Patrick Elphinston, who in his will asked in 1507 to be buried on the north side of St Serf's altar, was probably a weaver. Durkan's evidence throws considerable light on how the altars and graves served as focal points for religious observance and for the display of social status. An impression of how the nave with its altars and paving of gravestones might have looked it is be found in 17th-century paintings of the interiors of Dutch cathedrals (Figure 5.1).

Patterns of burial shifted significantly after the Reformation. In the middle of the 17th century the W end of the nave was transformed into a separate parish church after which burial was restricted to the three eastern bays of the nave, where it continued through the 18th century. These late burials were always in coffins, which were sometimes embellished with elaborate fittings. A significant proportion of the bodies had been treated with lime at the time of burial and had consequently dissolved. By the 19th century, burial in the upper church was all but abandoned, but several under-used spaces elsewhere in areas not then used for worship (the treasury, the base of the NW tower and the lower church) were divided into burial lairs. In the crypt there was limited evidence of medieval burials near the tomb of St Kentigern. This is probably because in this period burial *ad sanctos* had been restricted to only the most worthy. It is hard, however, to be certain about medieval burials here because, essentially, most earlier features were removed in a series of 19th-century interventions: from around 1801 elaborate burials were made to the W of the tomb, while in 1898 MacGregor Chalmers dug trenches along the N and S sides of the tomb. One consolation is that some of the elaborate early 19th-century coffin furniture, which escaped MacGregor Chalmers, was well preserved and provides unique insights into the burial practices of the 19th-century Glasgow élite.

Two 12th-century cathedrals

Evidence for two distinct building campaigns was recovered below the nave. The *in situ* traces of John's cathedral make it clear that, with respect to position and orientation, the subsequent cathedrals were indebted to decisions made in the early 12th century. Since only the bottom courses of the W nave wall survive, it is impossible to say much about the plan of this building. Fortunately, in addition to this *in situ* masonry, significant architectural elements were re-used in later masonry. The most impressive were the half-column drums. These and the other fragments

suggest a Romanesque church of some ambition, featuring a reasonable array of sculpted architectural elements. At its dedication in 1136, John's cathedral may have been the most ambitious church in western Scotland.

The re-used column drums were found, along with fragments of moulded stone, in the remains of the nave of the second cathedral, started by Bishop Jocelin about 1181 and dedicated in 1197. A second set of remains included two E–W running walls which survive as foundations supporting the piers of the nave. Despite being made of old masonry, these walls were exceptionally well built, even below ground level. Jocelin's nave was never finished and shortly after the dedication, the programme for this second cathedral was abandoned, but not before establishing a precedent which has resulted in the most outstanding feature of the 13th-century cathedral: its crypt. On the N side of the nave the foundations were about 3m below floor level. The depth of these foundations would seem to confirm that the E end of Jocelin's cathedral was on two levels with a large crypt. The foundations tie in with the crypt where the only visible fabric of the second cathedral can be seen, in the SW corner of the lower church.

Our knowledge of the visual appearance of Jocelin's cathedral was poor prior to the excavations. The cutting of ducts for the new heating system through the foundations of the 13th-century cathedral released two dozen sculpted and painted stones. The painted stones are of particular importance: not only do they reveal the intellectual and cultural environment of the cathedral in the late 12th century, they also offer a vision of the interior. Although not enough of the painting survives to allow full reconstruction, it is clear that at least some parts of the cathedral were very brightly painted in complex polychrome designs and figurative scenes.

This new evidence indicates that decorative schemes of the two 12th-century cathedrals were more advanced than had been previously presumed. The half-columns suggest that John's church was built on an impressive scale requiring cylindrical piers in some places, while the richly-carved details and painting from Jocelin's church invite comparison with the other major Scottish transitional buildings at the abbeys of Jedburgh and Holyrood, and with Durham Cathedral. The cross-head was one of the rare discoveries of sculpted stone made in the nave. The two fragments join to form a distinctive disc-headed cross (Figure 5.2) which probably marked either an important burial or the boundary of the churchyard.

High medieval to post-medieval

The construction of the existing cathedral took most of the 13th century, and evidence for a prolonged building campaign was seen in the nave. The arcade

FIGURE 5.2

The 12th-century cross-head (sf 174)

footings showed three stages of building. The earliest being the incomplete walls of Jocelin's nave used to support the columns. This was supplemented with an extension of the foundations of the arcade in two phases, the latter phase beginning W of the fourth column, where there is evidence for what was probably a temporary W front of timber, supported in socketed stones set in a raft of dry-stone work. There was no substantial evidence for later medieval construction work in the nave, despite reported repairs in the 14th and 15th centuries.

Major new building work did not take place until after the Reformation, when the interior was substantially remodelled to accommodate the reformed worship and the ecclesiastical needs of the growing 17th-century burgh. A massive partition wall was erected to create a parish church in the W bays of the nave about 1659, but was not carried all the way to the roof until 1713. The main partition wall was tied into the third column from the crossing and served as the E wall of the Outer High Kirk. A number of smaller walls, which presumably served as footings for the internal partitions and as supports for the galleries were also present. A few of the masonry features on the north side of the nave between the fourth and fifth columns seem to have served as footings for the other elements such as the pulpit and communion table. These footings provide the evidence for the tentative reconstruction of the internal plan of the Kirk, which is otherwise unknown.

Finds

Apart from the architectural discoveries the number of finds was not large and there was very little which could not be attributed directly to burial activity. The principal exception was a hoard, consisting of two massive bronze mortars and a large iron pestle, recovered from a pit in the crypt. The two mortars are of similar design and size but differ in detail. The smaller bears a cast inscription which links it to a William Wishart, either the bishop of Glasgow (1270–72), or more likely his namesake and younger contemporary, the archdeacon of Teviotdale (c1273–c1319). The larger mortar is nearly identical to a mortar discovered in nearby Bell Street at the former site of the Dominican Friary (Anderson 1879), perhaps suggesting that they were made locally. The pestle was made, unusually, of wrought iron and is especially notable for having been found in association with a mortar.

Mortars of this large size are very unusual and their interpretation is somewhat problematic. There were no residues within the vessels, and thus no direct evidence survives as to their function. The inscription and, above all, the manner of their deposition suggest, however, that their use was liturgical, probably for the preparation of incense. The mortars were carefully placed below the floor of the crypt, on the north side of the Lady Chapel. It is hard to imagine any motive other than safe-keeping. The burning of incense had no place in the reformed worship and liturgical items such as these would undoubtedly have been the object of public hostility if left unprotected. The exceptional size of the mortars, significantly larger than most other surviving mortars from the period, may be accounted for by the great quantities of incense which were apparently required in the cathedral on important feast days.

The other noteworthy find was a late 13th-century bronze seal-matrix recovered from one of the nave lairs. From its stratigraphic position it could have accompanied the earliest burial in the fourth bay on the N between the altars of St Manchan and Corpus Christi. The shield-shaped seal carries the arms of 'Adem Le Portier', which feature a castle surmounted by a pair of birds with fleurs-de-lis. The seal is equipped with a suspension loop, which may indicate that this was a badge of office, rather than a personal seal.

Wider implications

Because of its unique crypt and its remarkable good fortune in having come down to the modern age largely intact, Glasgow Cathedral has been widely recognised as one of Scotland's architectural treasures. The extensive modern excavations have further set Glasgow apart from the other Scottish cathedrals, none of which have been excavated on a large scale. The results of these excavations have, if anything, enhanced the cathedral's 'completeness' in so far as they have shed light upon the site's origins and 12th-century development.

The evidence for the pre 12th-century activity should be seen in the context of other churches in this area, in particular Govan. The earliest Christian burials at Govan have been radiocarbon dated to the 5th and 6th centuries (GU 9024 and 9025). The quality and quantity of the 10th- and 11th-century sculpture from Govan is strong evidence for regarding it as the principal religious centre on this stretch of the Clyde at the time of the foundation of the cathedral by David I. Although the discovery of a possible cemetery at Glasgow which might go back to the 7th century is a welcome confirmation of the antiquity of the site as a religious focus, no evidence was discovered which could be used to challenge Govan's claim to superiority. Admittedly the excavations were small in comparison to the size of the church and certainly foundations that have comfortably consumed two other churches could easily contain a collection of early sculpture equal to Govan's. But no trace of early medieval sculpture has ever been found at the cathedral site. This rather suggests that prior to its elevation by David I to the seat of a diocese, Glasgow was a church of relatively local significance.

The elevation of Glasgow was clearly a political act which sought to establish a new religious authority. The importance of this enterprise in the 12th–13th century can be measured by the scale of the architectural effort, as reflected by the rapid sequence of three cathedrals; the earliest extravagantly replaced as the diocese and cult grew in importance. The archaeological evidence reveals the quality and scale of the discarded predecessors. This rapid growth, which saw the size of the cathedral more than double in the course of 150 years, coincided with the period in which Glasgow emerged as one of Scotland's major religious and administrative institutions. In this respect, given that the see was established by royal initiative and that the bishops of Glasgow were dependable ministers of the Crown, the sequence of cathedrals can be read as a triumph of Scottish state building.

The cathedral served as the burgh church and much of the evidence from the 13th century onwards relates to the use of the church by the community, particularly as a privileged place of burial. These changing burial practices carry with them significant social and liturgical implications which cannot be elaborated upon here. The most substantial community influence was to seize control of the church building and remodel it for Presbyterian worship. In the nave this transformation involved both major building and a reorganisation of the burial regime. The most recent archaeological evidence documents the reclamation of the church by the state, its restoration to its medieval configuration and its transformation into an historical monument. The elaborate final-phase burials of the 19th century underscore this transformation into a focus of civic pride.

THE RADIOCARBON DATES
by S T Driscoll

There were not many suitable samples; those analysed were selected on the basis of their stratigraphic position (Figure 1). The two samples from phase 1 consisted of human bone from a grave and charcoal from a hearth. The hearth 359 was cut into the subsoil at the W end of the nave and represented the earliest feature in this area, probably the earliest on the site. In theory it could have been of prehistoric date. Stratigraphically it certainly predated any of the buildings and the burial within the nave. The burial 455 was the earliest grave encountered, in stratigraphic terms. The grave had been partially cut away by the construction of the wall, which was interpreted as the W wall of John's Cathedral, consecrated in 1136 (phase 2).

The third sample also consisted of bone from a burial (462) which was early. The grave was well stratified 2m below the existing floor level. Unfortunately on stratigraphic grounds alone, it was not possible to determine whether the burial belonged to phase 1 or 2. The grave was selected because it had a

direct stratigraphic link with the phase 3 building work. It had been disturbed by the construction of the deep wall interpreted as the N wall of Jocelin's nave, which was built between 1181 and c1200.

The radiocarbon date-ranges for the samples from the earliest burial (455) and the hearth 359 almost certainly predate the documented construction programmes of the 12th century. At a 95% level of confidence, the samples can be said to predate the building by between one to five centuries. This not only confirms the approximate chronology and interpretation of the earliest masonry discovered, but it is the strongest physical evidence for the existence of an Early Christian presence in Glasgow. The earliest likely age for the burial implies the existence of a cemetery, and presumably a church, within a couple of generations of Kentigern's death (c614).

The other burial (462) is significantly later than the other dates. Minimally burial 462 was made 150 years later than the early one (455). The burial 462, however, could equally have been made before any of the historically attested building work began. In theory, the burial could have been made within the nave of the

Lab No.	Phase/Context/Material	Radiocarbon age in years	Cal age one sigma (68.2 % confidence)	Cal age two sigma (95.4 % confidence)
Kentigern's obit, c614				
GU-4746	Ph1/455/bone	1250 ± 60 BP	AD 677–860	AD 660–890
GU-7301	Ph1/359/charcoal	1160 ± 90 BP	AD 772–980	AD 670–1020
Phase 2 — Dedication of John's cathedral, 1136				
GU-4747	Ph2/462/bone	820 ± 50 BP	AD 1169–1263	AD 1047–1280
Phase 3 — Construction of Jocelin's cathedral, 1181 — c1200				

FIGURE 1

Radiocarbon age estimates

first cathedral (dedicated in 1136), but cannot be demonstrated stratigraphically that it was part of the cemetery which predated the 12th-century building work.

PLASTERWORK
by S Bain

Catalogue

Each of the following entries is headed by the phase, area, context and small find number (sf).

4 CE (129) sf 279
5 fragments of painted plaster, with traces of red, black and mustard paint.

4 CE (129) sf 54
5 fragments of painted plaster in red and green.

4–5 CE (110) sf 207
Plaster with red paint.

4–5 CE (111) sf 292
Moulded plaster in a linear design on a stone fragment.

4–5 CE (139) sf 77
Fragment of painted plaster. 29 x 28x 12mm.

6 NN (322) sf 90
6 fragments from a linear motif, including 2 frag from a half-column (30mm diameter); 1 frag from a fluted design (115 x 80 x 35mm); 1 frag of simple linear design, perhaps from cornice (130 x 75 x 40mm).

6 NN (322) sf 391
3 small unpainted plaster fragments.

7 NN (316) sf 81
2 fragments from a sub-circular detail comprising 5 concentric rings forming a raised border.

7 NN (316) sf 94
Plaster circular architectural detail.

7 NN (324) sf 390
2 fragments of ornamental plaster with raised decoration.

7 NS (524) sf 102
Painted plaster fragment.

8 CE (105) sf 197
Plaster with red paint.

8 CH (002) sf 1
Plaster fleur-de-lis. 92 x 64 x 27mm (Figure 3.47).

8 CH (002) sf 24
3 pieces of plaster: 1 with traces of floral (?) carving. 67 x 31 x 25mm (largest).

8 CH (002) sf 26
Curving fragment of unworked plaster, perhaps for capital. 128 x 54 x 6mm.

8 NN (302) sf 89
Plaster circular architectural detail.

8 NN (302) sf 393
Fragment of plaster.

8 NN (302) sf 394
Gypsum on rough plaster with wood impression.

8 NN (302) sf 396, sf 428, sf 453
3 fragments of ornamental plaster.

8 NN (302) sf 689
Fragments of plaster on stone.

8 NS (501) sf 451
Ornamental plaster fragment.

MORTAR ANALYSIS
by S Bain

Catalogue

Phase 2

1 NN (368) Sample 20
Sample from the W wall front of the cathedral dedicated in 1136. The mortar is pale brown (10YR 6/3) with a visibly gritty texture; there were visible flecks of charcoal (max 7mm). The aggregate consisted mainly of sand of predominantly fine sub-rounded quartzite particles and occasional rounded sandstone pebbles. The mortar was still quite firm and was bonded to a cream sandstone.

2 NS (589) Sample 16
Sample from the W wall front of the cathedral dedicated in 1136 consisting of two distinct mortars, perhaps reflecting a repair or batch change. One type was essentially the same as sample 20 with a darker patch of sand. The second type was a finer texture with a lower sand content and was very pale brown (10YR 7/3) in appearance with only occasional charcoal flecks (max 2mm). The aggregate consisted mainly of rounded, fine-particle sized sand and sub-rounded small pebbles (max 4mm).

Phase 3

3 NN (303a) Sample 18
Sample from the N wall of the unfinished late-12th-century nave. The mortar was pale brown (10YR 6/3) and appeared to have lost most of its adhesive properties and was crumbly to the touch. The aggregate consisted mainly of fine particle sized sand with occasional quartzite pieces, occasional sub-rounded sandstone pebbles (max 15mm) and occasional pieces of shale. Shale can be added along with slaked lime to cements and mortars to give a semi-hydraulic cement. There also appeared to be flecks of burnt clay within the mortar.

4 NS (607) Sample 23
Sample from the corresponding S wall of the 12th-century nave. The mortar appeared to be the same as sample 18.

Phase 4

5 NN (325) Sample 4
Sample from a mortar spread abutting wall 303 in the nave and relating to the construction of the 13th-century cathedral. This sample is cream in colour (10YR 8/3) with a very distinctive mottled appearance caused by the large number of inclusions, including charcoal (17mm), rounded pebbles and burnt clay. The mortar was very firm and had a gritty texture. There was a moderate amount of rounded quartzite particles.

6 CH (005) Sample 26
Sample from the vaulting of the crypt. The mortar was pale brown (10YR 6/3) in appearance with a moderate amount of small charcoal flecks. The aggregate was of coarse sand with visible pink/brown, opaque quartzite grains with shell fragments.

7 CE (128) Sample 28
Sample from an early-13th-century context in the crypt. The mortar was still firm and appeared to be quite homogenous in texture and colour. The mortar was light yellowish brown (10YR 6/4) with sub-angular quartzite sand particles with occasional charcoal fleck.

8 CE (130) Sample 27
Sample from an early-13th-century context in the crypt. The mortar was slightly soft and crumbly to the touch. The mortar was very pale brown (10YR 7/3) in appearance with a moderate amount of fine charcoal flecks. The aggregate was composed of sub-rounded opaque brown quartzite sand containing fragments of sea shell and sub-angular pebbles (20mm).

Phase 5

9 NN (320) Sample 3
Sample from a mortar spread cut by wall 328 and may relate to the construction of the 13th-century cathedral. The mortar was very banded in appearance with bands of coarser and finer mortars. Overall it was light grey (10YR 7/2) in appearance and was composed of rounded pebbles (10mm) and had visible charcoal inclusions up to 7mm.

10 NN (328) Samples 17 and 19
Sample from wall 328, a later-13th-century construction. The mortar was light yellowish brown (10YR 6/4) in appearance because of a yellow ochre within the mortar mix. The aggregate was composed of quartzite sand with larger sub-angular sandstone pebbles (15mm) and very occasional pieces of shale. This mortar is similar to sample 21.

11 NS (606b) Sample 21
Sample from a later-13th-century construction. The mortar was light yellowish brown (10YR 6/4) in appearance because of a yellow ochre within the mortar mix. The aggregate was composed of sub-rounded quartzite sand with visible shell fragments and very occasional angular pebbles. This sample is similar to samples 17 and 19.

Phase 7

12 NN (307) Sample 25
Sample from a post-Reformation dividing wall. The mortar is a very pale yellowish brown (10YR 7/4) with a uniformly flecked appearance caused by small pieces of charcoal, burnt clay and perhaps iron sulphide.

13 NS (508) Sample 24
Sample from a post-Reformation dividing wall. The mortar is a very pale yellowish brown (10YR 7/4) with a uniformly flecked appearance caused by small pieces of charcoal, burnt clay and perhaps iron sulphide.

14 NN (315) Sample 22
Sample from a post-Reformation dividing wall The mortar is a very pale brown (10YR 7/3) with occasional small pieces of charcoal (3mm). The aggregate is composed of medium textured sand with a moderate quartzite content.

15 CW (201) Sample 30
Sample from a post-Reformation feature in the crypt. The mortar is cream (10YR 8/3) with flecks of charcoal and shell visible to the naked eye. The aggregate is composed of medium textured sand with a moderate quartzite content.

BIBLIOGRAPHY

ABBREVIATIONS

American J Anthropol: American Journal of Anthropology

BAR Brit Ser: Bristish Archaeological Reports British Series

BAR Int Ser: Bristish Archaeological Reports International Series

Brit Archaeol Ass Trans: British Archaeological Association Transactions

CBA: Council for British Archaeology

CBA Res Rep: Council for British Archaeology Research Report

Archaeol J: Archaeological Journal

Int J Osteoarchaeol: International Journal of Osteoarchaeology

J Archaeol Science: Journal of Archaeological Science

J Brit Archaeol Ass: Journal of the British Archaeological Association

J Forensic Sciences: Journal of Forensic Sciences

Archaeol Soc: Archaeological Society

Medieval Archaeol: Medieval Archaeology

Proc Royal Philosophical Soc Glasgow: Proceedings of the Royal Philosophical Society of Glasgow

Proc Soc Antiq Scot: Proceedings of the Society of Antiquaries of Scotland

Soc Antiq Scot Monogr Ser: Society of Antiquaries of Scotland Monograph Series

Trans Ayrshire Archaeol Nat Hist Soc: Transactions of the Ayrshire Archaeological and Natural History Society

Trans Dumfriesshire Galloway Natur Hist Antiq Soc: Transactions of the Dumfriesshire and Galloway Natural History Antiquaries Society

REFERENCES

Alexander, P and Binski, P, 1987 *Age of Chivalry. Art in Plantagenet England 1200–1400,* London

Allen, J R, 1903 *The Early Christian Monuments of Scotland*, Edinburgh

Anderson, J, 1879 'Notices of a mortar and lion figure of brass dug up in Bell Street, Glasgow, and of six lion-shaped ewers of brass the manilia of the Middle Ages, exhibited at the meeting', *Proc Soc Antiq Scot* 13 (1878–79), 48–66

Apley, A G, and Solomon, L, 1988 *Concise System of Orthopaedics and Fractures,* Oxford

Ash, M, 1990 'The Church in the reign of Alexander III', in N H Reid *Scotland in the Reign of Alexander III 1249–1286*, 31–52, Edinburgh

Bailey, T, 1971 *Of Sarum and the Western Church*, Toronto

Barrow, G W S, 1996 *King David I and the Church of Glasgow,* Glasgow

Barrow, G W S (ed), 1999 *The Charters of King David I*, Woodbridge, Suffolk

Bass, W M, 1987 *Human Osteology: a Laboratory and Field Manual*, Missouri

Black, G F, 1946 *The Surnames of Scotland*, New York

Blair, K G, 1922 'Notes on the life history of *Rhizophagus parallelocollis* Gyll.', *Entomologist's Monthly Magazine* 58, 80–83

Bowen, E G, 1969 *Saints, Seaways and Settlements,* Cardiff

Boyd, W E, 1988 'Cereals in Scottish antiquity', *Circaea* 5(2), 101–110

Breviarum Aberdonense, 1510, Edinburgh (reprinted 1854, Spalding and Maitland Clubs)

Bridges, P S, 1993 'The effect of variation in methodology on the outcome of osteoarthritic studies', *Int J Osteoarchaeol* 3, 289–295

Bridges, P S, 1994 'Vertebral arthritis and physical activities in the prehistoric southeastern United States', *American J Physical Anthropol* 93, 83–93

Brodrick, A, 1993 'Painting techniques of early medieval sculpture', in *Romanesque: Stone Sculpture from Medieval England* (catalogue of an exhibition at Leeds, 1993), 18–27, Leeds

Brooks, C, 1980 'Medieval pottery from the kiln site at Clouston, E Lothian', *Proc Soc Antiq Scot*, 110, 364–403

Brothwell, D R, 1981 *Digging up Bones*, Oxford

Buckland, P C, 1979 *Thorne Moors: a Palaeoecological Study of a Bronze Age Site (a Contribution to the History of the British Insect Fauna)*, University of Birmingham Dept of Geography Occasional Paper 8, Birmingham

Buckland, P C, 1995 'A beetle fauna from the organic deposit F23 in the stone-lined pit (F22)', in F McCormick 'Excavation at Pluscarden Priory, Moray', *Proc Soc Antiq Scot* 124, 417–418

Burgh Records: *Extracts from the Records of the Burgh of Glasgow AD 1573–(1833)*, Scottish Burgh Records Soc, 31 vols, 1876–1916

Caldwell, D H and Dean, V, 1992 'The pottery industry at Throsk, Stirlingshire, in the 17th and early 18th century', *Post-Medieval Archaeology* 26, 1–46

Cameron, N M, 1986 'The painted Romanesque voussoir in Glasgow Cathedral', *J Brit Archaeol Ass* 139, 40–44

Cameron, N M, 1989 'A Romanesque cross-head in St Machar's Cathedral, Aberdeen', *J Brit Archaeol Ass* 142, 63–66

Cardy, A, 1997 'The Human bones', in P Hill (ed) *Whithorn and St Ninian: the Excavation of a Monastic Town, 1984–91*, 516–562, Stroud

Catalogue 1975 *The Secular Spirit: Life and Art at the End of the Middle Ages*, Metropolitan Museum of Art Exhibition, New York

Cather, S and Howard, H, 1994 'Romanesque wall painting in the apse of St Gabriel's Chapel, Canterbury Cathedral: their technique, condition and environment reassessed', in *Forschungsprojekt Wandmalerei-Schäden* (Arbeitshefte zur Denkmalpflege in Niedersachsen, 11) 141–156, Hanover

Chalmers, P M, 1905 'A thirteenth-century tomb in Glasgow Cathedral', *Proc Royal Philosophical Soc Glasgow* 36, 184–189

Chalmers, P M, 1914 *The Cathedral Church of Glasgow. A Description of its Fabric and a Brief History of the Archi-episcopal see*, Bell's Cathedral Series, London

Clouston, R W M, 1949 'The church bells of Ayrshire', *Trans Ayrshire Archaeol Nat Hist Soc* 2nd ser 1 (1947–49), 200–260

Cocke, T, Findlay, D, Halsey, R and Williamson, E, 1996 *Recording a Church: an Illustrated Glossary*, CBA Practical Handbook in Archaeology, London

Collie, J, 1835 *Plans, Elevations, Sections and Views of the Cathedral of Glasgow*, London

Craig, D, 1991 'The sculptured stones from Hoddom 1991', *Trans Dumfriesshire Galloway Natur Hist Antiq Soc* 66, 27–35

Craig, G Y (ed), 1991 *Geology of Scotland*, London

Craigie, W A, 1931 *Dictionary of the Older Scottish Tongue from the Twelfth Century to the end of the Seventeenth*, Oxford

Cramp, R, 1984 *Corpus of Anglo-Saxon Stone Sculpture, 1. Durham and Northumberland*, Oxford

Cronyn, J M, 1989 *The Elements of Archaeological Conservation*, London

Cross, J F and Bruce, M F, 1989 'The skeletal remains', in J A Stones (ed) *Three Scottish Carmelite Friaries: Excavations at Aberdeen, Linlithgow and Perth Edinburgh*, Soc Antiq Scot Monogr Ser 6, 119–141, Edinburgh

Cruden, S, 1986 *Scottish Medieval Churches*, Edinburgh

Dainton, M, 1987 'A quick, semi-quantitative method for recording nematode gut parasite eggs from archaeological deposits', *Circaea* 9, 58–63

Davey, P J, 1992 'Dutch clay tobacco pipes from Scotland', in D Gaimster and M Redknap (eds) *Everyday and Exotic Pottery from Europe: Studies in Honour of John G Hurst*, 279–289, Oxford

Davidson, A N, 1938 *The Cathedral Church of St Mungo: a Short History and Guide with Illustrations*, Glasgow (revised *c*1960)

Dickson, J H, 1993 'The yew tree (*Taxus baccata* L) in Scotland; native or early introduction or both?', *Dissertationes Botanicae* 196, 293–304

Dimbleby, G W, 1975 'The seeds', in C Platt and R Coleman-Smith (eds) *Excavation in Medieval Southampton, 1963–69*, vol 2, 344–349, Leicester

Dowden, J, 1899 'Inventory of the ornaments, jewels, relicks, vestments, service-books, etc. belonging to the Cathedral Church of Glasgow in 1432, illustrated from various sources and more particularly from the inventories of the Cathedral of Aberdeen', *Proc Soc Antiq Scot* 33 (1898–99), 280–329

Dowden, J, 1908 'The bishops of Glasgow', *Scottish History Review* 5, 76–88, 202–213, 319–331, 447–458

Dowden, J, 1910 *The Medieval Church in Scotland: its Constitution, Organisation and Law*, Glasgow

Dowden, J, 1912 *The Bishops of Scotland*, (ed J Maitland Thomson), Glasgow

Driscoll, S T, 1993 'Glasgow Cathedral Excavations, 1992–1993', *Glasgow Archaeol J* 19, 63–76

Driscoll, S T, 1998 'Church archaeology in Glasgow and the kingdom of Strathclyde', *Innes Review* 49, 95–114

Düco, D H, 1981 'The clay tobacco pipe in seventeenth century Netherlands', in P Davey (ed) *The Archaeology of the Clay Tobacco Pipe, V. Europe 2*, BAR Int Ser 106, 118–468, Oxford

Duffy, E, 1992 *The Stripping of the Altars. Traditional Religion in England c1400–1580*, London

Duncan, A A M, 1998 'St Kentigern at Glasgow in the twelfth century', in R Fawcett (ed) *Medieval Art and Architecture in the Diocese of Glasgow*, Brit Archaeol Ass Trans 20, Leeds, 9–24

Durkan, J, 1970 'Some notes on Glasgow Cathedral', *Innes Review* 21, 46–76

Durkan, J, 1986a 'The Bishops' Barony of Glasgow in Pre-Reformation times', *Records of the Scottish Church History Society* 22, 277–301

Durkan, J, 1986b *The Precinct of Glasgow Cathedral*, Glasgow

Durkan, J, 1998 'Cadder and environs, and the development of the Church in Glasgow in the twelfth century', *Innes Review* 49, 127–142

Durkan, J, 1999 'Glasgow Diocese and the claims of York', *Innes Review* 50.2, 89–101

Edgar, A, 1886 *Old Church Life in Scotland*, Paisley

Eyre-Todd, G, 1890 'The old arrangements of the Glasgow Cathedral', *Trans Glasgow Archaeol Soc* n ser 1 (1885–90), 477–497

Eyre-Todd, G (ed), 1898 *The Book of Glasgow Cathedral*, Glasgow

Fawcett, R, 1985a *Glasgow Cathedral*, Edinburgh

Fawcett, R, 1985b *Scottish Medieval Churches: an Introduction to the Ecclesiastical Architecture of the 12th to the 16th Centuries in the Care of the Secretary of State for Scotland*, Edinburgh

Fawcett, R, 1985c 'The Blackadder Aisle at Glasgow Cathedral: a reconsideration of the architectural evidence for its date', *Proc Soc Antiq Scot* 115, 227–295

Fawcett, R, 1988 'Kirkwall Cathedral: an architectural analysis', in B E Crawford (ed) *St Magnus Cathedral and Orkney's Twelfth-Century Renaissance*, 88–110, Aberdeen

Fawcett, R, 1990a 'Glasgow Cathedral', in E Williams, A Riches and M Higgs (eds) *The Buildings of Scotland. Glasgow*, 108–136, London

Fawcett, R, 1990b 'Ecclesiastical Architecture in the second half of the thirteenth century', in N Reid (ed) *Scotland in the Reign of Alexander III 1249–1286*, 148–181, Edinburgh

Fawcett, R 1994a *The Architectural History of Scotland: Scottish Architecture from the Accession of the Stewardts to the Reformation 1371–1560,* Edinburgh

Fawcett, R, 1994b *Scottish Abbeys and Priories*, London

Fawcett, R, 1995 'The architectural development of the Abbey Church', in J H Lewis and G J Ewart *Jedburgh Abbey: the Archaeology and Architecture of a Border Abbey*, Soc Antiq Scot Monogr Ser 10, 159–174, Edinburgh

Fawcett, R, 1996 'Current thinking on Glasgow Cathedral', in T Tatton-Brown and J Munby (eds) *The Archaeology of Cathedrals*, Oxford University Committee for Archaeology Monograph 42, 57–72, Oxford

Fawcett, R, 1997 *Scottish Cathedrals*, London

Fawcett, R (ed), 1998 *Medieval Art and Architecture in the Diocese of Glasgow*, Brit Archaeol Ass Trans 20, Leeds

Fernie, E, 1983 *The Architecture of the Anglo-Saxons*, London

Finnegan, M. 1978 'Non-metric variation of the infra-cranial skeleton', *Journal of Anatomy* 125, 23–27

Forbes, A P, 1874 *The Lives of S Ninian and S Kentigern Compiled in the Twelfth Century*, Edinburgh

Forrester, D M and Brown, J C, 1987 (3rd ed) *The Radiology of Joint Disease*, Philadelphia and London

Fredskild, B, 1978 'Seeds and fruits from the Neolithic settlement at Weier, Switzerland', *Botanisk Tidsskrift* 72, 189–201

Frere, W H, 1898 *The Use of Sarum, 1. The Sarum Customs as Set Forth in the Consuetudinary and Customary*, Cambridge

Gallagher, D B, 1984 'Scottish three letter basal stamps', *Society for Clay Pipe Research Newsletter* 3 (July 1984), 9–11

Gallagher, D B, 1987 'Tobacco pipemaking in Glasgow, 1667–1967', in P Davey (ed) *The Archaeology of the Clay Tobacco Pipe, X. Scotland*, BAR Int Ser 178, 35–109, Oxford

Gallagher, D B and Harrison, J, 1995 'Tobacco pipemakers in seventeenth century Stirling', *Proc Soc Antiq Scot* 125, 1131–1142

Gardner, R, 1998 '«Something contrary to sound doctrine and Catholic faith»: a new look at the Herbertian fragment of the Life of St Kentigern', *Innes Review* 49, 115–126

Garton, T, 1987 'The transitional sculpture of Jedburgh Abbey', in N Stratford (ed) *Romanesque and Gothic: Essays for George Zarnecki*, Woodbridge, 69–81

Gilbert, B M, and McKern, T W, 1973 'A method for aging the female os pubis', *American J Physical Anthropol* 38, 31–38

Girling, M A, 1981 'Beetle Remains', in J C Thorn 'The Burial of John Dygon, Abbot of St Augustine's', in A Detsicas (ed) *Collectanea Historica: Essays in memory of Stuart Rigold*, Kent Archaeol Soc, 82–84, Maidstone

Glasgow *Registrum: Registrum episcopatus Glasguensis*, 1843, (ed C Innes), 2 vols, Maitland Club, Edinburgh

Godwin H, 1975 *History of the British Flora*, Cambridge

Goodman, A H, 1991 'Stress, adaptation, and enamel developmental defects', in D J Ortner and A C Aufderheide (eds) *Human Paleopathology: Current Syntheses and Future Options*, 280–287, Washington DC

Gordon, A, 1980 'Excavation in the Lower Church of Glasgow Cathedral', *Glasgow Archaeol J* 7, 85–96

Gordon, A, 1984 *Death is for the Living*, Edinburgh

Gordon, J F S (ed), 1866 *Glasghu Facies I,* Glasgow

Grauer, A L, 1991 'Patterns of life and death: the palaeodemography of medieval York', in H Bush and M Zvelebil (eds) *Health in Past Societies: Biocultural Interpretations of Human Skeletal Remains in Archaeological Contexts,* BAR Int Ser 567, 67–80, Oxford

Grauer, A L, 1993 'Patterns of anemia and infection from Medieval York, England', *American J Physical Anthropol* 91, 203–213

Greig J R A, 1976 'The plant remains', in P C Buckland (ed) *The Environmental Evidence from the Church Street Roman Sewer System,* The Archaeology of York 14.1, 23–28

Haggarty, G, 1984 'Observations on the ceramic material from Phase I pits BY and AQ', in C Tabraham 'Excavations at Kelso Abbey', *Proc Soc Antiq Scot* 114, 10

Hall, A R and Kenward, H K, 1990 *Environmental Evidence from the Colonia,* The Archaeology of York 14.6, London

Halsey, R, 1980 'The Galilee Chapel', in N Coldstream and P Draper (eds) *Medieval Art and Architecture at Durham Cathedral,* Brit Archaeol Ass Trans 3, 59–73, Leeds

Hamilton, D N H, 1981 *The Healers: A History of Medicine in Scotland,* Edinburgh

Hammond, P W, 1993 *Food and Feast in Medieval England,* Dover

Hardwick, J L, 1960 'The incidence and distribution of caries throughout the ages in relation to the Englishman's diet', *British Dental J* 108, 9–17

Harrison, R K, 1987 'Geology, petrology and geochemistry of Ailsa Craig, Ayrshire', *British Geological Survey Report* 16.9, London

Harvey, P D A and McGuinness A, 1996 *A Guide to British Medieval Seals,* London

Hawthorne, J G and Smith, C S (eds), 1979 *Theophilus. On Divers Arts,* New York

Hay, G, 1957 *The Architecture of Scottish Post-Reformation Churches 1560–1843,* Oxford

Hedrick, U P, 1972 *Sturtevant's Edible Plants of the World,* Dover

Helbaek, H, 1950 'Botanical study of the stomach contents of Tollund man', *Aarboger for Nordisk Oldkyndighed og Historie,* 329–341

Helbaek, H, 1958 'Grauballemandens sidste Maltid', *Kuml,* 83–116

Hillson, S, 1986 *Teeth,* Cambridge

Hoffmann-Axthelm, W, 1981 *History of Dentistry* (transl H M Koehler), Chicago

Holden, T G and Núñez L, 1993 'An analysis of the gut contents of five well-preserved human bodies from Tarapaca, Northern Chile', *J Archaeol Science* 20, 595–612

Honeyman, J , 1898 'The Cathedral Church', in G Eyre-Todd (ed) *The Book of Glasgow Cathedral,* 226–274, Glasgow

Horion, A, 1960 *Faunistik der Mitteleuropäischen Käfer, 7. Clavicornia, Sphaeritidae — Phalacridae,* Uberlingen-Bodensee

Howard, H, 1988 *Blue Pigments in English Medieval Wall Painting,* unpublished dissertation, Conservation of Wall Painting Department, Courtauld Institute of Art

Howard, H, 1990 '«Blue» in the Lewes Group', in S Cather, D Park and P Williamson (eds) *Early Medieval Wall Painting and Painted Sculpture in England,* BAR Brit Ser 216, Oxford, 195–199

Howard, H, 1991 *Cormac's Chapel, Cashel: Analysis of Paint Samples,* unpublished report

Howard, H, 1992 All *Saints' Church Witley, Surrey: Scientific Examination of the Romanesque Wall Paintings,* unpublished report

Howard, H, 1995 'Techniques of the Romanesque and Gothic wall paintings in the Holy Sepulchre Chapel, Winchester Cathedral', in A Wallert, E Hermens and M Peek (eds) *Historical Painting Techniques, Materials, and Studio Practice* (preprints of a symposium at the University of Leiden, June 1995), 91–104, Los Angeles

Howard, H, 1998 *Glasgow Cathedral: Scientific Examination of the Romanesque Wall Painting Fragments Excavated from the Crypt,* unpublished report

Howard, H and Gasol, R, 1996 'Scientific examination of the "Losinga Cycle" of Romanesque wall paintings in Norwich Cathedral', *Technologia Artis* 4, 19–24

Howard, H and Park, D (forthcoming) 'The painted wall plaster', in forthcoming report on the excavations at Sherborne Abbey

Hubbard, R N L B and Clapham, A, 1992 'Quantifying macroscopic plant remains', *Review of Paleobotany and Palynology* 73, 117–132

Jennings, S, 1982 *Eighteen Centuries of Pottery from Norwich,* East Anglian Archaeology 13, Norwich

Isçan, M Y, Loth, S R, and Wright, R K, 1984 'Age determination from the rib by phase analysis: white males', *J Forensic Sciences* 29, 1094–1104

Isçan, M Y, Loth, S R, and Wright, R K, 1985 'Age determination from the rib by phase analysis: white females', *J Forensic Sciences* 30, 853–863

Jackson, K H, 1958 'Sources for the life of Kentigern', in N Chadwick (ed) *Studies in the Early British Church,* 273–357, Cambridge

Johnson, C, 1962 'Ten British species of the genus *Rhizophagus* Herbst (Col, Rhizophagidae)', *Transactions of the Manchester Entomological Society* (1961–63), 3–9

Johnston, F E, and Zimmer, L O, 1989 'Assessment of growth and age in the immature skeleton', in M Y Isçan and K A R Kennedy (eds) *Reconstruction of Life from the Skeleton,* 11–21, New York

Jurmain, R D, 1990 'Palaeoepidemiology of a central California prehistoric population from CA-ALA-329: II. Degenerative disease', *American J Physical Anthropol* 83, 83–94

Katz, D, and Suchey, J M, 1986 'Age determination of the male os pubis', *American J Physical Anthropol* 69, 427–435

Kauffmann, C M, 1975 *Romanesque Manuscripts 1066–1190,* A Survey of Manuscripts Illuminated in the British Isles 3, London

Kennedy, K A R, 1989 'Skeletal markers of occupational stress', in M Y Işcan and K A R Kennedy (eds) *Reconstruction of Life from the Skeleton,* 129–160, New York

Kenward, H K and Hall, A R, 1995 *Biological Evidence from 16–22 Coppergate,* The Archaeology of York 14.7, London

Klackenberg, H, 1992 *Moneta nostra: monetarisering i medeltidens Sverige,* Lund

Koch, K, 1989 *Die Käfer Mitteleuropas, Ökologie* 2, Krefeld

Lai, P and Lovell, N C, 1992 'Skeletal markers of occupational stress in the fur trade: a case study from a Hudson's Bay Company fur trade post', *Int J Osteoarchaeol* 2, 221–234

Larsen, C S, 1984 'Health and disease in prehistoric Georgia: The transition to Agriculture', in M N Cohen and G J Armelagos (eds) *Palaeopathology at the Origins of Agriculture,* 67–83, New York

Lawson, J, 1990 'Topography and building materials', in E Williamson, A Riches and M Higgs (eds) *The Buildings of Scotland. Glasgow,* 18–28, London

Leask, H G, 1977 *Irish Churches and Monastic Buildings, 1. The First Phases and the Romanesque,* Dundalk

Lempiäinen, T, 1992 'Early occurrence of *Sambucus racemosa* L (Caprifoliaceae) in Finland', *Annales Botanica Fennici* 29, 35–39

Lightfoot, J, 1777 *Flora Scotica,* London

Litten, F, 1991 *The English Way of Death,* London

Lorimer, D H, 1994 'Human bones', in J O'Sullivan 'Excavations of an early church and a women's cemetery at St Ronan's medieval parish church, Iona', *Proc Soc Antiq Scot* 124, 327–365

Lovejoy, C O, Meindl, R S, Pryzbeck, T R and Mensforth, R P, 1985 'Chronological metamorphosis of the auricular surface of the ilium: a new method for the determination of adult skeletal age at death', *American J Physical Anthropol* 68, 15–28

Lovell, N C, 1994 'Spinal arthritis and physical stress at Bronze Age Harappa', *American J Physical Anthropol* 93, 149–164

Lukacs, J R, 1989 'Dental paleopathology: methods for reconstructing dietary patterns', in M Y Işcan and K A R Kennedy (eds) *Reconstruction of Life from the Skeleton,* 261–286, New York

Lunt, D, 1986 'Mediaeval dentitions from St Andrews', in E Cruwys and R A Foley (eds) *Teeth and Anthropology,* BAR Int Ser 291, 215–224, Oxford

MacAskill, N, 1987 'The pottery', in P Holdsworth (ed) *Excavations in the Medieval Burgh of Perth, 1979–1981,* Soc Antiq Scot Monograph 5, 89–120, Edinburgh

Macaulay, J, 1997 'The demolition of the western towers of Glasgow Cathedral', in D Mays (ed) *The Architecture of Scottish Cities,* East Linton, East Lothian, 115–124

MacGibbon, D and Ross, T, 1896 *The Ecclesiastical Architecture of Scotland from the Earliest Christian Times to the Seventeenth Century,* 3 vols, Edinburgh

Mackie, J D, 1954 *The University of Glasgow 1451 to 1951,* Glasgow

MacQuarrie, A, 1992 'Early Christian religious houses in Scotland: foundation and function', in J Blair and R Sharpe (eds) *Pastoral Care before the Parish,* 110–136, Leicester

MacQuarrie, A, 1997 *The Saints of Scotland AD 450–1093,* Edinburgh

Mairinger, F and Schreiner, M, 1986 'Deterioration and preservation of Carolingian and medieval mural paintings in the Müstair Convent (Switzerland). Part I: materials and renderings of the Carolingian wall paintings', in *Case Studies in the Conservation of Stone and Wall Paintings* (preprints of the contributions to the IIC Bologna Congress, September 1986), 195–196, London

Manchester, K, 1983 *The Archaeology of Disease,* Bradford

Manchester, K, 1991 'Tuberculosis and leprosy: evidence for interaction of disease', in D J Ortner and A C Aufderheide (eds) *Human Paleopathology: Current Syntheses and Future Options,* 23–35, Washington DC

Manchester, K, 1992 'The palaeopathology of urban infections', in S Bassett (ed) *Death in Towns: Urban Responses to the Dying and Dead, 100–1600,* 8–14, Leicester

Martin, P F de C, 1987a 'Clay pipes from the wreck of the HMS Dartmouth, 1690', in P Davey (ed) *The Archaeology of the Clay Tobacco Pipe, X. Scotland,* BAR Int Ser 178, 225–232, Oxford

Martin, P F de C, 1987b 'Pipemakers in the rest of Scotland', in P Davey (ed) *The Archaeology of the Clay Tobacco Pipe, X Scotland,* BAR Int Ser 178, 167–182, Oxford

Mason, R A, 1988 *The Glasgow Assembly 1638,* Glasgow

Massaler, M and Shour, I, 1994 *Atlas of the Mouth and Adjacent Parts in Health and Disease,* Chicago

Mayhew, N, 1993 'Medieval bread', *ROSC: Review of Scottish Culture* 6, 91–94, Edinburgh

McBrien, H, 1988 'Excavations at Cathedral Square, Glasgow', *Medieval Archaeol* 32, 307

McBrien, H, 1989 'Excavations at Cathedral Square, Glasgow', *Medieval Archaeol* 33, 236

McKern, T W and Stewart, T D, 1957 *Skeletal Age Changes in Young American Males,* Quartermaster Research and Development Command Technical Report EP-45, Nantick, Massachusetts

McRoberts, D, 1959 'Material destruction caused by the Scottish Reformation', *Innes Review* 10, 126–172

McRoberts, D, 1966 'Notes on Glasgow Cathedral', *Innes Review* 17, 40–47

McWilliam, C, 1978 *The Buildings of Scotland: Lothian, except Edinburgh*, London

Megnin, P, 1894 *La faune des cadavres. Application de l'entomologie à la medicine legale*, Paris

Meindl, R S and Lovejoy, C O, 1985 'Ectocranial suture closure: a revised method for the determination of skeletal age at death based on the lateral-anterior sutures', *American J Physical Anthropol* 68, 57–66

Mentel, R, 1998 'The twelfth-century predecessors of Glasgow Cathedral and their relationship with Jedburgh Abbey', in R Fawcett (ed) *Medieval Art and Architecture in the Diocese of Glasgow*, Brit Archaeol Ass Trans 20, Leeds, 42–49

Molleson, T, Cox, M, Waldron, A H, and Whittaker, D K, 1993 *The Spitalfields Project, 2. The Anthropology: The Middling Sort*, CBA Res Rep 86, York

Morley, J, 1971 *Death, Heaven and the Victorians*, Pittsburgh

Nash-Williams, V E, 1950 *The Early Christian Monuments of Wales*, Cardiff

NSA: *The New Statistical Account of Scotland 1841. Lanarkshire*, vol 6, Edinburgh and London (15 vols)

Ortner, D J, 1991 'Theoretical and methodological issues in palaeopathology', in D J Ortner and A C Aufderheide (eds) *Human Paleopathology: Current Syntheses and Future Options*, 5–11, Washington DC

Ortner, D J, and Putschar, W J G, 1981 *Identification of Pathological Conditions in Human Skeletal Remains*, Washington DC

O'Sullivan, J, 1994 'Excavations of an early church and a women's cemetery at St Ronan's medieval parish church, Iona', *Proc Soc Antiq Scot* 124, 327–365

Palm, T, 1959 *Die Holz und Rindenkäfer der sud- und mittelschwedischen Laubbaume*, Opuscula Entomologica Supplement 16

Park, D, 1983 'The wall paintings of the Holy Sepulchre Chapel', in T A Heslop and V Sekules (eds) *Medieval Art and Architecture at Winchester Cathedral*, Brit Archaeol Ass Trans 6, 38–62, London

Park, D, 1991 'The wall paintings in the Galilee Chapel of Durham Cathedral', *Friends of Durham Cathedral Annual Report* 1990, 21–34

Park, D, 1998 'Late twelfth-century polychromy from Glasgow Cathedral', in R Fawcett (ed) *Medieval Art and Architecture of Glasgow and Environs*, Brit Archaeol Ass Trans 20, 35–41

Peacock, E R, 1977 *Coleoptera Rhizophagidae*, Handbooks for the Identification of British Insects V, 5(a), Royal Entomological Society of London

Pennant, T, 1772 *A Tour of Scotland and Voyage to the Hebrides*, Chester

Pevsner, N, 1983, *County Durham*, The Buildings of England, rev E Williamson, Harmondsworth

Phenice, T, 1967 'A newly developed method of sexing the os pubis', *American J Physical Anthropol* 30, 297–301

Pryde, G, 1958 'The city and burgh of Glasgow', in R Miller and J Tivy (eds) *The Glasgow Region*, 134–139, Glasgow

Radford, C A R, 1970 *Glasgow Cathedral*, Edinburgh

Radford, C A R and Stones, E L G, 1964 'The remains of the cathedral of Bishop Jocelin at Glasgow (c1197)', *Antiquaries Journal* 44, 220–232

RCAHMS 1920: Royal Commission on the Ancient and Historic Monuments of Scotland, 1920 *An Inventory of the Ancient and Historical Monuments of Dumfriesshire*, Edinburgh

RCAHMS 1951: Royal Commission on the Ancient and Historic Monuments of Scotland, 1951 *The City of Edinburgh. An Inventory of the Ancient and Historical Monuments of the City of Edinburgh*, Edinburgh

RCAHMS 1963: Royal Commission on the Ancient and Historic Monuments of Scotland, 1963 *An Inventory of the Ancient and Historical Monuments of Stirlingshire*, Edinburgh

RCHME 1980: Royal Commission on the Historic Monuments of England, 1980 *Ancient and Historical Monuments of the City of Salisbury*, vol I, London

Redman, C, 1997 *Dryburgh Abbey, The Borders, Scotland: A Report on the Extent and Condition of the Wall Paintings in the Chapter House, Sacristy and North Transept*, unpublished report by the Courtauld Institute for Historic Scotland

Redford, M, 1988 *Commemorations of Saints of the Celtic Church in Scotland*, unpublished MLit dissertation, University of Edinburgh

Reed, I W, 1990 *1000 Years of Pottery and Analysis of Pottery, Trade and Use*, Trondheim

Reeve, J and Adams, M, 1993 *The Spitalfields Project, I. The Archaeology: Across the Styx*, CBA Res Rep 85, York

Reinhard K J, Geib P R, Calllahan M M and Hevly R H, 1992 'Discovery of colon contents in a skeletonised burial: soil sampling for dietary remains', *J Archaeol Science* 19, 697–706

Renwick, R, 1908 *Glasgow Memorials*, Glasgow

Renwick, R, Lindsay, J and Eyre-Todd, G, 1934 *History of Glasgow*, 3 vols, Glasgow

Rickerby, S, 1990 'Kempley: a technical examination of the Romanesque wall paintings', in S Cather, D Park and P Williamson (eds) *Early Medieval Wall Painting and Painted Sculpture in England*, BAR Brit Ser 216, Oxford, 249–61

Rodwell, W 1989 *Archaeology of the English Church*, London

Sager, P, 1969 *Spondylosis Cervicalis: a Pathological and Osteological Study*, Copenhagen

Saunders, S R, 1992 'Subadult skeletons and growth related studies', in S R Saunders and MA Katzenberg (eds) *Skeletal Biology of Past Peoples: Research Methods*, 1–20, New York

Sawdy, A, Heritage, A and Cather, S, 1998 *St Botolph's Church, Hardham: Conservation of the Wall Paintings. Phase I: Investigations, Recording, Treatment Testing and Assessment*, unpublished report by the Courtauld Institute for English Heritage

Scotichronicon: Taylor, S and Watt, D E R with Scott, B (eds and transl), 1990, *Scotichronicon by Walter Bower, 5. Books IX and X*, Aberdeen

Scott, J G, 1991 'Bishop John of Glasgow and the status of Hoddom', *Trans Dumfriesshire Galloway Natur Hist Antiq Soc* 66, 36–45

Shead, N F, 1969 'The origins of the medieval diocese of Glasgow', *Scottish History Review* 48, 220–225

Shead, N F, 1975 'Diocese of Glasgow: parish churches c1320, in P McNeill and R Nicholson (eds) *An Historical Atlas of Scotland c400–c1600,* 41–42, 154–155, St Andrews

Shead, N F, 1976 'The administration of the diocese of Glasgow in the twelfth and thirteenth centuries', *Scottish History Review* 55, 127–150

Shead, N F, 1988 'Glasgow: an ecclesiastical burgh', in M Lynch, R M Spearman and G Stell (eds) *The Scottish Medieval Town*, 116–132, Edinburgh

Simpson, W D, 1965 *The Ancient Stones of Scotland*, London

Sloan, D 1972 'Pollockshields, Hagg's Castle', *Discovery and Excavation in Scotland,* 35, Edinburgh

St Hoyme, L E, and Isçan, M Y, 1989 'Determination of sex and race: accuracy and assumptions', in M Y Isçan and K A R Kennedy (eds) *Reconstruction of Life from the Skeleton,* 53–93, New York

Stace, C, 1991 *New Flora of the British Isles*, Cambridge

Stafford, F, 1971 'Insects of a medieval burial', *Science and Archaeology* 7, 6–10

Steele, D G, and Bramblett, C A, 1988 *The Anatomy and Biology of the Human Skeleton*, Texas

Stones, E L G, 1969 'Notes on Glasgow Cathedral: the burials of medieval bishops with particular reference to the bishops of Glasgow', *Innes Review* 20, 37–46

Stones, E L G, 1970 'Notes on Glasgow Cathedral', *Innes Review* 21, 140–152

Stones, J A (ed), 1989 *Three Scottish Carmelite Friaries: Excavations at Aberdeen, Linlithgow and Perth Edinburgh*, Soc Antiq Scot Monogr Ser 6, Edinburgh

Stuart, M, 1989 *The Encyclopaedia of Herbs and Herbalism*, Novara

Stuart-Macadam, P L, 1989 'Nutritional deficiency diseases: a survey of scurvy, rickets, and iron-deficiency anemia', in M Y Isçan and K A R Kennedy (eds) *Reconstruction of Life from the Skeleton*, 201–222, New York

Suchey, J M, Brooks, S T, and Katz, D, 1988 *Instructions for Use of the Suchey-Brooks System for Age Determination of the Female os pubis*, Instructional materials accompanying female pubic symphyseal models of the Suchey-Brooks system

Sundick, R I, 1978 'Human skeletal growth and age determination', *Homo* 29, 228–249

Sutherland, L D, and Suchey, J M, 1991 'Use of the ventral arc in pubic sex determination', *J Forensic Sciences* 36, 501–511

Talbot, E J, 1975 'An Excavation at the site of the north-west tower of St Mungo's Cathedral, Glasgow', *Innes Review* 26, 43–49

Thompson, R T, 1995 'Raymondionymidae (Col, Curculionoidea) confirmed as British', *Entomologist's monthly Magazine* 131, 61–64

Thurlby, M, 1981 'A 12th-century figure from Jedburgh Abbey', *Proc Soc Antiq Scot*, 111, 381–87

Thurlby, M, 1994 'St Andrews Cathedral-Priory and the beginnings of Gothic architecture in northern Britain', in J Higgitt (ed) *Medieval Art and Architecture in the Diocese of St Andrews*, Brit Archaeol Ass Conference Trans 14, 47–60, Leeds

Thurlby, M, 1995 'Jedburgh Abbey, the Romanesque fabric', *Proc Soc Antiq Scot* 125, 793–812

Todd, T W, 1920 'Age changes in the pubic bone: I. The white male pubis', *American J Physical Anthropol* 3, 467–470

Trotter, M, 1970 'Estimation of stature from intact limb bones', in T D Stewart (ed) *Personal Identification in Mass Disasters*, 71–83, Washington DC

Ubelaker, D H, 1989 *Human Skeletal Remains*, Washington DC

Ure, D, 1793 *History of Rutherglen and East Kilbride*, Glasgow

Waldron, T, 1992 'Osteoarthritis in a Black Death cemetery in London', *Int J Osteoarchaeol* 2, 235–240

Watson, T L, 1901 *The Double Choir of Glasgow Cathedral*, Glasgow

Watson, W J, 1926 *The History of the Celtic Place-Names of Scotland*, Glasgow

Watt, D E R, 1977 *A Biographical Dictionary of Scottish Graduates to AD 1410*, Oxford

Watt, D E R, 1991 *Series Episcoporum Ecclesiae Catholicae Occidentalis: ab Initio Usque ad Annum MCXCVIII. Ser 6: Britannia, Scotia et Hibernia, Scandinavia. Tomus I. Ecclesia Scoticana*, Stuttgart

White, T D, 1991 *Human Osteology*, San Diego

Wilson, C A, 1973 *Food and Drink in Britain*, London

Wilson, C, 1998 'The stellar vaults of Glasgow Cathedral's inner crypt and Villard de Honnercourt's chapter-house plan: a conundrum revisited', in R Fawcett (ed) *Medieval Art and Architecture in the Diocese of Glasgow*, Brit Archaeol Ass Trans 20, 55–76

UNPUBLISHED SOURCES

Scottish Records Office (SRO), West Register House, Edinburgh, Files Consulted:

Ministry of Works files
SRO MW.1.188, 1836–57 Condition and repairs of fabric
SRO MW.1.287, 1860–71 Burial Lair Oswald Family

Files of Crown Estates Commissioners
SRO CR4/143, 1829–58 Crypt as Burial Place
SRO CR4/144

Plans
SRO RHP6503/36–37, 1857–64 Plans of Crypt by Matheson

INDEX

Peter Rea